A GUIDE TO GOOD SINGING AND SPEECH

KU-207-517

A GUIDE TO GOOD SINGING AND SPEECH

*

JULIAN GARDINER

CASSELL * LONDON

M 13736 63|- 9.70

CASSELL & COMPANY LTD
35 Red Lion Square, London WC1
Melbourne, Sydney, Toronto,
Johannesburg, Auckland

© Julian Gardiner 1968
First published 1968

S.B.N. 304 91847 4

Printed in Great Britain by
The Camelot Press Ltd., London and Southampton
F.1167

In memory of Franklyn Kelsey

A good deal of nonsense has been talked at one time or another about artistic theories. The artist is told that he should have no theories, that he should warble native wood-notes wild, that he should 'sing', be wholly spontaneous, should starve his brain and cultivate his heart and spleen; that an artistic theory cramps the style, stops up the helicons of inspiration, and so on, and so on. The foolish conception of the artist, to which these anti-intellectual doctrines are a corollary, dates from the time of romanticism and survives among the foolish and sentimental of today. A consciously practised theory of art has never spoiled a good artist, has never dammed up inspiration, but rather, and in most cases profitably, canalized it. Even the Romantics had theories and were wild and emotional on principle. . . . The only occasions, in fact, when the artist can afford entirely to dispense with theory occur in periods when a well-established tradition reigns supreme and unquestioned. And then the absence of a theory is more apparent than real; for the tradition in which he is working is a theory, originally formulated by someone else, which he accepts unconsciously and as though it were the law of nature itself.

On the Margin: Aldous Huxley
CHATTO & WINDUS

To Mr Bland's, where M. Povey and Gauden and I were invited to dinner. . . They had a kinswoman they call daughter in the house, a short, ugly, red-haired slut, that plays upon the virginals and sings, but after such a country manner I was weary of it, but yet could not but commend it. So by and by after dinner comes Monsr Gotier, who is beginning to teach her, but, Lord! what a droll fellow it is to make her hold open her mouth, and telling this and that so drolly would make a man burst; but himself I perceive sings very well.

Diary of Samuel Pepys: 24 July 1663

My imagination and emotions always ran hand in hand, but technique at first was almost a friendly enemy. In later years one comes to depend on it much more, like a companion whom one did not understand at school and only in middle life begins to lean on, appreciate and trust.

Forsaken Altars: Marguerite D'Alvarez
RUPERT HART-DAVIS

ACKNOWLEDGEMENTS

A number of people have given me helpful advice and criticism. In particular I would like to thank Sumner Austin, Douglas Blakely, Peter Brough, Rupert Donovan, Leon Goossens, Edward Hain, Professor J. M. Tanner and Dr. A. V. R. Watkins. In seeing the book and its writer through the long period of gestation, and the even greater agony of getting it into readable shape, my wife has been incomparable. Finally, I must not forget to mention my pupils; I have always encouraged them to speak their minds, and they have responded nobly.

I am also indebted to the following:

Chatto & Windus for an extract from *On the Margin* by Aldous Huxley; Rupert Hart-Davis Ltd. for an extract from *Forsaken Altars* by Marguerite D'Alvarez; Miss Collins and Messrs Methuen for an extract from 'The Rolling English Road' by G. K. Chesterton; Oxford University Press for an extract from *War and Peace* by Leo Tolstoy, translated by Aylmer Maude; and Editions Bernard Grasset for an extract from *L'Art de Chanter une Chanson* by Yvette Guilbert.

PREFACE

This book is for singers and speakers of all kinds—and for the sake of brevity the word 'singers' here and throughout most of the book, should be taken to include speakers. No previous technical or musical knowledge is assumed. Theoretically it would be possible for a beginner to read it on his own, work through the exercises, and at the end find himself equipped with a perfect technique; in practice any attempt to learn to sing without a teacher would be disastrous. So long as this is understood, I can confidently say that the book is not simply for teachers. First, last and all the time it is a practical guide to good singing and speaking, and nothing more nor less.

Like all textbooks this one at first glance may appear somewhat intimidating, but the noble and highly skilled arts of speaking and singing deserve more than those popular handbooks which skate so beautifully round each and every difficulty, and a great deal more than some of the weird publications by writers with very little knowledge of anatomy or sound physics, and even smaller powers of exposition. Exasperation with these two classes of book, and the lack of any systematic method of teaching have persuaded many people that the less singers know about the technical side of their art the better. It has also given rise to a rather absurd saying that every singing teacher has his own method. In fact most contemporary teaching in the English-speaking world is based either on no method at all, or on what is known as forward production. This method, which has been made popular in the English musical world by Plunket Greene and in the world of the theatre by Mr Clifford Turner, aims primarily at a smooth flow of tone, similar in many respects to a sigh, and unimpeded by any tightness in the throat. No one could quarrel with such a blameless objective, so long as nothing is done to affect the actual means of producing the tone. But that is what invariably happens, since the pupil's attention is concentrated on bringing the tone forward on to the lips and teeth, and away from the place where the tone is created. A ridiculous but not altogether unfair comparison might be with a clarinettist who took infinite pains to keep his instrument free from dust or condensation, but who never bothered to screw up, adjust or change the reed.

Like almost all singers of today I was trained on forward-production methods. My very average baritone was never intended by nature to set the Thames on fire, and soon after the Second World War I started teaching. With a large number of students passing through my hands it did not take me long to realize that, in spite of having been to a number of different masters, the methods I was using were far from satisfactory. Practical experience and reading the available textbooks helped to some extent; but it was not until 1950 that real enlightenment came. In the autumn of that year a book based on the teaching of Manuel Garcia was published,★ and it is no exaggeration to say that this book caused the scales to fall from my eyes.

The method of singing associated with the name of Manuel Garcia was no invention of this great teacher, who worked in London from 1850 until his death in 1906. It was the technical method which prevailed in the Italian singing schools from about 1600 until the end of the nineteenth century, and which earned for itself the popular sobriquet of 'il bel canto'. Many people have the idea that it was a kind of singing in which words did not matter and a beautiful instrumental tone was the sole objective. Nothing could be more untrue. 'L'arte del canto' as it was called—the term 'bel canto' was never used by Garcia or by any master of the old school—embraces every variety of singing from florid to declamatory. The note is hit clean and full, instead of sliding up to it with more or less of a crescendo; the vowels are excellent, and invariably the tone is carried through to the end of the phrase. Furthermore you will find, if you listen closely, that the tone, in contrast to the sounds of the vast majority of modern teachers, singers and speakers, has a kinship not with sighing but with groaning—and remember that 'kinship with' is very different from 'similarity to'!

It was Franklyn Kelsey's interpretation of this method which took me in the next eighteen months on frequent journeys to Cardiff where he was living. Kelsey was too oracular to be a first-class teacher; but my lessons with him, and the long evenings in his studio when he backed up his theories by playing me some of the scratchiest records I have ever heard, were sufficient to revolutionize my whole technique and conception of singing. I was not however a blind follower. I was an

★Franklyn Kelsey, *The Foundations of Singing* (Williams & Norgate 1950; 2nd edn., Ernest Benn, 1960).

experienced teacher and had ideas and theories of my own, many of them quite unconnected with the Garcia method. Some were discarded under Kelsey's influence, but others survived and, to my way of thinking, continue to be of vital importance. Kelsey, in his devotion to Garcia, was content to dismiss such notions as trifling irrelevancies. No wonder he found me an awkward pupil at times! As a rule however I managed to keep my own counsel, for like so many rebels and pioneers Kelsey would brook no argument.

But these private counsels never for one moment affected my confidence in the fundamentals of his teaching. In fact there was nothing new in what he taught. It was all common knowledge, but he was the first and only person to make sure that I understood it and applied it properly. Like me he had learned singing in the wrong school and never fulfilled himself as an artist. Only recently had he seen the error of his ways; having mended them, he wanted nothing but to save others from vocal extinction. More than anyone I have known, he cared deeply, humbly and passionately for good singing. Certainly he would have fulminated against parts of this book, and letters—on his side of gigantic length—would have shuttled between us. Alas, it was not to be.

CONTENTS

[xiv]

Contents

ILLUSTRATIONS

1

THE PROSPECT BEFORE US

God pardon us, nor harden us; we did not see so clear,
The night we went to Bannockburn by way of Brighton Pier.
'The Rolling English Road': G. K. Chesterton

The full title of this book is *A Guide to Good Singing and Speech*, but for the sake of brevity I have addressed myself throughout to the singer. To avoid misunderstanding, let me say that brevity was the only reason and that, except for about six chapters, all the material is equally relevant to the speaker. I wish to make this especially clear because there has grown up an utterly false legend that singing technique is something quite different from speech technique. Actors in particular look upon singing as something richly esoteric, having nothing to do with speech. It might be so if we were concerned with the ordinary everyday speech of untrained speakers. But we are not. We are concerned with good speech and good singing, and they are different aspects of one single craft. Admittedly speech is a much less complicated business. The singer has to sustain a much higher level of pitch than the speaker and to exercise a far more exact control over the intensity of the tone and the accuracy of the intonation; but though the technical and aesthetic demands on the singer are enormously greater than on the speaker, all actors, no matter how modest their musical equipment, should study the basic technique of singing as intensively as if it was their principal study. In this way they will discover completely fresh potentialities in their speaking voice.

In our present relationship of reader and author, we shall not alas be meeting face to face. So you must help me by reading this book in the way in which I intended it to be read. Take each chapter as you come to it, and begin by reading it straight through, as you would a novel. Do not bother at this stage if you do not understand certain parts. All that is needed is to get a general idea of the scope of the chapter. Having done this, take one section at a time, reading it slowly and carefully. Of the ninety-odd sections into which the book is divided, each is short enough to be studied and applied in a session which need not last longer than three-quarters of an hour. The order of the sections has been arranged so as to equip the careful reader with the technique required to master each problem as it appears; therefore it is essential not to dodge about, but to work steadily through, reading not more than one section per day, and as a rule not more than three sections in a week. This applies particularly to the first nine chapters.

a. The road to Bannockburn

Before we get started, let me put in a word of warning in case any innocent reader imagines that, by mastering the technique herein outlined, he will automatically become a fine speaker or singer. Artistic technique is not simply a means to an end. If this were all it was, the musical world would be bulging with Tebaldis and Fischer-Dieskaus. Technique is a means of discovering ends which would not otherwise be clearly discernible. In every musical institution there are pianists and violinists of dazzling attainments, yet they remain amateurs because they are too self-centred to realize that it is not the successful negotiation of a difficult trick which is important, but the use they make of it in communicating the composer's message to the audience.

Perhaps this is obvious; but it is worth stressing in case a superficial reader jumps to the conclusion that, because I have written very little about interpretation and a great deal about technique, I consider technique all-important. I do not! It is the road to Bannockburn, but not Bannockburn itself. Let nobody accuse me of confusing the road with the place. But when cavalcades of budding singers take the road to Brighton Pier, what can anybody do but implore them to have a look at their maps? Each and every singer has a battle to fight which lasts throughout his career, but before he starts on his crusade, he really ought to see that he is heading in the right direction and is adequately armed. Otherwise the battle will be a bloody massacre.

b. The singer's equipment

However experienced you are, the study of this book is certain to involve some reconsideration of your present technique. Naturally you will wish to make the period of overhaul a quick and profitable one, but there can be no hope of progress if at the same time you continue to lead a busy life of music making. No harm will come of occasional singing for your own amusement and physical satisfaction, provided it is kept apart from your real work, but public appearances must be cut out altogether; if this is impracticable, they should be restricted to a bare minimum, until you are certain that they will not be a ghastly mixture of old and new methods. Nor should you—and this is most important—take part in any kind of sociable singing. It may seem a cruel deprivation, but compromise would be a disastrous mistake. To forestall any misunderstanding, let me make it clear that choirs, madrigal groups and operatic societies are vitally necessary parts of musical education. Anybody who has not taken part in them misses a tremendous amount of pleasure and opportunities for making friends, and seriously reduces his prospects of professional success. As soon as he is equipped to do so, he should, and indeed must, indulge in all these varieties of music making. But for the first year at any rate he must possess his soul in patience. The multifarious arts of reading the music, following the conductor's beat, and blending with other voices, would keep him far too busy to attend to matters of voice production. Genuine progress in the early stages would be out of the question, and time and money would be wasted.

But there will be more than enough to keep you occupied. In the first place all singers should be able to play the piano well enough to cope with simple accompaniments. Gerald Moore's books* *The Unashamed Accompanist* and *Singer and Accompanist* will give the best guidance possible, and at the same time help to lay the foundations of a repertoire. Without some ability in this direction a singer finds life pretty difficult, for a pianist who is patient, efficient, musical and friendly is hard to come by and somewhat expensive. An even more convincing reason for studying the piano is that it develops qualities in which English singers are outstanding. Uninteresting voices and poor technique they may have, but at least they are fine musicians, with an unrivalled capacity for reading music and learning new works at top speed. These accomplishments, which can only be acquired by constant practice, are indispensable for any singer who wants to get on. No matter what his ambitions—opera or oratorio, concert or crooning—a singer must be able to read a vocal line as easily as a book. His first

* Gerald Moore, *The Unashamed Accompanist* and *Singer and Accompanist* (Methuen, 1949 and 1953 respectively).

engagements will be in choir or chorus, and a quick and accurate reader invariably gets the job, even if his voice is not as good as those of the rival candidates. Later, as a soloist, he will be remembered by managers and conductors as a reliable person, on whom they can safely call at the last moment when somebody has gone down with laryngitis.

In addition to work at the piano, try to get some stage experience. If you have a local repertory, join it even if at first you are given nothing but walk-on parts. Merely being on stage gives you the chance of studying how different audiences respond and how actors make their effects in gesture, timing, variation of speed and pitch, emphasis and throw-away. Apart from the educational benefit, any work with a repertory company is an invaluable talking point when you apply for jobs. Producers are not particularly interested to hear of the parts you played in the school opera, but they will prick up their ears when they learn that you worked with such-and-such Repertory Company, and played Poltroonius in *The Belles' Stratagem* or Grace Trampleasure in *The Fourth Viscount*.

Since you will not at present need to spend a great deal of time in actual singing, now is the moment to start learning one or more of the three European languages which have been the inspiration of vocal music. Choose the one you know best, and take every opportunity of hearing it sung or spoken, live and on records, broadcasts and films. Apart from the demands of repertoire, the more knowledge you have of one or two foreign languages, the deeper will be your intolerance of smudgy slovenly vowels. Indeed it is no exaggeration to say that the most effective means of cultivating the beauty and expressiveness of your singing of English words is by studying foreign languages.

Most important of all, listen to as many singers as you can. Do not be content with the radio. Hear them in real life, and if possible at close quarters. Buy one or two records of singers you particularly admire or wish to emulate and make them repeat isolated notes and phrases again and again and again. Sooner or later the vocal organ will seem to react sympathetically to what you are hearing, and the accompanying sensations will bring to the technical and anatomical details of this treatise a new and exciting significance.

But there is another and even stronger reason for listening to singers. With proper training a voice does not simply improve. Unless it is a so-called natural voice, there are moments when it literally seems to leap into life. This is when you must carry in the mind's ear the memory of great singing. In comparison your newly awakened voice will be merely loud and ugly, yet in recognizing a similar physical origin you will sense that a finer quality is within your reach. Without this memory to serve as a guide and imaginative stimulus, your tone quality will remain as inexpressive as the noises of a deaf-mute, however faultless the production. Technique is a means to enable you to do this, but no more than a means. Beauty can only be born as a result of imagination, emotion and experience, and there are few memoirs of singers which do not include a poignant description of the young student crouching for hours beside a worn record of Caruso or Melba.

It may be tempting to put on a record of some favourite artist, and directly imitate it. This is a most undesirable practice. The closer the apparent resemblance between a recorded voice and your own, the more it should be avoided. It is not the sound which you have to imitate, but the means whereby the sound is produced. That is why it is almost impossible to learn singing without a teacher. The voices of great singers can in some strange way confirm or deny the authenticity of the sensations in your own body, so long as you listen carefully and analytically. They cannot do more. An individual voice is something unique and precious; as often as not its qualities and potentialities are half buried, and need as much care and labour in excavating as any pre-Roman settlement. Success can only be achieved by learning how to induce the correct sensations. Direct imitation of another singer means that you are leaving your voice still buried, unexcavated and undeveloped, and masquerading pathetically and ineffectually in borrowed feathers. Gramophone records are an inspiration; they may also be helpful signposts; they cannot and must not be treated as spring-boards or bandwagons.

Your taste in performers will naturally favour the great singers of the past as well as one or two present-day heroes. Nevertheless it is unwise to limit yourself severely to music of the highest class. Nobody can make a living unless he is prepared to work in every kind of musical production and enjoy doing so. This means that you must be able to tackle every style of music without turning a hair. Your brow may be high but it must also be broad. Popular music can boast many fine artists; their style of singing may be different, yet they can teach a great deal to anybody who has ears to hear. You should in fact cultivate a good taste and a keen sense of criticism in every field of music by attending as many rehearsals and performances of as many operas, concerts and plays as you can. If you run short of money or complimentary tickets, go to the law courts and study the barristers, the judges and the witnesses under cross-examination. All of them are performers. If some are bad, you will learn what not to do; and that is just as important.

c. Especially for actors and speakers

In acquiring a technical command of something which does not directly concern them, actors will find that they are automatically improving their skills in their own particular speciality. Not only this but they will enormously improve their chances of earning a respectable living. After all there are a great many singers and even more actors, but very very few good actor-singers or singing-actors! As for those unfortunate people who simply cannot pitch notes at all, there is no alternative but to give up singing, and to concentrate on speech; this means in effect disregarding Chapters 9, 15 to 19, and 22, but studying all the rest of the book, and in particular Chapter 12.

In the world of the theatre technical standards are every bit as rickety as in the world of song, and for precisely the same reasons. All over the country, boys and girls are being trained to speak at the very front of the mouth, and thereby being deprived of any potential beauty and sonority of tone. At the same time they are made to keep the ribs expanded in order to provide what is called 'rib reserve'. Thus there is no possibility of maintaining a compression against the vocal cords and breath is allowed to flow up the throat and out of the mouth. If there was any scientific justification for believing in the value of these instructions, one might be prepared to give them a little sympathetic consideration; but there is none. As for the consequences they are deplorably apparent in our theatres, where not one young actor in a hundred knows how to make his voice travel beyond the fourth row of the stalls.

The average actor or actress who embarks on this book might conclude that it may be all very well for singing, but that for ordinary speech on stage it is far too complicated and energetic. This is entirely untrue. The same technique has to be employed, just as the basic

[6]

technique of driving a car at breakneck speed on a motorway is precisely the same as when negotiating suburban traffic. The demands on the engine and on the driver's skill are not so great, and in the same way the physical demands on the speaker are not so great as on the singer. But the actor who thinks he has only to speak clearly and naturally will be in for a rude shock as soon as he finds himself in a big theatre. If he wishes to be true to his art, he must be master of the principles of posture, lung tension and nasal resonance. Only when these have become so automatic as to be habitual has he any right to think of himself as an artist.

Perhaps our chief national defect is the tendency to associate vocal tone with consonants. Many teachers of singing and elocution foster this association by means of exercises in which isolated consonants are pronounced. There is in fact a popular theory that all that is needed to ensure audibility in halls and theatres is a firm articulation of consonants, together with what is known as 'projection of the voice'. What the word 'projection' means in this context no one seems to know; and since it is a universally accepted fact that sounds of any kind cannot be projected, directed, floated or carried by any conscious means this is hardly surprising. A cellist can do nothing to help the sound waves to emerge from the *f* holes in the front of his instrument except to see that the holes are open and free from obstruction. The mouth is the singer's *f* hole, and the same rule applies. Sound waves can be reflected, or they can be dampened; they cannot be projected by any conscious effort.

To cultivate a healthy and truly natural speaking voice, a student needs first to give up associating it with the mouth and learn to speak from the apex of the chest. This will deepen his voice, so that he will tend to speak on a lower pitch level than before, while his speech tones will acquire more dominance and authority. Naturally this will take some time, and meanwhile he must give up all forms of crooning and whispering which are its very antithesis.

Secondly he must associate voice production not with consonants, but with pure vowel sounds. If his native speech accent stems from one of the big cities such as London or Liverpool, New York or Chicago he will have a tough job ahead of him; accordingly his second resolution should be to give up singing popular and music-hall songs in his native dialect, at any rate for the time being.

[7]

Thirdly he must aim for a fluent continuity of speech tone. If sound waves impinge on the ear drums of an audience, at one moment strongly, at the next feebly, the words will not be easily distinguishable, no matter how firmly the consonants are articulated; indeed the better the consonants, the more the voice will degenerate into a succession of tonal bursts. Accordingly his third resolution should be to give up all forms of barking, shouting, swallowing and slurring; and to remember that speech can be music just as much as good singing.

2
THE FRAMEWORK

Good singing means skilful playing on a well-tuned instrument—the human voice. This well-tuned instrument is suspended inside a complicated framework—the human body. Before attending to the instrument, the reader should make certain that the framework is put to its best advantage, otherwise the voice will no more realize and maintain its true potential than will an engine inside a bent or imperfectly aligned motor chassis.

Essentially the human body is an admirable structure. Its distinguishing physical characteristic is the fully erect posture. Many creatures can walk on two legs but man alone carries head, neck, trunk and pelvis in a nearly vertical line. This is particularly noticeable in the case of athletes, dancers and others who depend for their livelihood on physical fitness. Perhaps the best and most vivid examples are Spanish dancers whose posture embodies a strutting catlike sensuousness which every reader should strive to emulate. All these people hold themselves so as to bring their centre of gravity★ up to its highest level; in this attitude they are ready to move in any direction with the least effort at the shortest notice. In the same way, though he seldom moves about while singing, a singer who uses his body as an instrument of music, needs to bring it to the point of utmost all-round efficiency, so as to be able to contract and relax with ease and speed a number of muscles, most of which lie outside his direct conscious control. Their degree of response depends firstly on his awareness of the practical steps to be taken, and secondly on the readiness of his body to carry out his wishes. In this chapter we are concerned with the means of establishing the second of these conditions.

a. Three pyramids

As a geometrical shape the upright body may be visualized as a system of three pyramids with their bases uppermost, balanced on top of

★ The centre of gravity in a human body is the point where a man impaled on a skewer could be most easily twirled around by a hungry giant.

each other and corresponding roughly to the head, the trunk and the legs (Fig. 1). The lowest pyramid has for its inverted base the broad, basin-shaped pelvis into which the legs are set, and for its twofold apex the feet. The middle pyramid extends from above the pelvis to the shoulders, the lowest section of the spine forming the apex and the

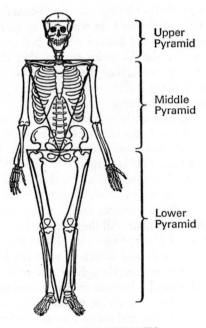

Upper Pyramid

Middle Pyramid

Lower Pyramid

FIG. 1. THREE PYRAMIDS

shoulders the base. In the top pyramid the apex is at the cervical vertebrae of the neck, and the base at the crown of the head. Each pyramid however is no mere example of solid geometry, but living substance supported by muscles on whose constantly co-ordinated activity the whole structure depends. In the act of singing all three pyramids must be kept stable, and the centre of gravity brought up to the highest possible level; in other words you must learn to sing on the stretch.

This might seem a comparatively easy task; but it is not as simple as it sounds. For all-round movement the human body is an ideal structure, but for standing still it is comparatively inefficient; that is why the average person prefers to walk about, sit down or lean against something. It is not just a matter of fatigue, but of sheer difficulty in keeping erect a structure so precarious as to resemble three inverted pyramids. In a standing position the body quite naturally starts to sag. This brings the centre of gravity down to a lower level than is athletically or vocally desirable. There is a sense of improved stability, but the power of swift movement and body control is lost.

In order to become a good singer, it is necessary to exchange the habitual posture for one which admittedly seems precarious, but which brings the body into the most favourable condition for versatility of movement. This position, which I shall be referring to as the position of readiness, is comparatively unstable and energetic owing to the circumstances of man's evolution. Since he started to walk and stand erect, the pull of gravity has caused the thorax to be pressed downwards against the abdomen. As a result the expansion of the lower ribs is more or less seriously inhibited, so that inhalation has to be in a downward rather than a sideways direction. It is of course a completely natural way of breathing, but it does not enable us to perform acts demanding unusual physical energy such as lifting a heavy weight. On these occasions we need to bring the chest away from the abdomen, in order to allow the muscles of the back, the ribs and the abdomen to work with maximum efficiency. Singing is not like weight lifting, but it is sufficiently strenuous to demand that we take similar steps to defy the pull of gravity. These will be outlined in the following sections.

b. The lowest pyramid

So long as the body is free to move according to its natural inclination, the average man's posture maintains a reasonable standard of efficiency. But if he is compelled to stand comparatively motionless or to sit for long periods, the body will be likely to sag at the apices of our three pyramids, where equilibrium is unusually precarious, i.e. at the feet, at the small of the back and at the neck. We should therefore begin by making certain that the apex of the lowest pyramid, on to which the weight of the body is thrown, is so balanced as to enable the two upper pyramids to maintain the most vertical alignment possible.

If you stand in bare or stockinged feet, you will find three points of contact with the floor, namely the heels, the balls of the feet and the toes. Almost everybody in a standing position allows the weight of the body to be supported by the heels. This may be all very well when waiting for the bus; a position of readiness however is impossible unless the weight is invariably on the balls of the feet. Exercises 1 to 5 are designed to make you aware of this. Their common denominator is an insistence on stretch, the benefits of which are evident in many everyday activities. If for instance you straighten out a kink in a hose-pipe, the chances are that another kink will appear in a different place. The only certain way of ensuring a steady flow is to pull the nozzle end away from the water supply so that the pipe straightens itself the whole of its length. Think of the body as something like the hose-pipe, and take steps to avoid kinks by keeping it long (Fig. 2). These first exercises should be done without shoes. Men should support their trousers with braces rather than a belt, not only in these exercises but whenever singing.

EXERCISE 1

Stand erect with the feet pointing forwards, and about two inches apart. The knees must on no account touch each other at any time in this or any of the Exercises 1 to 18.

Go up on tiptoe. Come down slowly without losing the feeling of stretch. The moment the heels touch the floor, stay in that position with the weight on the balls of the feet. To begin with you will have an almost irresistible impulse to let the weight of the body slip back on to the heels as you come down. Conquer this tendency by feeling that you go up in order to come down in order to go up again. If you maintain the stretch when the heels are on the floor, the body will have the same upward and slightly forward thrust as when you were on tiptoe. It is the attitude you instinctively take up before doing a standing jump, and has been already referred to as the position of readiness. From that position you are able to move in any direction without needing to make adjustments or intervening movements. Many people feel that they are leaning forwards with their heads tilted downwards as if they were peering over their spectacles, but this is a sensation that soon disappears.

[12]

Fig. 2 (*a*)   The
Singer's Stance—right

Fig. 2 (*b*)   The
Singer's Stance—wrong

EXERCISE 2

Stand in the same position, with feet pointing forwards and about two inches apart, and with knees bent slightly to avoid any possibility of their being locked back. Lift the heels and toes off the floor so as to balance solely on the balls of the feet. If you find this difficult, use the back of a chair to keep steady, but dispense with it as soon as possible. Walk up and down the room on the balls of the feet, taking care not to stiffen the knees.

EXERCISE 3

i. Stand with feet close together. Go on to the outside edge of the feet, so that the soles face inward towards each other, keeping the body stretched and upright. Go down on to the full flat of the foot, and back on to the outside edge.

ii. Walk up and down the room on the outside edge of the feet, keeping the knees flexed and the body long and erect.

In the position of readiness you find that the knees are rotated outwards, so that the legs seem to have an outward thrust; the big toe is still firmly on the floor, but rather more weight is thrown on to the outside of the foot and over towards the little toes. If you bring your weight away from the outside of the foot on to the inside so that only the big toe keeps close contact with the floor, you will find that the knees are rotated inwards and liable to be locked back. If you transfer more weight on to the outside of the foot, the knees regain their outward rotation, becoming flexible and slightly bent; this is the correct position. Be careful not to associate the desirable outward rotation of the knees with any idea of turning the feet outwards; this is invariably disastrous. Beginners will experience a distinct ache up the back of the legs.

EXERCISE 4

With knees rotated outwards repeat Exercises 1 and 2.

In the position of readiness with the weight on the outside of the feet, you find that the anterior bony projections of the hips seem to move outwards away from the navel. The moment you bring your weight

[13]

on to the inside of the feet, the hip-bones seem to move inwards towards the navel, and the feeling of poise is lost.

EXERCISE 5

Repeat Exercise 4, associating the outside of the feet, the knees and the hip-bones as parts of a common mechanism.

N.B. It is advisable not to read more than one section containing exercises on the same day, and not more than three in a week.

c. The middle pyramid: the gluteal muscles

In all three inverted pyramids the danger point, where care is needed, coincides with the apex. In the case of the middle pyramid the apex is at the lower end of the spinal column. The danger is intensified here by the absence of any protective bone structure at the front and sides, and also by the sort of life which most people lead. If they are keen on their job and in good physical training, their posture will be unlikely to deteriorate, but if the job forces them to sit or stand over it for hours on end, they will almost certainly lack the energy needed to keep the vertebrae of the spine properly erect. As a result the back will tend to become hollower, with the behind protruding and the abdomen sagging forwards and downwards. All this sets up new disturbances, for when something goes wrong at one weak spot, there is certain to be trouble elsewhere. Not surprisingly it will be at the apex of the top pyramid, where the neck muscles have to support an extremely heavy head.

The muscles governing the vertebrae of the spine and neck cannot be made to work efficiently unless the much more powerful group of muscles controlling the movement of the pelvis is properly employed. Of this group the gluteal muscles are the most important, and the only ones which need to be considered. Extending over nearly the whole of the buttocks, they are the strongest, coarsest and heaviest muscles in the body. In a standing position with the weight on the heels, or with the knees locked back, they will be comparatively relaxed, but in moving into a position of readiness these muscles perceptibly tighten (Fig. 3).

In the following exercises it is by no means enough simply to 'tuck your behind in'. You must be aware of the muscles in that region contracting and of the pelvis being pulled downwards in the back and

[14]

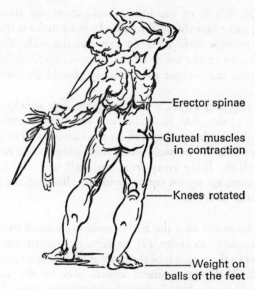

Erector spinae

Gluteal muscles
in contraction

Knees rotated

Weight on
balls of the feet

FIG. 3. THE GLUTEAL MUSCLES IN CONTRACTION

upwards in front. Only then will you experience the sensation of the spine and neck seeming to grow longer. The process might be compared to the act of pulling on a rope to hoist a flag or sail.

Except when you have been told expressly, or by implication, to do otherwise, the heels must remain in contact with the floor. Almost all beginners are inclined to go up on tiptoe when singing. If this is allowed to become a habit, it may easily be disastrous. The weight has to be on the balls of the feet, but the heels must stay on the ground.

Exercises 6 to 18 must be done in reasonable footwear. Women should wear flattish heels, or continue to take off their shoes when practising.

EXERCISE 6

i. With the lower back hugging the floor, lie with knees bent and pointed upwards. Keeping the back in this position, slowly straighten the knees so as to bring the legs into a nearly extended horizontal position. This is a preliminary exercise before tackling ii.

ii. Lean against a wall with the feet some eighteen inches out from

c

[15]

the wall. The whole of the lower back, from the shoulder blades downwards, must hug the wall so closely as to make it impossible for anybody to insert a hand between you and the wall. The feeling of growing a hump in the small of the back is most helpful. Throughout the exercise the weight of the body should be on the balls of the feet.

Keep the hugging position and bring the feet slowly towards the wall. In this way the spine, head and neck will seem to extend upwards, and there will be an increasing pull on the buttocks. When the feet are as near as possible to the wall while remaining in the same hugging position, push the body away from the wall with the hands; in the same movement go up on tiptoe, without allowing the spine to sag or the buttocks to relax.

It should be noted that the body position induced in this exercise, as also in Exercise 10 (page 18), is similar, not to the position of readiness, but to the position of the body in the act of singing. A notable characteristic is the pronounced contraction of the buttocks. No attempt should be made to induce this condition except in the course of the exercises.

EXERCISE 7

i. With your weight on the balls of the feet, place the hands on slightly bent knees. Lean right over so that the head is on a level with the knees. Come slowly into a position as upright as possible, with the feeling that you are pulling the hips away from the knees, and the ears away from the shoulders. This is a preliminary exercise before tackling ii.

ii. From a standing position swing over forward so that both hands touch or nearly touch the ground. Make sure that your weight is still on the balls of the feet and that the knees are not locked back, as in the ordinary exercise of touching the toes, but slightly bent. If you are doing this right, you will feel you are going to topple forward at any moment. Prevent this happening by an extraordinary contraction of the gluteal muscles. Come slowly into an upright position, as if you were unrolling the spine from the lowest vertebra up to the neck. Feel that the unrolling sensation goes right through the neck and out at the crown of the head. The exercise should make you feel very like a primitive man.

[16]

EXERCISE 8

i. With hands on ribs, and keeping the chest perfectly still, swing the pelvis from side to side like the pendulum of a grandfather clock.

ii. With hands on the pelvis, which remains still, swing the chest from side to side. Do both exercises in a dignified smooth rhythm. The secret is to feel that, by a contraction of the gluteal muscles, you lift the chest up and away from the pelvis, so that each can swing independently of the other.

iii. Standing erect, draw up the left knee, and clasp the hands round the left shin. Hop on the ball of the foot. Repeat on the other foot.

d. The middle pyramid: the rectus abdominis

The middle pyramid is supported only by a scaffolding of bones running up the back. The efficiency of this scaffolding depends on a correct stance and sufficient contraction of the buttocks to bring about a further muscular contraction along the abdominal wall. The muscle concerned, the rectus abdominis, extends the full length of the abdomen from the breast-bone down to the pelvis. Looking like a broad strap, it is easily distinguishable on the torso of athletic males.

It is perfectly easy to contract the upper part of the rectus abdominis with the gluteal muscles relaxed. This is far too often practised by students with the idea of supporting the tone; they are encouraged to do so by the common instruction to 'pull your tummy in'. Any such conscious contraction of the upper part of the rectus is disastrous. The act of singing demands a conscious contraction of the gluteal muscles only; this brings about a moderate contraction of the rectus abdominis, but it is an incidental result which must on no account be directly induced.

EXERCISE 9

i. Lie on your back with the feet under a heavy piece of furniture. With the hands at the sides, keeping the neck and head in line with the body and the legs flat, lift the trunk into a sitting posture. Return to the starting position, making each movement as slow as possible.

ii. Do the same thing with the hands clasped behind the head and elbows well back.

iii. Lying face downwards with hands on the buttocks, lift the trunk slowly up and down.

iv. Do the same thing with hands clasped behind the head.

[17]

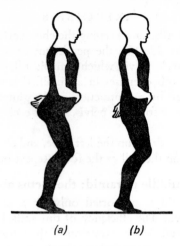

(a)   (b)

FIG. 4. EXERCISE 10

EXERCISE 10

Stand erect with the feet straight, the knees just apart and bent slightly so as to be over the toes, and still with the same outward tendency. Keep the heels on the ground, but feel as if you are ready to jump. Put one hand on the stomach and the other hand on your behind. Hollow the back and stick your behind up in the air as if you were an old barnyard fowl; the pelvis is now tilted in precisely the wrong direction, and there is no sensation of outward thrust in the front hip bones and knees. You are still perhaps on the balls of the feet, but the weight inevitably tends inwards on to the big toe (Fig. 4(a)).

By a vigorous contraction of the gluteal muscles tilt the pelvis in the opposite direction, keeping the knees bent and completely still. Nothing whatever should move above or below the pelvis. Feel that you have a sizeable tail which you are pulling down between the legs, in order to powder your nose with the tuft at the end of it. With the pelvis tilted into this new position the weight is properly distributed. The knees regain their outward thrust, and the front hip-bones point upwards and outwards. Your behind on the other hand will have descended, the buttocks being close together (Fig. 4(b)). In this position the lower section of the rectus is so contracted that the part

[18]

between the navel and the pubic bone seems to be lifted up and forward. There is also a moderate contraction of the upper sections of the rectus, resulting in an obvious stiffening and a slight retraction of the abdominal wall. The same condition is present in the act of launching a note.

Tilt back into the wrong position, and repeat. Do the exercise comparatively vigorously, but be careful to go gently back into the wrong position to avoid risk of strain.

Having tackled Exercise 10, repeat Exercises 6, 7 and 9, with particular awareness of the contraction of the rectus abdominis.

e. The top pyramid

Bad singers can be divided into two groups. In the first group are those who look forward eagerly to their top notes, regarding the rest of the aria as so much makeweight. They approach each pinnacle with the carefree enthusiasm of a lover home from distant lands. Their eyes light up, and they toss the head back so as to bring the crown well behind the imaginary continuation of the spine. Such ecstatic behaviour is most dangerous. A skilled tenor may stretch his neck up and back, but the crown of the head will remain the upper extremity of the body, though not necessarily its highest point. In the case of the less experienced tenor, you need only remember the analogy of the crooked hose-pipe on page 12, to understand why his climactic note too often emerges as a sonorous bleat.

The other group look upon high notes as the inevitable but necessary curse of music. Listening and watching them, one can sense the danger ahead from a distance of at least a line and a half. As they approach the precipice, their heads go into their necks, and their necks into their bodies. Everything shortens except for their eyes which seem to stand out as if on stalks. Both groups come to grief for precisely the same reason; they are shortening instead of lengthening. Most of us at some time have had affinities with one group or the other; and not surprisingly considering the mixture of emotion and calculated skill which are needed in good voice production.

In eliminating a wrong condition, the first thing to establish is that the crown of the head remains the topmost point; it must feel that it is being pulled up by an elastic cord attached to a hook on the ceiling.

[19]

The eyes may seem to be directed downwards, but this sensation soon disappears. The ears must be as far away from the shoulders as possible. Ladies can imagine themselves wearing very long earrings which they must keep from trailing over their shoulders. It is also helpful to remember your sensations when in swimming you have to keep the head above water.

But with all this emphasis on length, the spine must never become a ramrod. Like a highly flexible sword which never loses its resilience, each part of the body has to be sensitive and responsive to every other part. The slightest improvement in the condition of the neck will make the condition of the lower spine that much better and more secure. The body is a unity. The more this conception is established, the more efficiently the body will behave, not only in singing, but in the innumerable activities of daily life.

By practising Exercises 1 to 10 the reader can in a short time be confident of overcoming the difficulties relating to the apices of the two lower inverted pyramids, i.e. the feet and the lumbar vertebrae. The neck is not nearly so amenable to discipline. You may pull it upwards so as to make it feel like a piece of distended toffee, or you may stretch it up in the same way as you put a can on a high shelf, but you will not be using it correctly because neither toffee nor cans are analogous to necks. Each vertebra has to be lifted and supported by muscles, and these must be thought of as living entities, each one prepared to work at its highest potential. Maybe it will help if you remember that inside the neck is the vocal instrument—the larynx which contains the vocal cords, and the throat which amplifies their sound—and that the instrument must be treated right, and not allowed to warp. Remember this when you come to the next section. Remember also that when teachers, writers and colleagues talk about muscular relaxation, what they really mean is a balance of muscular tensions—a tensional equipoise. One can do no work whatever with a relaxed muscle.

EXERCISE 11

i. Taking care to keep a long neck, bring the head slowly forward and back as far as it will go in a smooth rhythm. Stop where it feels comfortable. This will be the correct position with the crown at the highest point of the body.

ii. Keeping the neck long and still, turn the head slowly from left to right as far as it will go. Do this five times, stopping where it feels comfortable; the head will now be in the correct position with the crown at the highest point, and the eyes facing forward.

EXERCISE 12

In an erect posture, with fingers interlaced and elbows wide:

i. Place the hands on the crown of the head. Press the head upwards against a downward pressure of the hands.

ii. Clasp the hands behind the back of the head. Press the head backwards, but prevent it moving by a counter-pressure forwards from the hands.

EXERCISE 13

Close the eyes and imagine that you are possessed of a long nose terminating in a pencil. On an imaginary board eight inches or so in front of your face, write your name and date of birth. This exercise is an admirable training for the carriage of the head and neck. It is also claimed to be effective in relieving general fatigue and strained eyes.

f. Ends and means

The rewards of good posture are enormous, but in early stages at any rate you will find the position of readiness exceedingly tiring. So much so that the body revolts from remaining in it for longer than is absolutely necessary. An artist should recognize this and take every opportunity of relaxing as completely as circumstances permit. 'Never stand when you can sit' is an excellent rule. Even so a good sitting posture is by no means easy to maintain over an extended period.

EXERCISE 14

Sitting: Sit in an ordinary straight chair in a relaxed attitude; now bring the front hip-bones away from the navel, and you will find yourself sitting on the two buttocks with the legs tending to go apart. This is the correct way to sit, no matter how the legs are arranged.

The remaining exercises in this section show how best to carry out some of the ordinary activities of daily life. You will of course be far too occupied physically and mentally to keep more than an occasional eye on your movements, but you can cultivate a sort of watchful second self. All good actors do this, thereby ensuring that, however uninspired their performance becomes as a result of nightly repetition, they never fall below a respectable standard of technical accomplishment.

EXERCISE 15

Rising from a chair: Have the left leg slightly in front of the right, and keep a strong sense of an outward rotation of the knees. Tell yourself that the small of the back is pushing against the chair, that the lower part of the abdomen is lifted up and forward, and that the head and neck are being pulled up to the ceiling by an elastic cord. With no further instructions to yourself, swing your weight over on to the left knee. You should now find yourself standing up. Repeat with the right foot forward.

If in the preceding exercise your first attempts were unsuccessful, it will have been due to lack of confidence and concentrated imagination. No doubt you were anxious to carry out instructions; you were even more anxious to get up from the chair, although such a common-or-garden act could not have the slightest significance. It is an all too human characteristic. We look on success in terms of concrete accomplishment, and are none too particular about the means whereby it is achieved. Ball games provide constant evidence of this. In all of them it is essential to keep the eye on the ball, yet you will have found by experience how peculiarly and surprisingly difficult it is to do just that. The underlying reason is invariably the same. Your real desire was not to make sure that the ball was met fair and square by the club, racquet or bat, but to watch it speeding to the boundary, or landing on a distant green. In other words you were out to gain your end, irrespective of how you achieved it. This is not the way to win championships. You can go on imitating Caruso's top notes till the cows come home, but any improvement will be purely temporary until you discover the means whereby he caused them to materialize.

EXERCISE 16

Sitting down: This is simply the reverse of Exercise 15. The spine, head and neck must remain long, and again it is important to let the knees go away from each other.

[22]

EXERCISE 17

Walking: With the same instructions to yourself as in Exercise 15, rise from the chair and, as part of the same movement, walk across the room. Imagine the body being pulled forward by a cord attached to the breastbone. The feet should point straight ahead, and be far enough apart to prevent the knee-bones touching. If you are doing it right, the legs and pelvis seem to be actually in front of the upper part of the body. You should also feel that you can stop, start again, or reverse direction without having to make any intermediate adjustment.

EXERCISE 18

i. Going upstairs: Giving yourself the same instructions as in Exercise 17, put the right foot on the bottom stair. Swing your weight on to the right knee, and in the same rhythm bring the left foot on to the next stair. Continue until you reach the top. Practise stopping, starting and reversing en route.

ii. Going downstairs: Give yourself the same instructions as in Exercise 17. Feel that the head and body are attached to the ceiling by elastic. Your legs are descending the staircase, but the head and body seem to be gliding horizontally forward.

Before doing these, and indeed many other exercises in the book, make someone press his hand gently but firmly downward against the crown of your head. The unfamiliar weight constitutes a challenge to all the anti-gravity muscles to exert an antagonistic upward pressure. But once again I must warn you not to go up on tiptoe. The importance of keeping the heels on the floor will be made more evident in later chapters.

In embarking on Chapter 3, do not imagine that you have finished with Chapter 2. The habits of a lifetime are not so easily overcome. Do the exercises which you find most effective, while waiting for the bath, washing-up, walking to work, standing in a queue or sitting in the bus. If people stare at you, don't bother. For all you know, they may themselves be on their way to or from a singing lesson, and applauding and secretly envying your artistic integrity.

𝟛

THE INSTRUMENT *

There can hardly be any small child who has not possessed a hollow rubber animal with a valve in some part of its anatomy. When squeezed the air inside presses against the valve and a squeak results. This is the principle underlying the tone production of nearly all woodwind and brass instruments. Like them, the voice is a wind instrument and consists of three components: the air compressor; the vibrator; and the resonator.

1. The air compressor consists of the abdominal muscles, which lift the diaphragm so as to squeeze the bottom of the inflated lungs, as the bottom of an inflated paper bag is squeezed in the act of popping it. In wind instruments, like the clarinet or oboe, the player blows directly against the reed, and to a greater or less extent varies the pressure of his breath according to the pitch of the note. A good singer works very differently. He does not consciously vary the breath pressure at all. As a result of using his body in a particular way, he can make the pressure already built up inside the chest act as a sort of power point from which he can draw whatever degree of breath pressure he may need at any particular moment. Changes in tone quality and dynamics are a matter mainly of subconscious adjustment, similar to those which trumpet players make in the approximation of their lips. They are a response to an emotional demand. Admittedly the singer has certain technical means of consciously assisting these adjustments, but they do not invalidate the basic principle that variations of breath pressure, tone quality and dynamics are almost entirely subconscious.

2. The vibrator consists of two flexible shelves protruding from the inner walls of the larynx. The edges of these two shelves, which are called the vocal cords (see Fig. 10, page 43), can be widely separated

* All the principal points referred to in this chapter are discussed in detail later on.

in a V-shape, or brought into close approximation. In the latter position, they resemble the double reed of an oboe, and can be made to vibrate merely by a subconscious command. Both the throat resonator and the vocal cords possess almost miraculous powers of adjustment, so that together they can produce any note within the two octaves which constitute the range of the average singing voice.

In other wind instruments the vibrating reed can do no more than cause an atmospheric disturbance to which the resonating tube responds by sounding a pitched note. This is due partly to the hardness of the instrumental resonator compared to the relative softness of the throat cavity, but more particularly to the inherent vitality and elasticity of the vocal cords. A clarinet reed vibrates as a result of a particular degree of breath pressure which varies according to the pitch and volume of the note. The player's compression is the only active element, the vibrating reed and the resonating tube being necessarily passive. But the human reeds, i.e. the vocal cords, are no mere slivers of split cane; they are part of a highly complicated, incredibly sensitive and responsive organ. If the singer wishes to attack a particular pitched note, he has only to issue the relevant mental command, whereupon the vocal cords will vary their length, thickness and tension, and start vibrating at any given moment. Admittedly there is at present no conclusive proof that the vocal cords can be made to start vibrating of themselves and independently of breath compression, but there is considerable evidence to suggest that this is what happens in good production. From the practical singer's point of view it is an invaluable conception, which he will be wise to adopt. He will thereby deprive himself of any excuse for a rough untidy start, or for beginning a note flat. Like the violinist who with a finger of his left hand makes a string vibrate before bringing the bow down on it, the singer animates his vocal cords by a mental command immediately before allowing the breath pressure, which he has already built up, to come in contact with them. Naturally the voice materializes only when puffs of breath, transmitted through the vocal cords, have passed through a resonating cavity and out of the mouth or nose.

However willing we are to accept the theory of the spontaneous vibration of the vocal cords, it is difficult to reconcile the idea of consciously building up breath compression against already vibrating vocal cords with the singer's ability to prevent breath from escaping through them; in other words how does he manage in these conditions to start his pitched note when and as he likes? An interesting theory which might account for this was developed many years ago by the great English baritone, Sir Charles Santley. Santley, who had been a pupil of Garcia, suggested that the vocal cords in vibration become thinner and sharper-edged, while their undersides form two conical bulges; and that these bulges constitute a valve which can release a thin blast of air on to the vibrating sections of the cords. Thus the vocal cords need never be overloaded with breath; moreover, like a car engine turning over in neutral or with the clutch pedal depressed, they could vibrate at any speed before a note was launched, and the attack would be smooth and firm on any pitch and at any dynamic. Since nothing whatever can be felt at the cords or anywhere in the larynx, it hardly matters to the singer whether this theory has any foundation or is just a load of rubbish—and at the present day there is no means of knowing which it is. But the very existence of such a theory proves that Santley must have used it as part of his technique and that from it came that wonderful velvety tone which right to the end of his life was so marked a feature of his singing. It was a technique, according to Neville Cardus, which would nowadays render him not only incomparable but unique.

By launching a note the singer seems to squirt the tone into the head much as a small boy squirts another by almost completely blocking the mouth of a running tap with his thumb. The greatest bar to progress is the usual notion that voice is something that must be projected towards the audience. So long as the mouth is open, the voice emits itself. The tone may leave much to be desired; it may be throaty, nasal or swallowed, but such as it is, it needs no auxiliary boost, and students are warned that the maximum degree of strain is imposed upon the larynx if they make any attempt to help the process of emission.

3. The singer's resonator actually extends over the whole body, but the main resonating tube is the throat or pharynx. From a practical point of view the ceiling of the throat is the soft palate, and the floor the larynx; both soft palate and larynx can be raised or lowered so as to vary the overall length of the throat. The front wall is formed by the back of the tongue root, which can be brought forward or backward as the singer desires. These adjustments enable him to make the throat

a responsive resonator of any sound coming off the vocal cords, but they are subconscious adjustments; if the reader tries consciously to manipulate the soft palate, larynx or back of the tongue, the consequences will be disastrous.

Behind and in the neighbourhood of the nose there is a group of cavities which are of great importance as upper resonators, but which cannot be consciously controlled. The singer can only provide the best possible conditions for them to realize their own individual glory, and then allow the emotions to colour his tone. This means in effect that he must make the tongue and soft palate as responsive as possible, and avoid any attempt to push the tone forward into the mouth, as many students are taught to do.

Because the superior flexibility of the vocal cords enables them to create pitched notes, the resonator possesses a further characteristic which is unique among wind instruments. This is its ability to form vowel sounds. The resonator of ordinary wind instruments actually creates the pitched notes and could not produce vowels at the same time; but with the mouth open it is impossible to sing, speak or whisper without uttering a vowel of some sort. The vowel is formed inside the mouth, and varies according to the position of the tongue, the soft palate and the lips, but the sound must always seem to spring to life simultaneously with the vocal tone in the apex of the chest. There should be no kind of sensation either in the throat cavity or in the mouth. Sensations in good singing occur below the larynx and above the cheeks; between these points is a no-man's-land.

Many students rightly associate vowel and note as a unity, but since the identifiable vowel is formed apparently in the mouth, they tend to look upon the mouth as the chief resonating cavity. This is something which must be corrected at the earliest possible moment. As an articulator of vowels and an articulator and resonator of consonants, the mouth is an extremely important part of the voice, but with regard to musical tone it is little more than a funnel for conveying sounds from throat to lips. In other words the beginner, forgetting about the mouth cavity and the subsidiary resonators, must concentrate on making the larynx a perfect begetter of sound waves, and the throat a resonator and transmitter appropriate to the vowel and note of his choice.

Figs. 5(a) and (b) show the locality of the three components of the

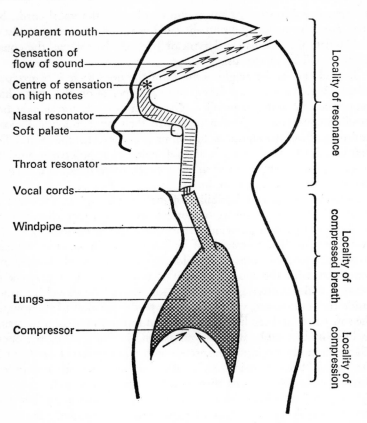

FIG. 5(a). THE VOCAL INSTRUMENT: APPARENT DIRECTION OF VOICE ON HIGH NOTES

voice. Below the soft palate the two diagrams are precisely similar and give an accurate impression of the functioning of the vocal instrument. The jaw has been omitted in order to show that, while the mouth is the actual outlet for the voice, it is not a resonator of vowel tone; and it is with vowel tone that the beginner will be at present solely concerned. Above the soft palate resonance occurs and can be felt all over the skull, but in aiming for good production the singer localizes his sensations of tone either at the bridge of the nose on high notes or above the temple on low notes. The tone should be felt as

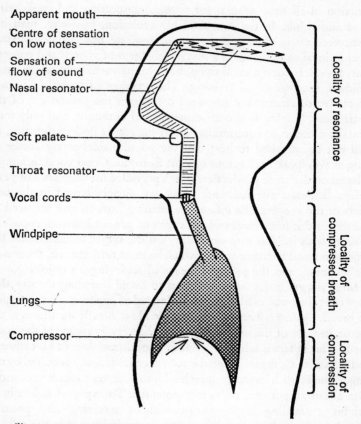

Apparent mouth

Centre of sensation on low notes

Sensation of flow of sound

Nasal resonator

Soft palate

Throat resonator

Vocal cords

Windpipe

Lungs

Compressor

Locality of resonance

Locality of compressed breath

Locality of compression

FIG. 5(*b*). THE VOCAL INSTRUMENT: APPARENT DIRECTION OF VOICE ON LOW NOTES

coming not out of the mouth, but out of a place a little behind the crown of the head. Note that these are not scientific assertions but a description in words and diagrams of a good singer's subjective sensations.

In addition to the three mechanisms common to all wind instruments, the voice contains a further mechanism which, if not unique, remains more or less undeveloped in any animal species and is not possessed by any musical instrument. This is the articulator, which consists of the mouth cavity, tongue, palate, lips and teeth. The primary function of all these parts is for tasting, masticating and swallowing food and drink. In the course of his evolution, however, man has discovered a way of using them to communicate, not merely by means of emotional sounds, but in a precise amalgam of vowels and consonants. Speech is not a natural thing, but a human artifice in which small children need years of training. The making of wordless sounds expressive of elementary emotions constitutes the natural use of the instrument. Singing is also an expression of emotions, and only incidentally a means of communication. If the reader understands this, he will not be surprised to hear that the popular catchpenny advice to 'sing as you speak' will get no support from me. Good vocal technique is based on the voice production which prevailed for thousands of years before language evolved, and which we ourselves used in the first years of life as speechless infants. In learning how to sing we need to rediscover this lost voice, and to adapt our present habits of speech to consort with it. This imposes a duty on the singer to understand the type of musical instrument into which he must turn himself, the reason for so doing, and the practical means of achieving his objective.

Most singers today are so anxious to avoid sounding throaty that they treat their voices like recorders. Instead of applying a compression of breath against vibrating reeds, they blow breath up through the throat and out of the mouth, ignoring the very existence of the vocal cords. This in fact is what the average Englishman does in his ordinary conversation. Compared with the 100 per cent efficiency required by the singer, the English larynx in speech seldom achieves a standard of more than about 20 per cent of its true potential. To expect it suddenly to exhibit a startling improvement without receiving any positive directions from the mind, is not merely optimistic; it is the wildest idiocy.

So far from even attempting to work along these lines, the method of voice training in most institutions in this country stands nature on her head. It persistently and wantonly deprives the voice of all richness and depth, and produces a shallowness of speech tone which exhausts the muscular system of the larynx in the shortest possible time. It is governed not by what is natural, but by what is considered to be genteel; it is the result of the English habit of emotional repression and tonal inertia, a relic of the Victorian belief that a naturally healthy and robust speech tone is somehow boorish and ill-mannered. The foreign pupil begins his voice lessons with a long start over his English colleague because he already articulates at the top of the chest. The English-speaking student must work much harder, not only during his practice hours, but at all times, not only to ensure correct vocalization, but to restore the tone of his laryngeal muscles.

To 'sing as you speak' is in fact just as idiotic as to suggest that you can learn ballet dancing by going for long walks!

4

THE COMPRESSOR AND
THE VIBRATOR

Wherever space is, there also is air; and wherever air is, there also is air pressure. It is a law of nature that the pressure of air inside a cavity is equal to the pressure of the outside atmosphere. A bicycle pump for instance is a hollow cylinder inside which a constant level of air pressure has to be maintained. By stopping up the hole and simultaneously decreasing the size of the container by pushing the handle inwards, you can build up an abnormal degree of air pressure inside the pump. Very much the same thing happens in singing. The chest is expanded, the hole at the top is blocked, and then the bottom of the chest is pushed upwards, so that an abnormal pressure of breath is built up inside the chest cavity. But whereas in a bicycle pump expansion is exclusively in a lengthwise direction, chest expansion is both sideways and lengthwise; in other words it is a combination of pump and fire bellows, as will be shown in the following sections.

a. The diaphragm

The trunk of the body may be compared to a cupboard, with a shelf dividing it into equal sections.

The lower section, called the abdomen, consists of the stomach, liver, gall bladder, spleen and so forth, together with yards of intestine. You will be relieved to hear that for the purposes of singing you will not need to study the lower chamber or its contents.

The upper section, the thorax or chest, extends from the collar-bone down to the bottom of the breast-bone. Although it can be contracted and expanded, the chest is not, like the bicycle pump, a box full of air, but a cavity containing the lungs. Each lung consists of an immense number of elastic air-sacs, somewhat similar to minute balloons, which vary in size according to the intake of air.

Separating the chest from the abdomen, and forming a partition

[32]

between them, is the diaphragm. This organ initiates, and to a great extent governs, the process of breathing. Its appearance is commonly compared to a dome, notwithstanding that such a description suggests enormous blocks of masonry. Actually the diaphragm resembles, both in appearance and flexibility, a thin shallow umbrella-shaped tent. Stretching clean across the body, it literally divides the body into nearly equal halves. The upper side is attached to the pleurae, the membranous envelopes containing the lungs; the underside is attached to the liver, and the peripheral edge to the ribs, breast-bone and spine; in this way the diaphragm forms the floor of the chest and the roof of the abdomen. Many singers think of the diaphragm as a single sheet of muscle, but this is not so. The centre is composed of limp fibrous tissue and cannot be contracted. Only the outside edge is muscular; this part, contracting on itself, produces a forward and downward pull which causes the centre to be flattened and lowered (Fig. 6 and Fig. 11).

As a result of the diaphragm's downward movement the size of the chest is increased, so that a vacuum inside the cavity is formed. This causes the air sacs of the lungs to be sucked outward towards the walls of the chest, and expanded so as to draw air into the newly created space (Fig. 6(*a*)). At the end of its contraction the diaphragm, reacting to an automatic impulse, relaxes, while the lung tissue, being no longer expanded because of the downward pull of the diaphragm, shrinks of its own elasticity to its natural dimensions. Since the upper side of the diaphragm is attached to the pleurae, the lung shrinkage causes the diaphragm to be pulled upwards into a domelike shape. Simultaneously a specific quantity of air is, under normal circumstances of rhythmical breathing, expelled from the lungs in order to keep the air pressure at a constant level (Fig. 6(*b*)).

The working of the lungs is a completely automatic process, the intake and expulsion of air being due simply to variations in the size of the chest cavity. If your previous ideas about inhalation have been confined to the single conception that you should breathe through the nose, I need only say that there is no sniffing apparatus which, by sucking in breath, pushes the diaphragm down and the ribs outward. It may seem so because it is all too easy to make an impressive noise at the top of the breathing tube, whereas the movement of the diaphragm is only noticeable in such exceptional circumstances as the following exercise:

[33]

EXERCISE 19

Sitting or standing in a relaxed posture, sniff inwards violently, as if you have a cold and wish to clear the nasal passages. The resulting diaphragmatic contraction manifests itself by a visible swelling immediately under the breast-bone. Now blow violently, as if blowing out candles on a birthday cake; this leaves you with a somewhat empty feeling, as a result of the diaphragm's sudden relaxation and the upward pressure of the abdominal muscles.

When relaxed, the act of inhalation causes a visible bulge from the breast-bone downwards as far as the navel. The reason for this will be obvious if the abdomen is compared to a hamper with a soft lid into which you are packing a quantity of china. Each article will be separately cushioned by paper and straw, and optimistically you fill the case to overflowing. If the sides of the hamper are sufficiently flabby to allow it to bulge when you close it, all will be well; but if they are unyielding, you may find yourself short of tea-cups. The abdomen similarly contains a number of fragile organs protected by layers of fat and covered by the diaphragm, which contracts on its outer edge so as to pull its central part forwards and downwards. Fortunately the skin is sufficiently elastic to bulge outwards and so compensate for the inevitable congestion. The resulting expansion is evident all round the body between breast-bone and navel, but should under no circumstances extend any lower than the navel.

The question in the minds probably of many readers at this moment is easily answered. When singing one always breathes through the mouth, never through the nose, and never through nose and mouth simultaneously. A very small amount of field-observation will provide overwhelming evidence that for speech or song the mouth is the only practical orifice for inhalation. If you watch two sopranos talking about a third one, you will notice that both do all they can to prevent the other getting a word in; they have to take breath extremely fast in consequence, and if they breathed through the nose, their conversation would be punctuated with colossal sniffs and snorts. This might be a source of merriment to the third soprano, but would not otherwise be a good thing. A lot of nonsense has been talked and written about the awful dangers of breathing through the mouth, but except as

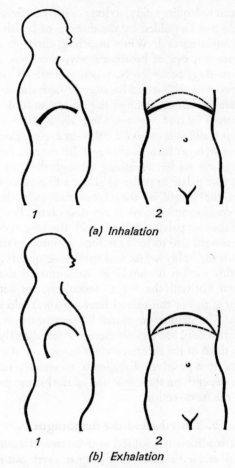

(a) Inhalation

(b) Exhalation

FIG. 6. THE DIAPHRAGM

regards variations in temperature these dangers are exaggerated. The one thing to remember is, that whereas the outside air on its passage through the nasal cavities is warmed and filtered clean before reaching the tonsils, throat and larynx, no such safeguard exists when breathing through the mouth. Consequently it is advisable, when going out of doors in chilly weather, to keep the mouth closed for a minute or two.

After that you can talk quite safely, so long as it is not freezing. In other circumstances do not be guided by the dictates of health-faddists, but by what seems most natural. When breathing through the mouth—assuming you are not out of breath already, you look as if you are about to speak or sing; accordingly, when you are about to speak or sing, do the appropriate thing and breathe through the mouth. On the other hand, when breathing through the nose, you look as if you are wrapped in thought or ready to stride into the night.

(At this stage it is difficult to give a coherent explanation why it is so essential for the singer to breathe through the mouth. For the benefit of the knowledgeable reader, breathing through the nose involves the lowering of the soft palate in order to allow a free passage for breath. This diminishes the length of the throat and seriously hinders its potential for becoming an effective resonating cavity. Furthermore the low position of the soft palate tends to block the space connecting the throat with the mouth and to send the tone up into the nasal passages. The result is an undesirably white and nasal tone quality.)

In studying this section it should be remembered that we are at present concerned, not with the singer's technique, but with the working of the diaphragm. For this reason Exercise 19 should be done in a relaxed position. The diaphragm under all circumstances initiates the movement of inhalation, but its contraction is not directly responsible for more than a third of the increased chest expansion of a good singer who is preparing, in a position of readiness, to attack a note. The real art of inhalation depends on the expansion of the lower ribs which will be described in the next section.

b. The ribs and the diaphragm

The position of readiness is adopted as a matter of course by good singers and by all trained athletes preparing to carry out a skilled act. Automatically the chest is lifted, the ribs expanded and the whole routine of breathing changed fundamentally from the simple diaphragmatic process described in the preceding section.

It has been shown that only the peripheral edge of the diaphragm is capable of contracting. This part is attached to the lower ribs in such a way that any contraction of the diaphragm causes them to be pulled upwards and outwards, like the ribs of an umbrella when held upright and in process of being opened. Their degree of mobility depends to a great extent on the singer's posture. In a relaxed sitting position the ribs move comparatively little, whereas in a position of readiness, in which the contraction of the gluteal muscles automatically produces a simultaneous contraction of the rectus abdominis, they have a very considerable field of movement. In fact there are two successive stages of inhalation, although in practice they seem to merge into one. In the first stage the centre of the diaphragm is pulled downwards and forwards, so as to produce a slight bulge of the upper abdominal wall. The diaphragm then reaches a point where, owing to the contraction of the abdominal muscles, it comes up against an unyielding barrier of viscera. Any further expansion downwards being now impossible, a second movement is initiated in which the edge of the diaphragm, continuing to contract on itself, pulls the lower ribs upwards and outwards. This causes a slight retraction of the upper abdominal wall. The two stages of inhalation follow one another so smoothly and imperceptibly that the singer himself is unaware of more than a single combined movement of ribs and diaphragm. On no account must he attempt consciously to induce the bulge and subsequent retraction of the abdominal wall.

EXERCISE 20

Stand with one leg forward and knees slightly bent. Lean over from the waist with the neck and head in alignment with the spinal column, hands stretched out in front of you with palms upward. Breathe into the back and sides of your waistcoat. The diaphragm will contract, and at the same time you will feel the ribs expanding upwards and outwards.

EXERCISE 21

Stand in the same position. Put the thumbs against the lower ribs a couple of inches away from the spine. This is where you want to feel that inhalation is concentrated. Come slowly into an upright position, breathing all the time in the same way. As you become more erect, you will, to begin with, find it increasingly difficult to maintain the expansion of the ribs.

The act of breathing here described is the so-called diaphragmatic-intercostal method, in which the contraction of the diaphragm is combined with an expansion of the lower ribs. The expansion is only effective in a position of readiness. Fig. 7 shows that, of the twelve pairs of ribs which are connected to the vertebral column and constitute the side walls of the thorax, all except the two lowest pairs, the eleventh and twelfth, are joined by cartilage to the breast-bone. The upper six ribs, which are joined to the breast-bone by separate cartilages, are

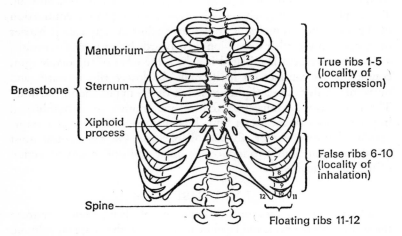

Manubrium
Breastbone { Sternum
Xiphoid process
Spine

True ribs 1-5 (locality of compression)

False ribs 6-10 (locality of inhalation)

Floating ribs 11-12

FIG. 7. THE THORAX

called the true ribs. The remaining seventh, eighth, ninth and tenth pairs, the so-called false ribs, all have the same connecting cartilage, and are considerably more flexible than the upper ribs. The eleventh and twelfth unattached pairs, the so-called floating ribs, are of no importance.

Chest expansion during inhalation must be confined to the lower or false ribs only. The slightest movement of the five upper ribs should be avoided. This can be done only if you draw an imaginary line of demarcation round the ribs on the level of the lower end of the breast-bone and confine all evidence of inhalation to the area below this line. Almost without exception beginners, and women in particular, take in too much breath in a movement which includes a notable expansion of the upper chest. A lifted chest is an essential characteristic of good

[38]

singing, but it is no part of inhalation, which is all that concerns us at
the moment.

Having studied this and the preceding section, the reader will rightly
conclude that in relaxation he inhales downwards like an extending
bicycle pump. In a position of readiness he inhales first downwards
then outwards; that is to say, he behaves first like an extending pump,
and then like an expanding bellows. In practice he need think of himself only as an expanding bellows.

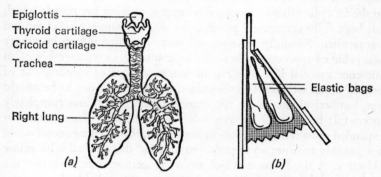

FIG. 8. THE HUMAN BELLOWS AND THE FIRE BELLOWS

Fig. 8 shows the trachea, bronchi and lungs side by side with an
ordinary pair of fire bellows. The two mechanisms are remarkably
similar. The bellows container corresponds to the thorax. Inside the
case are two elastic bags connected to the outside air by a nozzle; these
correspond to the right and left lungs which are joined to the outside
air by the trachea and throat. When the handles of the bellows are
pulled apart, the two bags expand and fill with air; when the handles
are closed, the bags are partially deflated. In the same way the lungs are
dilated and fill with air as soon as any diaphragmatic contraction takes
place. Both the lungs and the bag of the bellows are elastic; like
rubber balloons, though not nearly so violently, they shrink as soon as
the distending force is removed.

In a relaxed position, with the lower ribs not actively involved,
exhalation is a simple process of the expanded lungs contracting of
their own elasticity, expelling a proportionate amount of breath, and
simultaneously drawing the relaxed diaphragm, which is attached to

the pleurae, upwards. In a position of readiness, exhalation is equally automatic, so long as the lower ribs are allowed to move inwards; but if consciously or unconsciously you hold them up and out, the peripheral edge of the diaphragm to which they are attached must perforce remain contracted, and the lung tissue will remain in an expanded condition. In other words you will be unable to speak or sing.

Exhalation is impossible unless you allow the lower ribs to go completely lax. There are at least three reasons why this is difficult. In the first place there is a natural reluctance to relax any muscle which has been fully contracted, particularly when an impressive expansion has resulted. Secondly, whereas not more than one person in twenty is capable of appreciating beautiful tone quality, every member of an audience can tell if a singer is in serious danger of running out of breath. Small wonder if the beginner, in his anxiety not to be caught out, instinctively keeps the ribs expanded. He is of course completely successful; breath will be saved—but since the air pressure inside an expanded chest remains at atmospheric level, the resulting sound could not possibly measure up to good singing, and this after all is his prime objective. A third reason which makes relaxation difficult is that the beginner, rightly associating good posture with upheld ribs, assumes that ribs which are allowed to go lax will cause the spine to sag. In ordinary circumstances this is probably true, but not in the act of controlled exhalation or of good singing. If the spine seems to have an irresistible tendency to sag, try to feel it growing longer as the breath gets shorter. No self-respecting umbrella would be so inefficiently constructed as to allow the pole to collapse the moment you started to close it; in spines this is a regrettably common habit, but something which a little concentration can easily overcome.

In the context of singing or speaking, the diaphragm and the lower ribs should be regarded as a single entity. When the diaphragm is contracted the lower ribs are held up and out; when the diaphragm is relaxed the ribs must be allowed to swing inwards, as if to lift and support the diaphragm like tentpoles. The double pendulum-like movement is not at all easy. The reader has to train his body to assume a posture which is energetic, insecure and unfamiliar, and for the inward movement he has to overcome a curiously strong instinct to continue holding the lower ribs out. If he likes he may associate the outward swing of the ribs with the backward swing of his tennis racquet, which is merely a preparation for hitting the ball correctly. Any such conception can be immensely helpful in convincing the beginner that while both the outward and the inward swings are an integral part of voice production, the inward swing is infinitely more important.

EXERCISE 22

In a position of readiness take a breath, hold it a moment, then let it out on a whispered AH. The diaphragm, which on the inhalation was tough and resilient just under the breast-bone, will rise upward and inward; simultaneously the lower ribs seem to swing inward and upward. The spine remains long, and the abdomen feels satisfactorily svelte.

EXERCISE 23

Repeat Exercise 19 (page 34) in a position of readiness. Immediately after blowing, feel the lower ribs swinging back outwards. The sensation is as if they were bellows handles attached to springs, which pulled them outwards as soon as the inward pressure is relaxed.

Exercises in which one takes a breath, holds it for ten seconds or so and finally lets it out very slowly may be all right for underwater swimmers, but are of no practical help to singers.

c. The vocal cords

In Chapter 3 it was shown that voices, like nearly all wind instruments, possess a vibrating mechanism which transforms compressed breath into sound waves. The mechanism is in the larynx, which is connected to the lungs by the windpipe or trachea (Fig. 8). The windpipe is a hollow tube about five inches long and an inch wide, flexible in itself, but held firm by a series of cartilaginous rings. Surmounting the windpipe is the larynx. Here and only here is vocal tone created. Admittedly there have been people who, after their larynxes had been excised, were still able to talk in a more or less ordinary way, and even to sing; but these phenomena provide no conclusive evidence of the existence of any subsidiary vibratory mechanism.

The larynx is a hollow framework like a box without lid or bottom.

[41]

It consists of two cartilages one above the other. The lower smaller one, the cricoid, is generally said to resemble a signet ring with the seal at the back. Above it is the thyroid cartilage, popularly known as the Adam's apple, and visible in the neck of the recently adult male, particularly if he has a deep voice (Fig. 9; Fig. 10(*a*)).

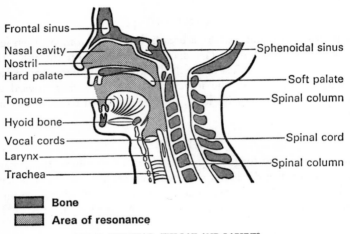

Frontal sinus

Nasal cavity
Nostril
Hard palate

Tongue

Hyoid bone

Vocal cords

Larynx

Trachea

Sphenoidal sinus

Soft palate

Spinal column

Spinal cord

Spinal column

Bone

Area of resonance

FIG. 9. THE HEAD, THROAT AND LARYNX

Half-way up the interior side wall of the thyroid cartilage are two shelves of muscular tissue, facing each other and projecting inwards. On the inside edge of each shelf is a white smooth ligament. These two ligaments are the vocal cords. In a man they are roughly half an inch long, and rather shorter in a woman or child. In appearance they resemble the ligament which connects the under surface of the tongue to the floor of the mouth. The position and functioning of the vocal cords can be illustrated by holding a hand in front of the chin, the palm facing you and the knuckles bent into a right angle so that the finger-tips are close to the neck. The part of the palm from the wrist to the knuckles may be taken to represent the front section of the lower half of the thyroid cartilage, the wrist the cricoid cartilage, and the forearm the windpipe. The thumb and the first and second fingers are held together as a unity, likewise the third and fourth fingers; the second and third fingers are free either to be drawn apart so as to create a

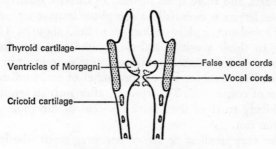

Thyroid cartilage
Ventricles of Morgagni
Cricoid cartilage
False vocal cords
Vocal cords

*(a) The larynx with the front of the
cartilages removed*

(1) *(2)*

Sound waves
entering throat

Breath pressure

(b) The vocal cords seen from above
(1) In the act of inhalation
(2) In the act of vibrating

*(c) The vocal cords in lateral
cross-section showing their
vibratory swing*

FIG. 10. THE VOCAL CORDS

V-shaped gap, or else to be brought together so as to leave only a
crack between their inside edges. These edges may be compared with
the vocal cords which are joined at the front of the larynx, and which
can be drawn apart or brought close together; in the latter position they
are said to be adducted. The movement is effected by muscles which
rotate the arytenoid cartilages, to which the cords are attached at their
posterior end. The crack between the vocal cords is called the glottis;
this important word must not be confused with the epiglottis, the name
for the upper part of the thyroid cartilage. Except for examinations
there is no need to remember the arytenoid cartilages or the epiglottis,
but the glottis, which will be frequently referred to in later sections,
must be readily identifiable (Fig. 10(*b*)).

During inhalation the vocal cords assume a V-shaped appearance
(Fig. 10(*b*) 1). In preparing to launch a note they are brought into
comparatively close approximation (Fig. 10(*b*) 2). The movement

[43]

cannot be felt, and there is no method of directly controlling them. Happily the larynx is essentially a compliant instrument, adapting its behaviour to whatever ideas we happen to hold about it. This obliges the singer to think about it realistically and logically. In ordinary English speech it is far too often treated, not as an instrument with a double reed like an oboe, but as the funnel of an insufflator for the production of consonants. To expect it, after such an ignoble assignment, suddenly to right itself with no kind of direction, is wishful thinking run riot.

With the very smallest degree of encouragement, the larynx will function as nature intended. Indeed, as a piece of mechanism, the vocal apparatus is truly amazing. A particular note is desired, and immediately the cords are adjusted to a certain length and tension. The process might be compared to a one-fingered man playing on a one-stringed fiddle, which he has had no opportunity to tune beforehand. From such an unpromising instrument one would expect an orgy of excruciating swoops, yet an untrained singer can execute intervals up to an octave with no apparent slurring. It is only when a gramophone record is played at slow speed that the voice's idiosyncrasy is easily noticeable.

A clear picture of the way in which sound is produced by the cords can be provided by a toy balloon. Having blown it up, you close the aperture by placing the finger and thumb of both hands just below the lip of the balloon. If you pull one thumb and finger gently but firmly away from the other so that the rubber is stretched, the pressure of air will cause the two edges to vibrate and produce a squeak. Further experiment will show that the two rubber edges must be held close together, but not so closely as to prevent them vibrating. Vocal cords in the same way must be closely but not tightly approximated. This is a mistake which many people make who, in learning a method of singing at total variance with their previous ideas, imagine that the closer together the vocal cords are, the better they will vibrate. Such an idea can only lead to a throaty, bottled production.

d. The technique of compression

In a position of readiness, the singer will automatically have enough breath to make an effective compression. If he takes in any more, he will find himself as heavily handicapped as in running a mile after a four-course luncheon; let all beginners take note of this, for there has never been a singer who has not at some period suffered from taking in too much breath. Next, by a mere act of will, he brings the vocal cords together. He then reduces the size of the chest cavity, lifting the relaxed diaphragm into an arched position by means of a particular contraction of the abdominal muscles. By itself the relaxed diaphragm could no more return into an arched position against a weight of compressed air than could a collapsed tent erect itself against the pull of gravity.

Except when you need to expel breath forcibly out of the nose or mouth, as when blowing the nose or extinguishing a candle, upward compression occurs only in moments of emotional stimulation; such moments can be pleasant or unpleasant, as when you unexpectedly encounter an old enemy; when you witness or are yourself involved in a near-accident; or in moments of physical pain or ecstasy. The movement on these occasions is quite involuntary. As the old saying goes, your heart comes up into your mouth. The condition is terminated as soon as the excitement is over, either by an emotional sounding 'oh' or 'ah', or else by a grunt or groan. Anyone who has attended a football match or a circus will be familiar with these reactions.

The technique of establishing compression in the chest cavity is unexpectedly elusive. This is not altogether surprising, since most abdominal compression is in a downward direction, as in urinating and defaecating. On these occasions there is a protrusion and hardening of the abdominal wall, but no contraction of the gluteal muscles. The sensation is felt more particularly to right and left of the rectus abdominis, whereas the sensation of upward compression seems to involve only the upper and central part of the abdominal wall (Fig. 11).

In creating a breath compression your first move is to imagine the centre of gravity high up the body near the top of the breast-bone. It is also helpful if someone lays a heavy hand on the crown of your head, so that you are compelled to think and to push upwards. You then make an inward and upward movement in the triangular area formed by the divergence of the lower ribs at the bottom of the breast-bone. The inward movement is not towards the interior of the abdomen. It is a pull on the corners of the lower ribs, as if you were drawing them together in a clench. The contraction must be as powerful and consistent as possible, and since the particular muscles involved

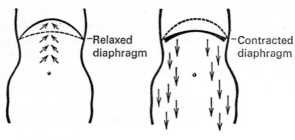

(a) Act of singing   (b) Act of defaecation

FIG. 11. THE DIAPHRAGM AND THE ABDOMINAL MUSCLES

will be unaccustomed to such hard work, they will probably ache to begin with. The movement is accompanied by a simultaneous contraction of the gluteal muscles and of the rectus abdominis; these contractions however are automatic and must not be consciously induced. The over-all physical sensation is as if you had lifted up a little trapdoor immediately behind the triangular division, and were pulling the intestines up through it. Pulling from above, you will have noticed, not pushing from below!

The physical evidence of good breath compression is felt and seen, not on the hard breast-bone, but at the apices of the lungs, just below the collar-bone and about an inch inside the line where shoulder-straps and braces are located. All good singers bulge at these points from the moment before attacking the note and throughout the sung phrase. The shoulders will inevitably rise in the same way as the upper part of an inflated paper bag bulges when squeezed from below, but there is no need to worry about this. Altogether too much stress has been laid by many teachers on the importance of keeping the shoulders down, and not nearly enough on the importance of pulling the neck high out of the body, and never allowing it to shorten. Nevertheless any lifting or hunching of the shoulders must be checked at an early stage. There is a world of difference between compression, which in this context is the singer's aim and objective, and upper chest expansion which is no more than corroborative but quite inconclusive evidence that compression has been established. A lifted chest can be induced by the contraction of certain neck, shoulder and intercostal muscles just as easily as by a contraction of the abdominal muscles; but Tarzan-like

[46]

poses have nothing to do with good voice production (Fig. 12(*b*)).

The sensation of inducing a compression of breath, when correctly managed, is a glorious one, but be careful not to go up on tiptoe. Keep the weight on the outside of the balls of the feet, and do not take the heels off the floor. As a result of the intake of breath your stance will seem to have become perilously insecure, and you will be tempted to sway backwards. Do not allow this to happen, and keep your behind well in and under.

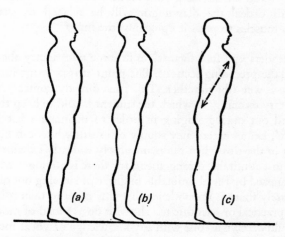

(a) Position of readiness
(b) Abdominal compression
(c) Compression with contraction of erector spinae

FIG. 12. COMPRESSION AND THE ERECTOR SPINAE (SACRO-SPINALIS)

The reader must not be put off by the apparently highly energetic nature of the act of compression. It is energetic, but once you have mastered it, you will be able to proceed to Section f, in which the secrets of the sacro-spinalis muscles are divulged. You will then find that compression can become an automatic and almost natural feeling. Energy admittedly will be involved, but a kind of subconscious energy which will not seem to demand any squeeze below the ribs or bulging of the upper chest. But all this is for the future and depends on your present skill in consciously attaining these very things.

EXERCISE 24

Keeping the rest of the body absolutely still, bring the left lower ribs forward towards the right; relax, then bring the right ribs towards the left. It will be difficult to do this without wanting to make some sort of grunt at the end of each movement.

EXERCISE 25

Imagine that you are inserting yourself into an extremely tight corset. During this ordeal the diaphragm will be relaxed to enable the abdominal muscles to press it up against the lungs.

[Many readers will find themselves in some uncertainty about parts of this and the preceding sections. The point at issue is my instruction to pull the lower ribs together. This runs directly contrary to most contemporary teaching, in which the student is told to keep the lower ribs up and out during singing in order to maintain what is called 'rib reserve', i.e. an emergency supply of breath which can be tapped by pulling in the ribs when the main supply is nearly exhausted. This sounds a most admirable arrangement, for there is no singer who is not for ever harassed by the abominable bugbear of running out of breath. Unfortunately there is no evidence that this is more than a beautiful idea. Any practical or scientific test shows it up as a load of moonshine, which would deceive no one with any knowledge of vocal mechanics.

Now I am not denying that it is perfectly easy to speak or to sing with extended ribs, but I do say first that this method does not enable the singer or speaker to sustain his tone for any long period; secondly that it is impossible to speak or sing in this way, except by allowing the vocal cords to go flabby, so that a great deal of air is allowed to pass into the throat without being converted into sound waves.

Try to make any sound you like other than speaking or singing; grunt, groan, cough, sneeze, whistle, whisper, shout, or blow any kind of musical instrument, and you will be unable to make any sound at all without the lower ribs moving inwards. Like the reeds of any woodwind instrument the vocal cords have to be energized by breath pressure. They may of themselves be able to vibrate, but air has to be passed between them before sound waves can be created, and at atmospheric pressure no energy is forthcoming. The top of the windpipe, i.e. the vocal cords, must be closed and the chest cavity made smaller by pressing the diaphragm upwards against the inflated lungs. Naturally the vibration of the vocal cords gradually exhausts the air, so that the air pressure against them is bound to drop unless compression is continually maintained. To ensure this happening the diaphragm must be allowed to ascend during singing. It cannot do so if the singer pushes outward or clamps downward upon his abdominal muscles.

The view of the modern school is expressed as succinctly as possible at the beginning of the article on 'Voice' in the 1926 edition of *Grove's Dictionary of Music*: 'We compress air by breathing out.' So we do; but we also open the vocal cords, and practice proves that whenever we sing by breathing air out through a closed glottis, the approximation of the vocal cords is inevitably imperfect and the tone shallow. Conditions at the bottom end are equally confused. If you spread a rug flat on the ground, anchoring it with stones, it is impossible to turn it into a tent; in the same way, if the ribs are held out, the abdominal muscles which are attached to them will be unable to make any kind of effective upward compression against the diaphragm.

In fact, was anything so plain daft as to try simultaneously to compress air at the top of the chest, and decompress it at the bottom? If you wish to use up the fluid in a garden syringe more slowly, it is no good trying to resist your own push on the handle. Obviously you will conserve the fluid, but you will not get much further in spraying your roses! Your only course is to continue to press the handle inwards, but to use a finer nozzle; and it will not take long to discover that the smaller the size of the nozzle, the harder you have to compress the fluid. Singing more softly is strictly comparable, for in good production it uses up the breath more slowly but demands, on high notes at any rate, a greater physical exertion.

To sum up: rib reserve (*a*) prevents the diaphragm from being lifted, and impedes the abdominal muscles in their upward and inward contraction; (*b*) compels the vocal cords to resort to the only way in which they can produce any kind of note, i.e. by going flabby and releasing unphonated air. It is the father and mother of all those tremolos that afflict our ears, and it has ruined the voices and expectations of thousands of students. For all our sakes let us kill it dead; then perhaps we shall be able to hear an occasional voice which is absolutely steady, perfectly in tune and capable of maintaining a true legato.]

e. The diaphragm in relaxation

The human body is founded on a system of complementary and antagonistic muscles. In other words the contraction of one muscle can be achieved only if its antagonistic muscle co-operates by relaxing. When singing one might reasonably say that the diaphragm and the breath-compressing muscles are antagonistic. Neither can contract unless the other has previously relaxed. In normal circumstances the mere idea of inhaling is enough to ensure that the correct muscles relax and allow the diaphragm to contract. But the inexperienced singer, in mid-song and bent on maintaining a glorious stream of bel canto, is understandably prone to take his technique of inhalation for granted; he keeps the abdominal muscles in a state of contraction or semi-contraction long after he has finished singing, and wonders why inhalation is such a long and exhausting business. This is the almost universal experience of singers who have just learned the technique expounded in these sections. It is a growing-pain but of a kind which a little systematic work will easily eradicate. At this stage however, before even a note has been uttered, it would be inappropriate to discuss it further.

A second and equally common failing is that students, in their anxiety to achieve a high degree of diaphragmatic relaxation, allow their act of contraction to deteriorate into a mere formality, ineffective as regards either diaphragm or lower ribs. Executed in this manner the double movement may be compared to the wild circular swing which a novice might make in trying to hit a golf ball. The essential characteristic of a golf stroke is that it is in two parts; the swing back and up being followed by a downward swing. At the top of the swing there is a moment when the club-head is stationary. The acts of taking breath and attacking a note are also two opposite movements; in the first movement the diaphragm pushes downwards, and in the second it is lifted up. Between the movements there must be a moment's pause. No golfer would dream of running two opposite movements into one; singers however are surprisingly apt to do this. It was perhaps an extreme case of telescoping not merely two but three movements into one, which prompted the great Madame Tetrazzini to make one of her more celebrated pronouncements; 'Do not,' she said, 'attack a note at the same time that you are inhaling. That is too soon.'

It is misleading to say that the better singer you are, the quicker you take breath. In certain respects this is perfectly true, but only when it is in terms of efficient technique. You certainly do not want to go slow, but it must be remembered that in breathing we are not working with a machine which can be artificially accelerated. The diaphragm is one of the largest muscles of the body, and can only contract in its own time; it is a cart-horse and not a grasshopper. When breath is needed in the middle of a phrase of music, diaphragmatic breathing is too slow to be practicable, and the singer takes what is commonly known as a catch breath. This consists of a partial contraction of the diaphragm, followed by an upward thrust of the upper ribs. It is perfectly simple; but for the time being the student should confine himself to the normal method of breathing. Once again he is warned not to take in too much breath. Provided his posture is correct, sufficient breath for an ordinary phrase of music will be available in the chest with no effort on his part. The golden rule in fact is to look after your posture—particularly the tendency to sag at the small of the back—and your breathing will look after itself.

If the act of inhalation presents no serious problems, the subsequent movement of breath compression, in which the function of the two muscular groups is reversed, is intensely difficult to maintain. The working of our bodies includes what is called the respiratory cycle. This is the rhythmical pattern in which the period occupied by the contraction of the diaphragm is preceded and followed by a period of relaxation; thus an unbroken rhythm is maintained in which breathing out follows breathing in. Good singing demands an interruption to this rhythm. Inhalation is followed, not by breathing out, but by a deliberate act of compression combined with a suppression of breath. If you refer to my analogy of the bicycle pump on page 32, you will have no difficulty in understanding this. In such conditions the respiratory cycle is broken, the diaphragm remains relaxed over a more or less extended period, while breath is at one and the same time compressed and suppressed. Needless to say, it is an unfamiliar and therefore an unnatural condition. It cannot be assumed and maintained unless the singer encourages it by consciously feeling that for the diaphragm the state of relaxation is the natural state, the condition from which it departs only for a moment, and to which it returns as a matter of course. This point of view enables his body to revert to, and if necessary to remain in, the condition of maximum efficiency described in Chapter 2. With the diaphragm relaxed, the heavy organs immediately underneath it are pushed upward by the action of the abdominal muscles. Since these organs include the liver, which lies under the right side of the diaphragm, a considerable upward shift in the position of the body's centre of gravity is to be expected; it will be increased when, as a result of a compression of breath inside the chest, the upper ribs are raised. Naturally the singer does not have to think of all this; he simply induces the sensation of a high centre of gravity.

The elusive nature of the diaphragm is a sore temptation for the reader to take the line of least resistance. But no matter how convinced he may be that the act of subconsciously inducing its relaxation is beyond his power, he is not going to help matters merely by paying particular attention to the contraction of his abdominal muscles. Unless the diaphragm stays relaxed there will be a juddering deadlock. It would be as if the upturned right hand were trying to lift a downward pushing left hand. The vocal consequences need not be described; they can be heard along the corridors of any musical institute.

One might compare the diaphragm and the abdominal muscles in the act of compression to a dance team in which the ballerina is lifted by her male partner. Skilful though the latter may be, he cannot carry through his routine unless the ballerina has previously distributed her weight so as to bring her centre of gravity as high up the body as possible. Not many singers have been ballerinas, but we can all remember occasions when our favourite uncle carried us pickaback, and in excited joy we turned ourselves into little feather-weights. There were other and sadder occasions no doubt, when on fine summer evenings we were dragged up from the beach howling blue murder, and taking particular pains to make ourselves as heavy as possible with an extremely low centre of gravity.

The following exercise will help to establish the sensation of a high centre of gravity, but the condition of the diaphragm is so much a question of attitude of mind that no exercise can be really effective.

EXERCISE 26

Read through this exercise two or three times before attempting it, and then do it without reference to the book.

You are a tightrope walker, and for this you need an extremely high and consistent centre of gravity. Having chosen a line on the carpet, mentally remove the rest of the floor, substituting a circus ring a hundred feet below you. Unless your shoes are soft and flexible, take them off. As you set foot on the imaginary wire, feel that your centre of gravity has shifted to half-way up the breast-bone. Instinctively you find yourself holding the breath. This is a characteristic of performing any skilled act, such as threading a needle, hitting a ball, jumping or walking a tightrope. Thereby one prevents any chance of equilibrium being disturbed as a result of the descent and contraction of the diaphragm.

Having walked some distance along the wire you wish to retrace your steps. If you are eager for a smooth journey, remember that the human body is put to its best use mechanically when it is held in such a way as to be capable of turning itself round with the least effort. This is why the bullfighter, who has learned to keep very straight, is able at the last moment to get out of the way of a charging bull. With pelvis, trunk and head piled vertically one above the other, the centre of gravity of the body is brought to the highest level and the muscular contraction sufficient to prevent him from falling is the smallest possible.

(The scientific reader may feel that, in discussing the diaphragm, I am attributing characteristics that do not belong to it. This has been intentional. To talk about the vagus or phrenic nerves, or the effects of neuro-muscular disturbances when all the reader wants to know is how to produce a stream of beautiful tone would be plain foolish. I have therefore directed his attention to the diaphragm, and allowed him to infer that it can of itself revert to a partially contracted condition. Experience has shown that this is the only practical way of tackling an extremely elusive aspect of voice production.)

f. Compression and the sacro-spinalis

As soon as the abdominal muscles have established an upward compression, a further group can be brought into conscious contraction. These are the sacro-spinalis muscles which are situated on either side of the lower spinal column. With the muscles contracted, the sensation at and a little above the small of the back is of being pulled outwards as if you were growing a hump. The contraction is most easily recognized in Exercises 6 (page 15) and 10 (page 18). In addition to the sensation of bulge below the lower ribs, there is a tendency for the arms to be held away from the body, and of a cave-man feeling about the carriage of the upper part of the body. The cave-man feeling is increased by the realization that it is impossible to have the knees locked back so long as the sacro-spinalis muscles are contracted. In this condition there is very little feeling in the front of the body; it is almost as if the abdomen had disappeared. In early stages the contraction may cause an ache in the lower back; needless to say the ache will disappear as soon as you have accustomed yourself to using these muscles.

The technique of keeping the sacro-spinalis contracted enables the singer to think of his upper chest as a kind of inflated motor tyre with an air compression kept constant by some automatic regulating mechanism below it. In launching a note it is as if a valve in the tyre was opened, so as to produce an immediate and steady compression which, as a result of the contracted sacro-spinalis, is never allowed to vary. There is no conscious pumping, pushing or squeezing, and at the moment of attack no bodily movement is perceptible.

In sustaining a note the upper chest and small of the back remain still and removed as far as possible from each other, as if a strut had been interposed between them; the abdominal wall is the only part of the body that moves, seeming to be pulled slowly inward towards the spine as the breath is used up, but this movement must on no account be consciously induced (Fig. 12(c)).

The contraction of the sacro-spinalis muscles is a particularly difficult habit to acquire and impossible unless the technique of breath compression has become completely automatic. My lurid analogy of pulling the intestines up through a little trap door will have helped to establish the sensation of breath compression, and on the assumption that it has served its purpose, I shall now introduce a further analogy which will ensure both an adequate compression and a steady contraction of the sacro-spinalis. Quite simply you imagine that you are preparing in two successive movements to shoot an arrow from the bow. Assuming that you are right-handed, you first extend the left arm; similarly, in preparing to sing, the upper chest bulges as a result of the compression below it. In the second movement the right-handed bowman draws back his right arm until maximum tension is achieved; in similar fashion the singer's sacro-spinalis muscles are tightened, so that the small of the back bulges outwards and upwards. With this double preparation, the work is to all intents and purposes done; the archer simply releases the arrow, and the singer his pitched note. It is a release from a condition of tension. There is no pushing or squeezing as in blowing a wind instrument, and the only difference between singing and archery is that the singer must maintain the tension throughout the sung phrase and until the moment after he has completed the final note.

In your endeavours to secure a consistent feeling of stretch between the upper chest and the small of the back, be careful to do things in the right order. Before launching the note, the singer must first have his perpendicular 'Spanish dancer' strut, then his upward and inward compression, and finally the diagonal 'bow and arrow' pull, which has to be maintained until the moment after his note or phrase is completed. The routine should be practised in slow motion until you feel that it has become automatic.

Emphasis on a particular body posture and the routine of breath compression can make you feel terribly stiff and unnatural. This is to be expected when learning a complicated technique, but once you have mastered the art of contracting the sacro-spinalis, you should give the body complete freedom of action. When practising, walk up and down the room, lean against the piano, sit in a chair or do anything rather than stand stiff and immovable. Never feel as if you were sending down roots into the earth, but rather as if two moving staircases, like the arms of an inverted V, starting from the front hip-bones and meeting at the bridge of the nose, were going up inside you. The centre of gravity must seem as high as possible so as to give the impression of continuous dynamic movement, easy body control and split second timing. It is like skating, or skiing down a gentle slope; you do not need to exert energy, but you have to keep the sacro-spinalis contracted to avoid landing on your bottom.

EXERCISE 27

This exercise does not involve the larynx at all; the glottis remains open throughout. The closed lips are made to act in the same manner as do the vocal cords in singing or speaking, a sufficiently strong and steady breath pressure being brought against them to produce a sound. Most people can only make spluttering noises at first; but among your friends there may be somebody whose admirable imitations of a mewing cat intrigues dogs and delights babies.

Just as there should be four distinct and successive movements in the act of launching a note, so also in this exercise there are four distinct movements, each of which must be separated from the preceding one by an appreciable pause. Apart from the fact that we employ the lips instead of the vocal cords, these movements are precisely similar to those used in singing; they are the indispensable preliminary to an efficient attack either at the lips or at the vocal cords. It is essential to acquire such a mastery of the four movements that they become completely automatic.

Movement I
Breathe in through the mouth, contracting the diaphragm and expanding the lower ribs.

Movement II
Close the lips. Relax the diaphragm and contract the abdominal muscles. A compression of breath has now been built up behind the closed lips. Evidence of a compression will be seen by a bulging of the skin all round the lips. The moment any attention is paid to the lips themselves, some demon causes them to relax and allow breath to escape. There is no particular skill in keeping the lips closed, nor does it matter whether they are thin or full, lipsticked or naked. It is a question purely and simply of steady breath pressure with the emphasis always on diaphragmatic relaxation.

Movement III
Contract the sacro-spinalis muscles. The compression will now feel stronger and more secure.

Movement IV
As soon as the breath pressure is firmly directed, start mewing. You don't do anything fresh; you just mentally say 'Go'. It is the same principle as when an archer shoots an arrow. He draws his bow and takes aim, and not until he has completed both acts does he release the arrow.

g. First sounds
For the vocal cords to vibrate in smooth and steady fashion, a routine of four separate movements, similar to those in Exercise 27, is required. This does not mean that the act of singing is enormously complicated. No doubt a great many skilled undertakings such as a high jump, a

tennis service or a ballet step could easily be broken up into a succession of as many separate movements, each of which was consciously realized and experienced in relation to the ones preceding and following it.

Sung notes should not at present be attempted. Every inexperienced singer, in his anxiety to hit the note perfectly in tune, is apt to let the breath pressure go. In grunting however there is no definite pitch. Consequently there is no difficulty in maintaining pressure and giving vent to perfectly produced, albeit primitive grunts. People only make such sounds in particular circumstances. They have just lifted a piano, or hit a tennis ball, and the grunt is an expression of their physical and emotional reactions. They are not giving out information but simply making a sort of animal noise. You hear the grunt joyous, the grunt surprised, the grunt of physical or mental effort and physical or mental pain, but never the grunt informative. The American reader with his wide range of noises expressing affirmation, denial, agreement or disagreement may consider this highly dubious. But such noises are not really grunts; they are merely substitutes for spoken words.

Movement I
By contracting the diaphragm, the singer draws in breath as it were through the back and sides of his waistcoat.

Movement II
Relax the diaphragm and with a contraction of the abdominal muscles, lift it up so as to produce a compression of breath. The shoulders will inevitably rise with the expansion of the upper chest, and no attempt should be made to prevent this. To forestall any sensation of the neck sinking into the body, feel that the neck is lengthening and lifting the head up and away or, if you like, that the ears are going away from the shoulders.

Movement III
The sacro-spinalis muscles are contracted. The overall sensation will be of a secure compression and a high centre of gravity. One experiences the same thing prior to and during big moments in athletics. In diving, for instance, or skiing, the body is poised as if leaning on air, and there is a physical and emotional sense of well-being which is far removed from the work-a-day world. Both activities seem next door to flying—and indeed the singer might well visualize himself as a

gigantic gull, speechless yet emotionally expressive, skimming above the water or soaring up the side of a cliff on a warm current of air. Literally and metaphorically he will be bursting to start, and the real difficulty is to pause for a moment—but only a moment with the steadiness of an expert bowman—before launching the note.

Movement IV

The sensation at the moment of launching is as if the larynx were gently tapped by a tiny hammer. Note that the sensation is the passive one of being tapped. In early stages the cessation of breath pressure, as the barrier of the glottis opens, leaves the throat with a tickling sensation which may set up an impulse to cough. There is absolutely no reason for doing so. Provided you are strong-minded, the sensation disappears very quickly, never to return.

EXERCISE 28

With special reference to taking a breath to begin with, and grunting at the end, do the following actions. Try to find out in each case whether you are using the abdominal muscles as you would in singing.

  i. Thread a needle.
 ii. Lift a table.
iii. Pull a cork out of a bottle.
 iv. Serve an imaginary tennis ball.
  v. Shoot an arrow into the air. Remember you are shooting with a full-sized bow; this calls for a strong contraction of the sacro-spinalis in drawing the string taut, and keeping the bow absolutely steady prior to releasing the arrow.

Note: Correct singing is the only activity I know of in which a compression of breath must be maintained at the top of the chest, i.e. in the apices of the lungs. In this respect even the specialized breathing exercises are comparatively ineffective. In normal life the full expansion of the upper part of the lungs is very seldom realized, consequently the fluid inside them becomes stagnant and a favourable breeding ground for bacteria. The incidence of tuberculosis, as well as most kinds of bronchial disturbances, is invariably found among these apices. It seems therefore that the best possible prevention of all such infections would be in learning the rudiments of correct voice production. Naturally the infection could only be arrested in the early stages.

5

THE VIBRATOR AND THE CHIEF RESONATOR

From the singer's point of view sound may be regarded as fundamentally a sensation. A pair of vocal cords are thrown into a state of vibration; the vibrations are communicated to the surrounding air and eventually reach the ear-drum of someone in the neighbourhood, setting up a nervous disturbance which we call 'sound'. Sound in fact exists only when there is an ear capable of receiving the sensation. Dr Percy Scholes, in his *Oxford Companion to Music*, illustrated this charmingly by observing that a brass band of stone-deaf players in a home for the deaf and dumb where only the patients were present would make no sound.

a. Pitch and intensity

The pitch of a singing voice is determined by the frequency of these vibrations. Gramophone records played at the wrong speed produce shrill or sepulchral noises as a result of the greatly increased or diminished frequency of the vibrations communicated to the sound box. In voices frequency of vibration depends partly on the variable length and thickness of the vocal cords, and mainly on the degree of elasticity in their inside margins; all these things are regulated by muscles inside the larynx, and are outside our conscious control. Little or nothing can be felt there, and it will probably be many years before we can say with any degree of certainty how the vocal cords function.

In the pitching of notes the reader must not relate breath pressure to variations either of pitch or volume; in other words he must not deliberately tighten the abdominal muscles on a crescendo or a rising passage, nor slacken the pressure on a diminuendo or a falling passage. In point of fact he cannot do so, since the contraction of the sacrospinalis will prevent any conscious increase or decrease in the contraction of the abdominal muscles. Breath management for singing is not

[59]

like stepping on an accelerator, or squeezing a bellows; it is like utilizing a power socket which can supply whatever degree of electric current is needed to switch on a fire, a vacuum cleaner or a radio. There is no possibility of pressing on the tone; simply because, with the sacrospinalis contracted, it is not possible to do so.

Naturally the reader has no chance of maintaining a correct technique unless his mental concepts are in line with his physical movements. In this respect the visual impression of 'up and down' which the singer cannot help deriving from written music is a most pernicious influence. When he sees a note above or below the stave, he should think of it not as a 'high' or 'low' note, but as a note of quick or slow vibration. In this way it is possible, at least to some extent, to crush the bogey of high notes.

Where the vibrations of any sound-producing element are ample, the sound is full; where the vibrations are less ample, the sound is softer. When a violin string for instance is plucked so as to give a strong pizzicato note, it can be seen vibrating an appreciable distance on either side of its normal straight line (Fig. 10, page 43). If the string is plucked gently, its vibration will be much less pronounced, but the number of vibrations per second will in each case be the same. Similarly, a garden swing will make the same number of backward and forward movements however violently you push it. With a vigorous push you send it high; with a lesser push you send it not so high. On the first occasion it travels quickly, on the second it travels slowly; but the time occupied by a complete back-and-forth motion is the same on both occasions, only the amplitude varying.

As in pitching the note, the manner of varying the vibratory swing of the vocal cords is subconscious. The voice is capable of a wide range of dynamics, but no conscious muscular effort should be made to produce a loud or soft grunt or note. Whatever the dynamic the singer should not do more, and certainly not less, than make sure that his preparation was correct. How then, you will ask, does one 'put in the expression'? The simple answer is that consciously one does nothing. Naturally one has some idea of the dynamic appropriate to the music, but generally speaking one should be guided solely by the inner emotional demands which are called forth by the physical and mental stimuli governing the act of singing. Admittedly this may seem farfetched. With the poor voice production of most of today's singers it is more than that; it is downright impossible. By contrast the physical act of producing sound, as described in the first six chapters of this book, inhibits conscious abdominal contractions, but seems to stimulate the emotions, so that the singer finds his musical expression being brought to life without any motivation on his part. This puts the solo singer into a class apart from choral singers or instrumentalists. Needless to say the emotional stimulus varies according to the music which he is performing. Nevertheless, if he is willing to recognize and encourage it, the stimulus will emerge in the trashiest ballad as readily as in *Tristan and Isolde*.

Like tuned violin-strings the vocal cords of a healthy person may be said to possess a normal degree of tension, which under certain circumstances become relaxed. It is a common sequel to inflamed throats, colds and other ailments, or when we are mentally depressed. Age of course affects the best of us; so also does the menstrual period, its effect on some women being comparatively severe and on others negligible. One of the chief factors in reducing the natural tension of the vocal cords is neglect, and this is one of the strongest arguments in favour of starting to learn to sing as soon as one is past the age of puberty. A second factor which may bring about either relaxation or undue tension is faulty technique; needless to say this is the main cause not only of defective intonation, but of the bulk of laryngeal and other vocal disorders.

EXERCISE 29

With the idea of quick and slow vibration in mind, grunt the following notes; the mouth should be kept half open, so as to make the sound of *ng*, as in 'thing'.

EXERCISE 30

Repeat each phrase of Exercise 29 first forte then piano.

b. Sound waves

The effect of the vibration of the vocal cords is to release a rapid succession of puffs, each of which throws the air particles in its immediate neighbourhood into a momentarily disturbed condition. These particles are pushed against adjoining particles, which in turn disturb momentarily their immediate neighbours. Thus a succession of disturbances, an energetic force moving in three dimensions through space, is produced. Yet the effect on the atmosphere through which the puffs travel is infinitesimal. In the same way, if you drop a succession of pebbles at very rapid and exactly regular intervals into a pond, you cause a series of ripples to spread outward in concentric circles from the point where the stones hit the surface of the water; but despite the furrowed appearance of the normally tranquil surface, the effect on the whole expanse of water would be negligible. Each disturbed drop of water disturbs the drops in its immediate neighbourhood, yet no single drop would be moved more than an infinitesimal distance. A leaf on the water for instance would be rocked up and down by the movement of the ripples, but would remain in the same place.

The phenomenon of energy moving in three dimensions through space without directly affecting the atmosphere constitutes what are called sound waves. Like ripples on water, sound waves move through the flame of a candle without making it flicker appreciably. This can be verified by singing AH while holding a lighted candle in front of the lips, but the experiment will only succeed provided the breath passes between the vibrating cords in a regular series of puffs and not otherwise. Unphonated breath, i.e. breath which does not produce any kind of voiced sound, will make the candle flicker; so too will consonants, nearly all of which are pronounced in the mouth cavity and necessarily involve momentary escapes of breath. Nevertheless, in the case of a good singer, interruptions to the tone stream are so short that they hardly disturb the steadiness of the candle flame.

Good singing depends on forming and maintaining first, a nobly resonating throat cavity, and secondly, a breath compression sufficient to enable a series of puffs of breath to pass between the vibrating vocal cords. The actual breath which forms the puffs, as soon as it finds itself above the vocal cords, has no more to do with the act of singing than have exhaust fumes with propelling a car. It is a waste product which merges with the breath already in the throat. Since the air pressure therein remains constant, an equal amount of breath has to be expelled from the mouth. The same outlet happens to be used by this breath and by the sound waves constituting the voice, but breath and sound waves are ill-assorted travellers; breath drifts upwards at per-haps an inch or two per second, while sound waves travel at over seven hundred miles per hour. No one has any business to confuse one with the other.

The original sound coming from above the vibrating vocal cords is extremely feeble, as would be the note of a violin-string detached from the instrument and stretched in mid-air. It is only when the tone is enriched by a resonator that it acquires any beauty or volume. Both qualities in fact depend mainly on the effectiveness of the resonator, just as the difference between a Stradivarius and a cheap violin lies in the respective instruments and not in the strings and bow. In the same way the tone quality of a good singer is due mainly to his superior resonating cavities, though there are many other factors to be taken into consideration.

c. Harmonics

Whatever the source of sound, vibrations are hardly ever the simple kind which one might expect from the action of a hammer on piano strings, or a bow on a violin. In nearly all musical instruments vibra-tions are invariably compound. This is best explained by practical experiment on a reasonably good piano. If you hold down middle C and at the same time, without using the loud pedal, strike the C one octave below with a firm sharp staccato, you will hear middle C quite distinctly. The reason for this is that in striking the lower C you cause its strings to vibrate, not only along their entire length, so as to sound the actual note, but also along their two half-lengths, each of which would vibrate at twice the rate of the complete strings. The half lengths in fact vibrate at the same frequency as middle C; this means that, provided the vibrations from the half lengths of the lower C strings are powerful enough to reach the requisite distance, the strings belonging to middle C on the piano would be brought into sympa-thetic vibration and sound an audible note.

As well as vibrating along its whole length and in half sections, the lower C strings on being struck are made to vibrate simultaneously in other and smaller sections. Along a third of their length they would sound the G above middle C. Accordingly, if you hold this G down and again strike the bottom C, the G would resonate in sympathetic vibration. By holding down middle C and the G together, you would hear the two notes simultaneously, for there is no question of sound waves resulting from one vibrational frequency being in any way disturbed by sound waves resulting from another. In similar fashion ripples on water cross each other's path without their progress being affected.

The cluster of sounds which are called into being as a result of the diverse vibrations of a single string is known as the harmonic series. The note originally struck is the first harmonic or the fundamental; the second harmonic vibrates at the same pace as do the sections of the strings of the fundamental when divided by two; the third harmonic vibrates at the same pace as do the sections of the fundamental when divided by three, and so on. Naturally the identity of the actual notes varies according to the pitch of the fundamental, but the relationship remains constant. Assuming that C below the bass clef is the fundamental, the notes of the harmonic series are as follows:

Just as sound can hardly be said to exist until there is an available ear-drum, so harmonics are only effective when a sympathetic resonator is to be found within a reasonably short distance of the place where the original sound is made. Any undampened piano string, provided it belongs to the harmonic series, is such a resonator. So is a properly shaped violin provided it is connected to the string by a bridge. So is the human throat together with the various cavities of the skull, and it is part of the singer's job consciously or subconsciously to make these resonators as sympathetic as possible to the vibrations coming off his vocal cords.

If a cavity is the right shape and sufficiently large it will pick up and reinforce the original vibrations on the fundamental; that is to say, it will sound the same note as the vocal cords in addition to the subsidiary harmonics. If the cavity is too small, it will sound only those harmonics compatible with its size. When for instance an average man sings a middle C, his throat cavity, being too small to resonate on this note, will respond to the second harmonic, i.e. the C in the middle of the treble stave one octave higher, but not to the fundamental. If he sings an F above middle C, the higher pitch calls for a relatively smaller cavity; this cavity would be of a size equivalent to our average man's throat, which would be able to resonate in unison with his vocal cords, as well as on the subsidiary resonances. A woman's throat is not as a rule big enough to resonate on any note lower than the G above middle C; consequently on F above middle C the second harmonic one octave higher is her lowest potential resonance.

In company with his audience, the singer hears only the fundamental. Harmonics in his voice are not as a rule individually distinguishable; but for the benefit of his musical taste and sensitivity he should at least have some idea of the lowest note on which the throat cavity can resonate. After all the throat is for him the only truly important cavity, inasmuch as it provides far the greater proportion of the tone and is the only resonator whose shape he can appreciably modify. The musical examples on pages 66–67 show the deepest harmonics of various voices in different sections of Handel's 'Where e'er you walk'. If he examines these, the astonished reader will observe that, though certain notes differ, the deepest range of potential throat resonance in all voices does not venture beyond the extremely narrow limit of about a seventh, and furthermore that the pitch lies within the soprano octave. A subconscious awareness of this may account for the universal preference shown by both composers and singers for baritone parts written in the treble clef; the upper harmonics of high baritones are in fact unusually distinct, so that on more than one occasion I have found them indistinguishable from the front door bell!

The greater part of a sung note is as a rule contained in one or more of its upper harmonics, and only a minute part in the fundamental. Supposing a man sings middle C, the sound of the actual note made by his vocal cords will be tiny. Much the largest proportion of the sound will issue from the throat cavity; this would consist of a combination of harmonics beginning with C in the treble stave, one octave above. Similarly a bass who sings a bottom G cannot resonate on any note below the fourth harmonic, i.e. G on the treble stave two octaves higher, but the listener is never in any doubt of the actual sung pitch. This mysterious faculty is not confined to sounds issuing from the human voice. It was found for example that on the open G string of the violin—the G below middle C—the second harmonic contained 26 per cent of the energy of the tone, the third harmonic 45 per cent, and the fourth, fifth, sixth and eighth harmonics proportions varying from 4 per cent to nearly 9 per cent. As for the fundamental, it contained just one-thousandth part of the complete tone.

The throat does not necessarily respond most readily on its lowest available harmonic. Much depends on the identity of the note and the vowel employed, on the context of the phrase, and the singer's skill in shaping and retaining an efficient resonator; but as a rule a voice sounds best when the throat cavity resonates on as deep a harmonic as possible. For this reason a singer with a large throat cavity invariably has the advantage over a singer with vocal cords of a similar length but with a smaller throat, no matter whether he is singing loud or soft.

Sympathetic vibration is not by any means confined to the insides of musical instruments, human or otherwise. It is the relative degree of sympathetic vibration contained in theatres, churches, bathrooms or tunnels which makes them favourable or unfavourable to the making of music. In all sorts of ways it is a familiar and not always welcome

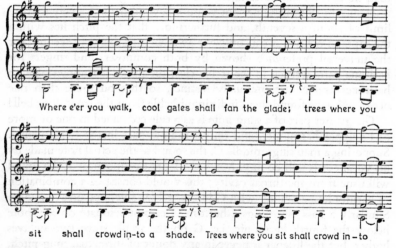

THE TOP STAVES SHOW THE DEEPEST POTENTIAL THROAT RESONANCES OF A MEZZO-SOPRANO, THE MIDDLE STAVES THOSE OF A BARITONE. THE BOTTOM STAVES SHOW THE ACTUAL SUNG NOTES.

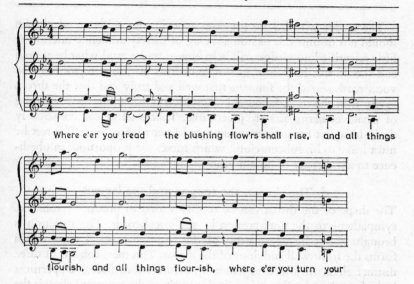

Where e'er you tread   the blushing flow'rs shall rise,   and all things

flourish, and all things flour-ish,   where e'er you turn your

THE TOP STAVES SHOW THE DEEPEST POTENTIAL THROAT RESONANCES OF A
SOPRANO, THE MIDDLE STAVES THOSE OF A TENOR. THE BOTTOM STAVES SHOW
THE ACTUAL SUNG NOTES.

phenomenon of everyday life. Readers of detective fiction may recall
a case in which the vibration of a thirty-two foot organ pipe brought
about the sympathetic vibration and subsequent collapse of a tottering
wall under which the victim was opportunely standing. Less lethal and
even more annoying are the ornaments on mantelpieces which start
vibrating sympathetically in the middle of piano solos. Occasionally
one finds oneself actually inside a resonating cavity. This happened to
me once in Lincoln, where I was staying in a hotel near the Close. It
was a still summer night and I was lying in a bath when the Cathedral
clock struck eleven. At the end of the quarters the hour is struck by a
noble old bell called Big Tom, which sounds a deep A flat. Immediately
Big Tom began to strike, the bathroom was filled with the sound of
middle C which seemed to come from everywhere at once. There was
no question of the sound issuing from the plumbing or anywhere outside
the room; for at midnight I was again in occupation of that bathroom,
this time with my wife. I did not have another bath, but I filled it up
with the same amount of water. Sure enough the same thing happened.

[67]

The reader who has no previous acquaintance with sound physics should not dismiss this section as being of merely academic interest. A little scientific knowledge will help him to understand what he should and should not be doing. In simplest terms his job is to see that the vocal cords sound the fundamental well and truly and that the throat cavity is in the most favourable condition possible for the resonating of whatever harmonics are practicable. That is all he can consciously do in his quest for greater volume and finer tone colour. The rest he must leave to his subconscious, which mixes the proportions in obedience to the dictates of his emotions.

d. The throat, the tongue and the larynx

The shape of the throat can be readily varied to produce resonances sympathetic to the note created by the vocal cords. The variation is brought about by adjustments of the large anatomical mass which forms the front wall and floor of the throat. This mass consists of three distinct elements joined together by membranous fibres. Uppermost is the large bunch of muscles which constitute the tongue; below is the small hyoid bone which supports the tongue and from which the larynx is suspended; finally there is the larynx itself, which consists of two superimposed cartilages (Fig. 10).

To get an idea of the general shape of the tongue, hold the forearm in a vertical position with the hand inclined backwards from the wrist; bend the fingers at the knuckles into a right angle, and bend them again at the middle joint so that the fingers project a little beyond the wrist. In this position the hand will resemble a sickle. The two end finger joints represent the part of the tongue enclosed by the teeth and hard palate, while the joint nearest the knuckles represents the part of the tongue lying under the soft palate. Hereabouts the tongue curves round in a roughly right-angled bend, though not nearly so sharply as the angle of the hand at the knuckles. The remainder of the hand, from the knuckles down to the wrist, represents the main part of the tongue. This part, generally known as the root of the tongue, takes up every bit of space inside the lower jaw; in fact, as far as singing is concerned, the jaw is the tongue, the jaw-bone being merely a wall encircling it on three sides.

If you put the first finger and thumb of the other hand round the wrist, they will represent the small hyoid bone which can be felt by a finger placed above the Adam's apple. Shaped like a horseshoe with its concavity facing backward, the hyoid bone supports and is attached to the base of the tongue. Below the hyoid bone and attached to it by ligaments, is the larynx. Thus the hyoid bone joins the tongue to the larynx making one combined mass. Harnessed together in this manner neither tongue nor larynx is free to go its independent way. Like two dogs attached to the same lead they must be trained to work together. As regards singing, the larynx is invariably the exemplary animal, whereas the tongue needs constant supervision. To look for good production by worrying about the larynx is idiotic. It is the refractory tongue which must be taken in hand.

The reason for the misbehaviour of the tongue is that in English conversation the emphasis is on articulation without much regard for tone quality. Accordingly the tongue, obsessed with its duties of articulating consonants, chooses a conveniently high, forward position close to the upper teeth. The larynx, concerned exclusively with tone production, would prefer to move to a lower position than is usual in ordinary conversation; in consequence the length of the throat would be increased, making the voice a deeper, nobler instrument. As a rule however this is not permitted. The larynx is pulled up to a higher level and all hope of beautiful tone is eliminated.

Consonants are not the only reason for this lamentable behaviour. Badly pronounced vowels and diphthongs are equally disastrous; particularly diphthongs, which abound in the English language, as will be shown in the following sections.

EXERCISE 31

Put your finger lightly on the larynx and say:

   i. Do we see you too?
   ii. Do be true to me.
   iii. He knew me too!

The larynx will sink on the OO vowel, and rise on the EE.

Rest a finger on the tongue root under the tongue, and say as well as you can 'OO-EE'. You will feel the tongue root as well as the tongue rise on EE and sink on OO. The whole anatomical mass, from the flapping part of the tongue down to the base of the larynx, is like a moveable platform; and it is on the free movement of this somewhat odd structure that good voice-production depends.

[69]

e. Italian and English vowels

So far from being an additional complication, the pronunciation of clear, clean vowels on the middle and lower notes is an essential requisite of fine tone quality. This is so, whether one sings in Italian, English or any other language.

The profusion of English vowels and diphthongs is presumably the reason why it has always been considered desirable to study songs in the Italian language. Few beginners have not had 'Caro mio ben' inflicted on them! But until they have acquired a technical command of the vocal organs, no amount of academic knowledge or skilful imitation can really eliminate the basic muddiness of the Englishman's normal manner of speech. Having made this point, let me say emphatically that the study of languages should be part of every singer's education. Nobody has any business performing in a language of which he is completely ignorant; but over and above the demands of the modern repertoire, the more knowledge a singer has of French, Italian and German, the deeper will be his appreciation of words, particularly English words, and the greater his intolerance of smudgy, slovenly vowels.

As a vehicle for singing, our own language has been unjustly maligned, but one has to admit that in many respects it is exceptionally difficult. In contrast to the five pure Italian vowels, English contains a number of diphthongs in addition to some thirteen supposedly pure vowels. I call them supposedly pure, because in spoken English many of them fall far short of anything approaching purity; the vowels in the words 'pay' and 'know' for instance are invariably pronounced 'peh-ĭ' and 'kno-uh'. From the point of view of spoken and sung English there is every reason why they should be pronounced in this way, for English is a language which derives much of its beauty from its abundance of diphthongs.

Diphthongs can be sung as easily and effectively as pure vowels but, since they require a special technique of pronunciation, the beginner should confine himself to the five Italian vowels. These will in future be represented as *A, E, I, O* and *U*. Two of these vowels, *I* and *U*, are plain sailing, since we have equivalent vowel sounds in English. The remaining ones, *A, E,* and *O,* are not so easy since their pronunciation varies according to context, and in any case does not occur among English vowel sounds. Here then is a table of Italian vowels:

[70]

A half-way between ah (as in 'father') and ŭ (as in 'but'), e.g. *dalla sua pace; questa quella; La Traviata.*
E (closed) like the French *è* or the Scottish 'cake', e.g. *mele, vedere.*
E (open) like the English 'red', e.g. *bello, vento.*
I (as in 'seem'), e.g. Gigli; Puccini; *si, mi chiamano Mimi.*
O (closed) like the Lancashire O in 'note', e.g. *sole.*
O (open) as in 'not', e.g. *donna.*
U (as in 'moon'), e.g. Caruso; Turiddu; *una furtiva lagrima.*

Of these five vowels *O* and *U* should not at present be attempted; they call for a special technique which will be explained in Chapter 7. The vowel *I* is also one which the beginner must avoid. This leaves *A* and *E*, both of which he may safely use. Two vowels may seem lamentably short commons; but the wisdom of these restrictions will be appreciated later. It should be noted that, like *O*, the vowel *E* has two distinct sounds, open and closed; very roughly they resemble the English vowel sounds in 'pen' and 'pain'. But whereas the Italian closed *E* is a pure vowel, the English vowel sound in 'pain' is invariably a diphthong; since this makes the pronunciation of the Italian closed *E* rather difficult for the beginner, *E* should be pronounced as an open vowel as in 'pen'. Incidentally, do not be unduly alarmed at the complications of the open and closed vowels. They are mispronounced as a matter of course by quite educated people in many parts of Italy. The important thing is to avoid any suspicion of a diphthong.

f. The spoken vowel

The voice of present-day man is produced chiefly to communicate with his fellows. He has no need of a high standard of beauty or clarity. If a certain amount of unphonated breath is allowed to slip through the cords to the detriment of the tone, he is not unduly distressed. It is only in genuinely emotional exclamations that the vocal organs of the average English person can be relied upon to work with real efficiency. Such situations can be arranged by treading on an old gentleman's toe as you enter the bus, and poking an elbow into a lady's eye as you get off.

In the animal world the voice is used more sparingly. Nearly all mammals have an efficient vocal apparatus; but except in circumstances of abnormal physical or emotional stress they use only as much voice as is needed for their day to day existence. In the same way primitive man could go about his affairs with a perfectly developed vocal organ of which, to all intents and purposes, he made no use as a means of communication. Emotional tension alone set off his organs of speech, and there is no reason to suppose that the resulting sound had any more significance for him than the twang which followed the release of an arrow from his bow.

Luckily for the world this by-product of emotional tension can be turned into an instrument of infinite variety and beauty; it is the source of music, and to this day remains the subconscious inspiration of all composers and players of musical instruments. But neither beauty nor variety can be realized if the singer is content merely to interpret the written notes. Interpretation is nothing unless at the same time he artificially reproduces in his body that state of emotional tension which inspired primitive man to utter his first cries. This fundamental aspect of singing will be unfamiliar to anyone who is not himself a performer, but readers of *David Copperfield* may perhaps remember an extraordinary description of the manner in which Rosa Dartle sang to Steerforth:

> I don't know what it was in her voice, that made that song the most unearthly I have ever heard in my life, or can imagine. There was something fearful in the reality of it. It was as if it had never been written, or set to music, but sprung out of the passion within her; which found imperfect utterance in the low sounds of her voice, and crouched again when all was still.

For years this passage amused me as a supreme example of a great novelist tying himself up in a description of the hopelessly indescribable. Middle age has brought me sufficient wisdom to realize the fund of insight beneath the rather turgid prose. Clearly Miss Dartle, who was a strange passionate woman, could not in the mood of that particular moment have sung otherwise than in that abnormal fashion. Quite certainly she must have sounded appalling. Even so the description suggests that she put her body into a condition in which, if she had the mind and the capacity, she could have made beautiful music.

The idea that emotional tension is literally the immediate means of producing vocal tone is as a rule acceptable, but extremely difficult to put into practice. You will find it easier after reading further sections. Meanwhile a helpful analogy is to compare the act of singing with the mechanism of a whistling kettle. For this admirable domestic appliance to give tongue, a certain amount of water has to be heated to a very high temperature. In due time the steam from the water comes in contact with the whistle, and the resulting vibration indicates that tea is almost ready. The kettle itself, being an inanimate object, does not do the whistling. Steam driven upwards against a valve by heat is the one and only sound producer. In the same way the singer should never feel, in the sense that the average member of a choral society feels, that he himself is energetically singing. Breath driven upwards by the abdominal muscles sets up a pressure against the vocal cords, and the pressure creates an emotional tension which urgently demands some form of audible self-expression. Without these physical conditions the singer should feel himself no more capable of making music than would a kettle of whistling after the heat had been turned off. In this context the only difference between kettle and singer is that the former can only whistle under the right conditions, and has no choice in deciding whether and when to do so. The singer unfortunately can sing after a fashion under any conditions; but it is only under special conditions that he can sing correctly. Furthermore he is free to decide, once the conditions have been established, whether to sing forthwith, to wait till a given moment, or to relax his pressure and eliminate the emotional tension.

The singer who models himself on the example of the whistling kettle must now decide on the kind of vocal sound this technique demands. Broadly speaking there are two methods of producing vocal sounds; either as in sighing or as in groaning. Obviously Miss Dartle chose the second method. Contemporary teachers, despite their alleged hatred of crooners, almost invariably favour the first method. This is understandable, for the sigh is a gentle, non-committal and highly refined sound, very different from the crude and primitive groan. But the more one uses the sigh as a basis for sung tone, the breathier and woollier and farther forward the sound will be. No true air compression would be possible, because the very nature of the sigh is a process of breathing air out. The groan on the other hand draws the vocal cords together excluding all air which is not phonated. It is in fact a sustained grunt and demands a similar technique and preparation. On a voiced note its characteristic quality remains the same.

In recommending the groan as a basic model, I must warn the reader against identifying desirable tone with the kind of sound associated with groaning. The groan is a positive gesture made in a positive way, and the very fact of its being an expression of revolt against the buffeting of fate prevents any likelihood of beautiful tone quality resulting. To transform the groan into something fit to be heard inside Covent Garden, we must ignore the kind of sound usually associated with it and think only of the peculiar technique required to produce it. This depends entirely upon what may be called the singer's overriding purpose. If he aims to express primitive emotion regardless of its effect upon his voice, then we may expect to hear the sort of sound usually associated with the word 'groan'. Indeed if his emotion is the result of overwhelming physical or mental distress, the cords will be drawn too tightly together for them to vibrate at all. But if his predominant purpose is to make beautiful sounds, the cords will not be approximated so tightly, and their spontaneous vibration will enable the voice to flow freely. The expression of emotion is the singer's secondary purpose; his primary purpose is to enchant his listeners.

EXERCISE 32

Breathe in through the mouth with the lips just parted. Give a short grunt; then say 'UH' (as in 'wood') in exactly the same way. Repeat the grunt and UH alternately five times, making sure the UH is located at the top of the lungs at points just above the nipples.

Now say two short UHs followed by one long UH, keeping the feeling of groan right through to the end.

EXERCISE 33

You are meeting your friend at a rendezvous by a wall which reaches just to eye level. Having rearranged your figure, you are able to peer over; and there he is. His smile of greeting induces an immediate glottal closure; the abdominal muscles contract and a relaxed diaphragm is lifted buoyantly. 'Ah', you say. (He should be taken to signify 'He' or 'She' since in such matters it is taken for granted that man embraces woman.)

g. Air and bone conduction

All sounds are received either by air conduction or bone conduction, or, as in singing and speaking, by a mixture of the two. In air conduction sounds are received as a result of sound waves entering the external passage of the ear. The end of this passage is completely closed by a thin membrane called the ear-drum, which can be thrown into vibration when waves of sound beat upon it. Behind the ear-drum is a small cavity called the middle ear. Across this cavity stretches a chain of three tiny bones which transmit the vibrations of the ear-drum to the inner ear. All sounds outside the body are normally received in this way, and a partially deaf person's hearing can be improved by an amplifier placed in the entrance to the ear.

In bone conduction sounds originating inside the body are received as a result of sympathetic vibrations of certain bones which are transmitted directly to the inner ear. In the case of extensive damage to the middle ear an amplifier placed against the mastoid bone provides satisfactory hearing by bone conduction. This kind of reception does not often occur in ordinary life, but owing to the characteristic position of their instrument violinists hear themselves to a greater or lesser extent through vibrations in the collar-bone.

The sounds which the singer or speaker makes come from inside the body and inevitably are heard by himself very largely through bone conduction. This is why nobody at first recognizes his own speaking or singing voice on a record or tape. At the recording session the voice may have sounded wonderfully rich and full, yet when played back it is a hollow mockery. We all have suffered agonies from hearing our own voices—and nobody hated it more than Caruso. That may be some small consolation!

The difficulty of learning to hear one's voice as it sounds to the audience is so great that it is almost impossible for a moderate singer to improve his technique without the help of a teacher. The fortunate people with so-called 'natural' voices have very often steered clear of any teachers, and wisely too because they are able to rely implicitly on their sensations to guide them. The rest of us have to learn to recognize and induce certain sensations of which we have had little experience hitherto. This calls for unusual qualities of patience and resolution. One has to remain comparatively indifferent to the changing sound of one's voice; but since this is a near impossibility, here is a small piece of advice: Do not cup your hand behind the ear when singing. Admittedly this will make the voice sound considerably better to yourself; far, far better than the way it sounds to the audience! To hear your own voice in any way remotely like its real self, put your open hands with the palms facing forwards in front of both ears. This will give an approximately accurate idea of your actual voice; but do not think that by doing this you will learn how to sing. The only reliable way is by inducing the correct sensations.

⑥

THE CHIEF RESONATOR
IN ACTION

Singing has been defined as the art of projecting words on a vocal line. If we accept this definition, three different methods may be distinguished. By using a heavy breath pressure against the vocal cords one can shout or scream. By using a low breath pressure against loosely approximated cords one can sing as one speaks; this produces many varieties of performance, all of which to a greater or less extent partake of the technique of crooning. Like the shouter and screamer, the crooner does not adjust his resonance cavities, and since his breath pressure is the same as in ordinary conversation, he has no difficulty in performing in a completely natural manner. With a good voice or a pleasing personality, the result will not be uplifting but can be very charming. His limitations however are glaringly obvious. He cannot sing loud, and in singing softly his voice changes colour and merges into a whisper. In any case the voice has no effective upper harmonics and cannot be projected beyond the length of a small room. For this very reason it sounds extremely well over the microphone which has a low ceiling of dynamic power.

I would not for one moment deny that a young singer with a fine throat may be able to use either of these methods, and still produce very pleasant sounds. The tragedy is first, that he could make much fuller, rounder, more significant and beautiful sounds; secondly, that he will not be able to go on for many years of professional work without losing his robustness and sympathetic quality.

The singer who uses the third method of projecting words adjusts his resonance cavities and keeps them firm and steady throughout the sung phrase; simultaneously he takes a breath. He then approximates the vocal cords so that they are able spontaneously to vibrate, and builds up sufficient pressure of breath for them to transmit sound waves up into the resonator. The approximation of the cords is voluntary but subconscious, and depends largely on the efficiency of his resonator and compressor. In Chapter 4 the techniques of inhalation and compression were discussed. Chapters 6 and 7 will be devoted to the rather more complex technique of adjusting the resonators, but before embarking on them, do make certain that the routine of inhalation and compression has been so thoroughly mastered that the muscles function subconsciously.

a. The soft palate

The roof of the mouth is divided into two parts. The front bony part is called the hard palate. Behind is the soft palate. It is indeed soft and spongy, as may be confirmed by an exploratory finger. At its rear end there is a grape-like protuberance called the uvula, which has intrigued the budding singer since time immemorial. One of my pupils thought it was the vocal cords!

The soft palate is like a movable flap. It can be raised to a horizontal position or lowered, as in the following exercise:

EXERCISE 34

Hold up a mirror close to a window with a good light, so that you can see the back of the throat.

With the mouth open, take a breath through the nose. This will feel very odd! If you watch in the mirror, you will find that the tongue humps itself up so as to meet the descending soft palate. Together they form an effective barrier against breath entering the mouth. If there were no such barrier, it would be impossible to breathe in through the nose with the mouth open, since air automatically enters the nearest and widest aperture.

On a whispered AH breathe out through the mouth. At the same time tell yourself that you are anxious to see right to the back of the throat. For breath to come out through the mouth, the tongue-soft palate barrier must be removed, the tongue flattening itself and the soft palate rising.

The mobility of the soft palate is an important element in voice production, but there is no question of consciously adjusting the length of the throat in the manner of a trombone. A deliberate lift of the soft palate causes a stiffening and distension which effectively cuts off all possibility of nasal resonance. The toneless hollow sound which results

[78]

Fig. 13 Exercise 35
(a)

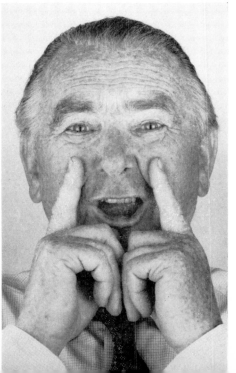

(b)

Fig. 14
The Italian Vowels
E and *A* (front view)
(a) E in good
production

(b) A in good
production

(c) A in bad
production

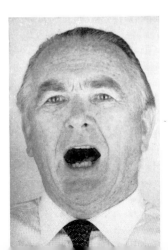

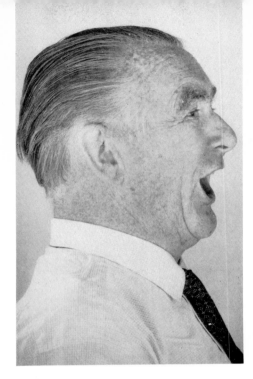

Fig. 15   The Italian
Vowels *E* and *A* (profile)
(*a*) in good production

(*b*) in bad production

Fig. 16 (*a*) (*b*) The Italian Vowels *E* and *A* on high notes

is a familiar characteristic of yawning. Equally there is no question of any downward pressure. In struggling to keep the larynx in a low position, you will smother the tone and build up a number of wrong habits; sooner or later damage will be caused which may be irreparable. Singing is an act of co-operation, not of conflict.

The next two sections will show how the soft palate can be brought into a high position without risk of distension and consequent hootiness. Meanwhile continue practising Exercise 34 until you are satisfied that the soft palate is sufficiently energetic. Then discard the exercise. If you keep on with it, your inhalations will be punctuated by sniffs and snorts and the audience will be amused in the wrong places.

b. The jaw and the cheeks

The length of the throat depends on the positions of the larynx and soft palate. With a low larynx and high soft palate the throat will be long and deep, and the tone likely to be good. Contrariwise a short throat with a high larynx and low soft palate will certainly produce poor tone. But a long throat is not in all circumstances correct. The act of yawning for instance calls for a long throat, but produces a condition in which the throat is dilated and the soft palate stiffened; this causes poor resonance in the throat cavity and none in the nasal and head cavities, as we all know when weariness or boredom overtakes us. The sensation of being about to yawn is however a most desirable one. It is symptomatic of a raised soft palate and low larynx, but with none of the stiffness and dilation which accompanies the actual moment of yawning. It can be induced without difficulty, but is not easily dissociated from the act of yawning of which it is the prelude. A more reliable method of building an efficient resonance cavity is demonstrated in the following exercise:

EXERCISE 35(a)

Put one finger behind the upper front teeth, so that it stands almost vertically in front of and touching the chin (Fig. 13a). The lower lip will now be in more or less a straight line with the upper front teeth. Lift the tongue so that the sides are against the upper back teeth; the position of the front of the tongue is of no importance. The part of the cheeks immediately below the pupils of the eyes when looking straight ahead should be lifted and slightly bulging, and the nostrils wide open.

Instead of feeling down and forward and heavy and determined, the jaw will now feel back and up and lightheaded and stupid. The movement may be associated with the sensation of being about to yawn.

In addition you will notice the following characteristics:

(a) The expression suggests not smiling but laughter.
(b) The point of the chin feels blunter and less protrusive than usual.
(c) The lower lip is relaxed.
(d) The upper lip curls a little up and forward, so as to reveal about six teeth.
(e) There should be about a finger's breadth between the teeth.
(f) With the nostrils dilated, the nose feels shorter and broader.
(g) With the cheeks lifted, the lower eyelids are pushed upwards. High cheeks and wide nostrils are in fact as indispensable to good singing as firm pegs to good violin playing (Figs. 14 and 15).

Without allowing the jaw to disturb the position of the finger, say the following:

    i. O.K.! Cook a cake
   ii. Go gay
  iii. King Kong
  iv. Grow grey
   v. Going, going, gone
  vi. Cowlick
 vii. Cockcrow
viii. Lacking glue
  ix. Crow on a log

Since this facial arrangement opens the door to good production, the reader should determine to get his features accustomed to it as speedily as possible. Accordingly he will be well advised to keep a finger behind the teeth, while reading this and other sections, and while watching television. In this position the throat becomes long and deep as a result of the soft palate being raised, while the larynx is so favourably disposed that forward production is virtually impossible. This can be verified by first whispering, which is most difficult and uncomfortable; and then grunting and groaning which is correspondingly easy.

(The methods of holding a pencil laterally between the teeth, or inserting a bone prop perpendicularly between the upper and lower front teeth are both positively harmful. The jaw is not properly retracted; moreover the resulting contraction of the muscles of the lower lip and neck will have deplorable consequences.)

EXERCISE 35(*b*)

Keeping the face in the condition established in Exercise 35(*a*), place the two thumb-nails against the chin, and the tips of the first fingers against the cheekbones immediately underneath the pupils of the eyes. In this position the pupils, the fingertips and the corners of the lips will now find themselves in more or less a straight line (Fig. 13(*b*)).

Repeat Exercise 35(*a*) (i to ix), keeping watch that the jaw does not revert to its habitual position. As soon as you feel confident of saying these correctly, continue with the following examples:

    x. Topper took a trip.
   xi. Dad adored Edward.
   xii. Twice ten are twenty.
  xiii. Nonagenarian nun nurtures Ned.
  xiv. Saucy Sally sails Saturday.
   xv. Thousands throng theatre.
  xvi. Fee, Fie, Fo, Fum.
 xvii. Many a man may call me Madam.
xviii. A babel of people.

Stiffness of the jaw is a contributory cause of most bad singing. Habitually the jaw remains in the position most convenient for talking. Since the English language is usually pronounced in terms of consonants rather than vowels, the English or American jaw position is normally the one in which consonants can be pronounced with the least possible effort. It is not however a position in which it is possible to form an efficient resonating cavity, and since the jaw is extremely reluctant to change its habits the importance of Exercise 35 will be appreciated. The singer is likely to be additionally handicapped by the curious ideas he may be harbouring about the mechanism of the jaw. Almost everybody labours under the delusion that the jaw moves up and down. In fact it does nothing of the sort; it swings like the handle of an inverted bucket. The reader will corroborate this, as soon as he has examined other people's jaw movements and forgets his own misleading sensations. When the mouth is opened, the jaw should feel as if it went down a little and then back and up. The sensation is rather as if you were putting on spectacles upside down, with the sides going back under the ears instead of over them. In any case the two ends of the jaw-bone should feel as if they were being pulled backwards and upwards, as a rider pulls on his horse's reins. On no account should there be any sense of pushing the front of the jaw-bone into place.

EXERCISE 36

Place the right finger and thumb on the cheek-bones. With the left fingers on the chin, pull the jaw down as far as it will go. Feel the cheeks rising at the same time, and see that the lips do not spread sideways. There is no difficulty in doing this, but many people will find that they have never opened their mouths so wide before, and that they are making ominous crackly noises. The stiffness wears off very quickly, and in a few minutes you will be able to move the jaw through its complete stretch silently and smoothly. A helpful dodge is to forget about the lower jaw, and to feel that, by raising the cheeks, you lift the upper jaw.

In singing, as indeed in speaking, eating, swallowing or any movement, the jaw drops a short distance down to a point where it can be either protruded or retracted. From there, in good voice production, it should swing backwards. On medium and low notes the distance it travels is only enough to leave a little more than a finger's breadth between the teeth; on high notes the distance is considerably greater. In any case the cheeks are lifted as if they were being pushed up into the eyes.

It is possible that some readers may confuse retraction of the jaw with the instruction that many teachers give, to drop the jaw. This is the position in which one falls asleep in the train; the upper teeth are covered by a long upper lip, the nostrils are slits and the countenance is suffused with a gentle melancholy. Such a position has no claim to serious consideration. Nor has the crackbrained suggestion that the singer's jaw should resemble the village idiot's. It derives from the facile association of good singing with relaxation. This is a half truth which has done an incalculable amount of harm. Singing demands the relaxation of certain muscles and the contraction of others; it suggests not so much the village idiot as a tiger about to spring (Fig. 16).

[82]

An even commoner panacea is the plea for smiling faces; beloved of choirmasters, it is the signal for their flock to respond with wide and ghastly grins. A smile is usually an indication of love and friendship, but by no means always. It may express other emotions, such as pity, surprise or sarcasm. It may even suggest polite defiance, as when an animal bares his teeth in a snarl.* The expression induced in Exercise 35 suggests none of these things. You look in fact as if you are laughing, and with this expression goes a certain loss of co-ordination which is invariably characteristic of laughter. A group of people at a theatre for instance show by their smiles that they are enjoying themselves, but they are still able to disturb us with their irrelevant chatter; their world is still a rational one, founded on communication by speech. The moment they start to laugh this rational world disappears. In short, smiling is rational, while laughter is essentially emotional. Singing is also emotional and demands an emotional expression; for this reason the singer should look to the expression of laughter as a guide to beautiful tone quality.

It is obvious why choirmasters, knowing nothing of mandibular retraction, hesitate to recommend laughter as a guide to voice production. With the best will in the world it is difficult for the ordinary person to assume a laughing expression. It demands an absolute release from self-consciousness. Even when he has found how to do so without trouble, his efforts will be in vain unless the correct kind of laughing expression is assumed. The normal laughing smile is not desirable, because there is a tendency for the lips to spread sideways and the lift of the cheeks to move in an easy-going outward, rather than an upward, direction. The correct expression will suggest not so much the cosy associations of laughter, as the tragi-comic mask of the classical theatre.

All these directions may seem inordinately complicated and elaborate. But they are needed, because they are the only means of enabling the singer to recognize and manipulate certain tongue muscles which control the shape of the throat cavity. These muscles, which are described in the next section, are probably the most important and certainly the most neglected element in good voice production. When

* The reader will have had this experience when, in collecting examples of vocal cord adduction (see page 71), he felt it advisable to offer a token apology.

properly contracted they turn the throat into a highly efficient resonating cavity, and at the same time they bring about, in a much less exaggerated degree than the reader has probably been inducing, the various facial characteristics already described; consequently if you induce these characteristics, you will sooner or later find that the tongue muscles have gone into contraction. You will then be able to recognize the sensation, and contract the tongue muscles at will. Once you can do this, you may forget all about any facial manipulation. The general expression will be the same, but the feeling of artificiality will disappear.

The reader may wonder how the expression of laughter can possibly be reconciled with each and every vocal interpretation—with Musetta's tantrums and Mimi's decline, with Carmen's scorn and Brahms' 'Four Serious Songs'. Obviously it would be ridiculous if the audience received a visual impression of laughter; but provided instructions are followed, both voice and face will simply feel and look truly alive. If, on the other hand, the face remained in a natural reposed state, the mere act of singing would tend to make it look heavy and stiff, with very little impression of vitality. Needless to say, the impression would be intensified by the comparatively poor vocal quality.

A singer conveys the various emotions suggested by the song or role which he is interpreting primarily with his voice; secondly, by movements and attitudes of the body which express and amplify his vocal conception; thirdly, and only very occasionally, by facial expression. On the concert platform he, and especially she, may greet the audience with smiles, curtsies and kisses, but from the moment before the music begins both he and she depend on their voices, and not their faces, to convey each and every emotional expression. This is equally true in operatic work. Naturally, while listening to other singers a good artist allows his face to reflect the appropriate emotion; but when he himself is singing, it is more than enough if he manages to sing well. Students who disregard this principle do so to the detriment both of the musical and the dramatic tension. They distract the audience and themselves from what should be their sole preoccupation. So far from creating a masterly interpretation of their role, they merely provide an exhibition of what is commonly known as 'mugging'. On the musical stage there is no exception to the rule that one acts with the body, and keeps the

[84]

face for singing. More often than not, performers who disobey this rule end by stepping half-way out of their assumed character, saying in effect to the audience 'Watch me acting!' Or even worse, 'You may be bored by this, but I'm an awfully nice person!'

It is not surprising that the growing tendency intentionally or unintentionally to make faces coincides with a steady decline in vocal technique. The awful grimaces of so many singers are clear evidence that their technique is defective. Almost as invariably the mugging which we see so often is due to subconscious efforts to compensate for a poor performance. Admittedly all kinds of attempts are made to seduce the poor singer from the paths of righteousness. Photographers in search of glamour, producers in search of easy dramatic effects, and the media of film and television which can blow up a small, unresonant voice into something both rich and strange—all of them clamour in their different ways for features which portray but do not express, which may be lively enough but are not truly emotional, which pronounce words on pitched notes, but do not make and project a vocal line out of whatever words are sung.

c. The tongue muscles: I

When sound waves come up against a hard surface, they do not flatten themselves against it, nor do they flow alongside it like water; they rebound in all directions. In order to achieve the finest possible resonance, the passage through which they travel must be as smooth and round as possible. This is a condition which very many singers have never experienced in their lives, owing to the tendency of the back of the tongue to encroach into the throat cavity. Of all vocal defects this is perhaps the commonest and the most disastrous. So far from travelling up a straight pipe, simple, unangular and of a width appropriate to the demands of the vocal cords, the sound waves encounter a combination of kink and bottleneck (Fig. 17). The resulting rake's progress is easily imagined. Aware that the tone is not altogether satisfactory, the bad singer instinctively increases his breath pressure; in order to maintain their vibration, the vocal cords become tighter, making the quality thin and the intonation sharp. The singer thereupon reinforces his breath pressure, the cords in turn increase their tension, and so the vicious circle gathers momentum.

Operative muscles for securing a fine resonance cavity are available

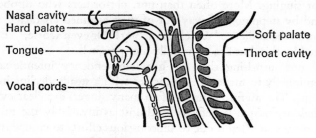

Nasal cavity
Hard palate

Tongue

Vocal cords

Soft palate
Throat cavity

(a) Right position

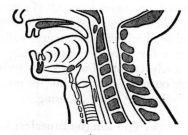

(b) Wrong position

FIG. 17. THE EFFECT OF THE TONGUE MUSCLES I

of course, and employed even by the most lachrymose crooners. The trouble is that, with our slovenly speech habits and unfamiliarity with the vocal mechanism, we do not use these muscles as efficiently as we might. They are not easily identifiable, but if you have studied the previous section, and practised Exercise 35, you will have certainly discovered that one of the characteristics of the retracted jaw is that the tongue seems to be curled up. It is a familiar feature of the sensation not of yawning, but of being about to yawn. There is a pull on the underside of the tongue close to its root, as if to lift the sides and bring them inwards towards its central point. This brings the back of the tongue farther forward, although we are not aware of it. One effect of the contraction is plainly visible if the tongue is put into a perpendicular attitude, as in Fig. 18. In this position the veins and blood vessels overlying the muscles concerned can be seen to bulge, as the contraction takes place. With a little practice in front of a mirror you will be

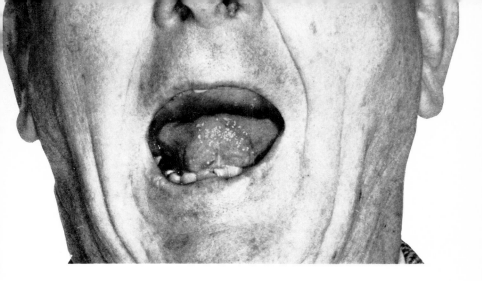

Fig. 18   The effect of the Tongue Muscles I
(*a*) in contraction

(*b*) in relaxation

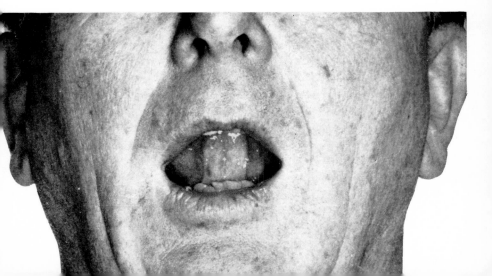

Fig. 19   The effect of
the Tongue Muscles II
(*a*) in contraction

(*b*) in relaxation

able to control these muscles, and to recognize the accompanying sensations.

EXERCISE 37

Open the jaw as wide as possible, as in Exercise 36 (page 82). In this position the tongue muscles will be contracted. Close the jaw slowly, taking care to maintain the contraction. It will be found that in the closed position the jaw remains retracted.

Put the tongue out as far as it will go. In this position the muscles will be contracted. Without closing the mouth, draw the tongue back in, but do not allow the muscles to relax.

The importance of the tongue muscles can hardly be overstressed. Admittedly the throat is a highly adaptable and efficient chamber for conveying air, food and drink from mouth to windpipe or gullet, and for resonating on spoken, shouted, coughed and other noises. It is a good all-round article but without special training cannot be expected to give more than good all-round service as a resonator of vocal tone. In the same way a soap-box is a good all-purpose article, far more useful than a Stradivarius. Nevertheless, though it might be possible to play the Beethoven concerto on a soap-box, a Stradivarius would be infinitely preferable. Anatomically the throat is an all-purpose soap-box, but can be transformed into a Stradivarius if the owner so wishes. But the singer must set about his work with the right tools; in other words he must be ready and able to manipulate the tongue muscles at the drop of a hat. In this way the throat is made flexible; yet with all its flexibility it should seem as hard and firm as any instrument of sounding brass (Fig. 19).

Compared with the singer an orchestral player has a very easy task. His instrument, having been already prepared for action, will remain, apart from occasional adjustments, a reliable apparatus for making music. Admittedly the voice, without any kind of preparation, will emit the requisite sounds, but these will be merely pitched notes coming out of a speech-producing instrument. To make beautiful sounds, the singer must first transform his throat from a speaking instrument into a musical one, and no amount of aesthetic sensitivity can compensate for this elementary need.

The reader who is unaware of the tongue muscles needs to keep a constant watch to prevent the clarity of the vowel sound being obscured. He may be successful if he is a good artist, but the expenditure of concentration and nervous anxiety is more than the average student can sustain over a protracted period. A comparison might be drawn between the steering mechanism of a very old car (in which the play was so great that constant adjustment was needed) and that of a modern racing model. In this day and age far too many vowel mechanisms resemble the steering of the Dodgem cars of the fair-grounds.

The position of the tongue when lying flat and relaxed with the front and sides against or close to the lower teeth may be compared to that of a dog lying flat on the hearthrug. With contracted tongue muscles the tongue and the tongue root are like the same dog in an erect begging position. The tongue root is lifted up, and the back of the tongue finds itself against or very close to the back upper teeth, with the sides drawn together into a compact round mass. In short, like a miniature edition of the body in a position of readiness, the tongue must be lifted up and kept narrow.

With the tongue muscles contracted the mouth resembles a lozenge-shaped hexagon. The lips are slightly apart, and the sides—not the corners or the centre—of the lips protrude very slightly up and out; in this condition they will fold themselves half or three-quarters over the opened mouth quickly and easily when pronouncing O or U. It is in fact impossible, with the tongue muscles contracted, for the upper lip either to be loose and relaxed, or to spread sideways; it is equally impossible for the tone quality to degenerate into a wide, white or catty sound. The position of the front part of the tongue is usually considered to be immensely important in tone production. It is not. The front part of the tongue is needed for articulation, but has absolutely no effect on tone quality. It should not be flat, and the tip need not be behind or indeed anywhere near the lower teeth. The insistence on these two points by many teachers has, I am sure, done enormous harm to music. The front of the tongue must be left free to move about as it chooses. Just as the tail of an airborne squirrel helps it to bring off miracles of balancing, so the front of the tongue enables the back part to achieve an exact adjustment in the size of the throat resonator.

The most practical way of achieving a correct position of the tongue is to rely on the consonantal sound *ng* (as in 'thing'). In pronouncing *ng* the tongue will be found to be against the back teeth, and the mere act of singing *ng* seems to send the sound in a backward and upward direction; the sensation is part and parcel of good voice production, as will be explained later. In singing the Italian vowel *E* it is perfectly easy to keep the tongue in precisely this same position. On the Italian vowel *A* almost everyone will find that the tongue wants or in some cases has to leave the upper back teeth, but in flattening itself it must not be allowed to move backwards. It should move as little as possible and, once the *A* is completed, should return to the same position against the upper teeth as if it were attached to a powerful spring.

EXERCISE 38

i. Keeping the back of the tongue against the upper teeth, say:

(*a*) *ng—E—ng*
(*b*) *ng—A—ng*

ii. Keeping the back of the tongue against the upper teeth, repeat Exercises 37(*a*) and *(b)*.

iii. Say the following Italian vowels with the tongue muscles first relaxed and then contracted:

(*a*) *A—E—A*
(*b*) *E—A—E*

d. Emotion and expression

Singing is the vocal expression of an emotional mood. The function of the words of a song is to indicate the particular mood, and to identify it with some experience which the listener can comprehend and share; the function of the music is to reflect this mood, and to intensify its impact.

The reader need not be alarmed. He will not be expected to induce a lot of trumped-up sentimentality. He is not even going to be told to 'put his soul into it' when he sings! Emotion is created as a result of a combination of the two elements which go to make up good voice production. Of these the first is a well-wrought resonating cavity, which with the indispensable aid of the tongue muscles remains completely firm and defined; the second is an upward breath compression, reinforced by the contraction of the sacro-spinalis. Together the two elements set up an emotional condition which will stay throughout the sung phrase. Without either one of them the emotion will not be induced, and the tone quality will be poor and lacking in vibration.

The following analogy from an old fairytale may help you to understand and apply this correctly. The Sleeping Beauty was aroused first, because she herself was ready for love and, secondly, by the arrival of her insistent prince. In singing the readiness corresponds to the condition of the throat when the tongue muscles are contracted and the Prince's arrival to a breath compression against the vocal cords. With these two preconditions an emotional stimulus is automatically aroused; the technique is merged with the emotion to become one driving force, and this is what causes the musical phrase to be initiated and to continue to its very end. Emotion and technique must never be segregated mentally or physically; they become a union out of which sound materializes. The masculine element is the act of compressing breath, while the feminine element is the far more difficult and subtle business of shaping the throat so as to make it a favourable resonating cavity. From their union comes the emotional condition which sets off the act of singing.

Curiously enough the feminine element seems to come much more easily to men singers than to women. In any case all singers tend to favour one element rather than another, for reasons which are not necessarily psychological. Some may find one side of their faces peculiarly intractable, so that the right cheek may rise easily while the left hardly stirs. Consequently their resonating or feminine element is so disabled as to ruin any hope of success. The remedy, which is to concentrate on the cheek less easily movable, may seem to result in hideous grimaces; but it is well to remember that the worst grimaces are found in those parts of the anatomy which are not doing their job, and either look dead or meaninglessly contracted. Muscles that are working properly may not result in the most ravishing expression possible, but will at least give the comfortable assurance that as a singer you will be looking all right.

Once you experience the emotional condition, you have to remain inside it, no matter how strange you may feel. It is a condition in which you will be unable to think clearly and logically, and in which you will be reluctant to examine near or distant objects. Not surprisingly, like a cautious guest who likes cocktails but is scared of getting drunk, the beginner instinctively shies away from the one thing that is essential to good singing. Yet of all conditions it is the most enviable. He seems to be freed from the shackles of earth, and to be wafted into the air. Once off the ground he need not expend any unusual energy. Like a gull, who may remain confidently airborne so long as he does not fold his wings, the singer will preserve his emotional condition so long as he keeps the tongue muscles and the sacro-spinalis contracted.

But although it is created primarily by physical means, you must at the same time help the process by inducing an appropriate emotional condition. In Section b the expression resulting from laughter was found to be a reliable means of securing a good resonating cavity. The emotion giving rise to genuine laughter is however not readily susceptible to the physical movements connected with the act of singing. Much more easily induced is the opposite emotion of weeping. It is easy to understand why this is so, for whereas laughter is of most frequent occurrence on sociable occasions, weeping is a very personal affair, intimately associated with the groan which has been found to be one of the keys to good singing. In short the expression of laughter and the emotion of weeping is the singer's ideal.

You may feel a little apprehensive at the prospect of mixing your emotions so extravagantly. It is not particularly complicated. The face maintains its laughing appearance, but the compression of breath against the vocal cords produces a personal and emotional stimulus which is miles away from the easy relaxation of most instances of laughter, but similar to many conditions of weeping. It is in fact the same condition as precedes the first sounds we utter as new-born babies. Since these sounds are made in conformity with the laws of nature, it is not surprising that a baby's cries are in many ways an object lesson in the art of producing tone. All singers who have been trained in forward production should make a point of examining one such specimen in their immediate neighbourhood. You no doubt possess a more than average voice and a great interest in the technique of tone production; yet if you try at any pitch you like to imitate that infant, you will probably be utterly baffled. Having become accustomed to treat the voice as a kind of recorder, you will be unable to reproduce even in imitation the most natural, simple, effective and primitive method of making vocal noises. It seems that we should take a closer look at our instrument.

[91]

Reduced to its simplest terms the human voice is a device for transforming air pressure into vibratory movement. In the same way the whistling kettle of page 73 contains a device for transforming steam pressure into a vibrating movement of the valve inside the whistle. Like the kettle with its gas ring the voice has a boiler (the lungs) where the pressure is raised, a valve (the larynx) where the compressed breath is transformed into sound waves, and a funnel (the throat and opened mouth) where the used air is passed out to the atmosphere. If this is understood, it needs no great insight to realize that the natural and proper place from which to work the voice is the boiler and not the funnel. And that is how a speechless infant utters its very first cry at birth. The clench of its abdominal muscles sets up an impulse for the diaphragm to contract, so as to fill the lungs and start the respiratory cycle. If the baby does not cry, the midwife gives it a sharp slap.

Because its body functions in conformity with the laws of nature, the voice of a healthy baby is strong, clear and untiring. But as the months go by, the voice seems gradually to lose its robust quality, and to become shallower and shriller. One hears a lot about the shrill voices of children, but the voice of a speechless baby is never shrill; it only becomes so in the course of learning to pronounce consonants nearly all of which have to be formed in the front of the mouth. 'Say "daddy", sweetie pie,' says the mother. 'Tat,' says the baby. 'No, darling, "daddy". D-d-d-daddy.' And so it goes on week after week, month after month. All too soon the infant ceases to associate the making of voice with the lungs and begins to regard the air in the funnel as that which sets the voice going. The boiler is left to look after itself; the voice rises in pitch, and the tone deteriorates in quality.

As a result of this gradual disintegration, the natural voice disappears and is superseded by what may be called the habitual voice. The orthodox teacher of forward production tries to make this habitual voice more musical and pleasing to listen to. No doubt much of his advice will be excellent, and very probably his musicianship and sense of style beyond reproach. But when all is said and done, a lot of his instruction is apt to be curiously vague. Every teacher, it is said, has his own method. This oft repeated saw is itself pretty good evidence that something must be wrong. And so it is. The first and by far the most important duty of the teacher of singing is to restore the strictly *natural* voice, the voice that is the birthright of every baby. Having done this, he trains his pupils to articulate their consonants clearly, but not so as to interfere with the correct pronunciation of vowel sounds. In this way the bel canto teacher brings his pupils' voices back to nature; the forward production teacher, confusing what is habitual with what is natural, cultivates a vocal technique which contravenes nature at almost every point.

Much of this may seem bewildering or wildly controversial to some readers. They will, I feel sure, come to understand and agree with it as they read further. At present it is enough if I can convince them that the sounds and behaviour of the new-born baby are enormously revealing. One characteristic, which the memories of even the oldest and most hard-bitten among us will corroborate, is that babies seem to create their tone at the top of the chest, directing it upwards and back-wards towards the crown of the head. The backward direction is in fact illusory; it is simply that adults are so used to trying in some degree to throw their voices towards the person whom they are addressing, that any kind of sound which is not produced in this manner seems to be directed at least partially backwards. The sensation of upward and backward projection is what the singer, as he builds up his compression, must take pains to induce; furthermore, he must maintain it to the end of each phrase. Irrespective of outward appearances the singer must never think of the mouth of his instrument as anywhere else but at a point a little behind the crown of the head. As for his own personal mouth, it is merely an outlet, like the *f* holes on the front of a violin; the sound must never seem to himself to issue out of it or anywhere near it.

Fig. 20 shows the apparent direction of the voice as the reader should feel it. Very probably he may at the same time experience a lot of vibration behind the nose and up in the forehead. So much the better. It is a sign that he is working along the right lines, and the last thing he should do is to try and suppress it. But since I shall not be discussing the frontal resonators at present, I advise him not to pay any attention to these sensations for the time being.

e. Eyes and the act of singing

Mentally and physically, the singer must be constantly aware that the throat is the central point of his voice. If the vocal cords as the initiators of the voice represent the royal bedchamber, the throat is certainly the

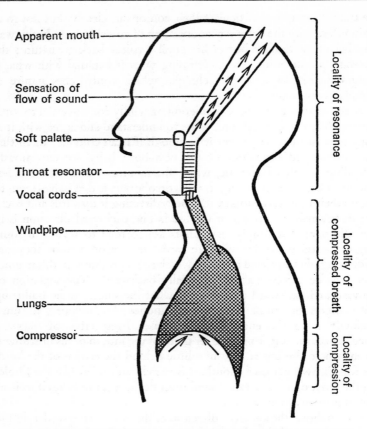

Apparent mouth

Sensation of
flow of sound

Soft palate

Throat resonator

Vocal cords

Windpipe

Lungs

Compressor

Locality of resonance

Locality of
compressed breath

Locality of
compression

FIG. 20. THE DIRECTION OF THE VOICE, EXCLUDING FRONTAL RESONATORS

throne room from which the might of an ancient dynasty stems. The preceding sections describe certain methods of realizing this condition; but they will only be effective if the reader has a clear idea of what is needed for good tone quality. If he dutifully keeps a finger behind the upper teeth, with no more idea of its practical purpose than that it is a means of improving the voice, the jaw will continue to feel like a caged animal awaiting its opportunity to escape. The finger constitutes a reminder that the duty of the jaw is wholly towards the well-being of the throat. The jaw, so to speak, turns inward to its lord and master.

Every relevant muscle in the singer's body must be prepared to act in similar fashion, relaxing or contracting in such a way as to ensure the finest conceivable resonance cavity.

Particular attention should be paid to the muscles governing the eyes. As collectors of visual impressions the eyes are in a state of habitual movement of which we are unconscious. Abnormality sets in if the movement is inhibited. This happens when we try to achieve an objective by bringing the eyes forward, as if they could be projected outwards in the manner of a snail's eyes. It is a characteristic of L drivers in their early stages, and of incompetent golfers who with bated breath and terrific concentration try to stare the ball out of countenance.

If after taking breath in the ordinary way you continue to stare at some particular object, the voice will seem to remain obstinately heavy; but as soon as you allow the eyes to shift from point to point, it will feel dynamic and buoyant. In this way the singer will recover, if only for a moment, the emotional condition described in the previous section. But there is no need to forestall vocal shortcomings by an attitude of shifty-eyed restlessness. A healthy condition can be ensured by making a habit of occasional blinking, and of doing a certain amount of quick light butterfly blinks at intervals during the day.

Eyes straining to see distant objects are incompatible with good tone production and can play havoc with the most carefully trained voice. Nearly all singers make a habit at rehearsal of reading their part over the accompanist's shoulder; and a most pernicious habit it is, because hardly anybody can read easily at such a distance. If during performance they start trying to identify people in the audience, they again will be projecting the eyes, and it will only be a question of time before the breath, infected with the same virus, is projected also. All such tendencies can be counteracted by occasional blinking. An even more effective remedy is deliberately to bring the eyes to what seems to be a near-sighted focal length, keeping them there throughout the act of singing. People with normal vision can do this quite easily, but it is difficult, maybe impossible, when wearing spectacles. Short-sighted people who live in this sort of world should not make a virtue of their defect. It may be a joy for them to go out in front of a large audience which they are unable to see, and whose existence they can blandly ignore, but it is not a satisfactory solution. Between them and the audience there must be a bond of communication, and in establishing it they have a choice of two techniques; they can only choose one and they cannot mix the two together. In one case they are pea-shooters, and in the other they are magnets. Human nature being what it is, most of us have gone pea-shooting in our time. Let us have done with such childish ways, and turn ourselves into gigantic magnets to draw the audience towards us.

The habit of closing the eyes, particularly on high notes, stems no doubt from a subconscious awareness that visual concentration cannot be associated with good singing. Nevertheless it is a bad habit. Closed eyes tend to lapse into a state of muscular immobility, which may not be as disastrous as the condition of staring, but which induces a passivity that accords ill with the demands of good voice production. Physically the act of compression will be less complete and less rigorously maintained; mentally the singer may drift into an ostrich-like conviction that, since he can no longer see his audience, he must be making beautiful sounds. He will be doing no such thing! As for the audience, nothing is more depressing than a singer who shuts his eyes. It is as though he were deliberately excluding them from any share in the act of re-creation which is the one and only object of artistic performance.

The following exercise is valuable for two classes of readers. First, for those who have been trying to bring the tone up against the hard palate, or into the nose or the head, or to project it forward and out to the audience. Secondly, for those who appear to rely on their eyes to see them safely through their ordeal. Very likely they will be people with good eyesight who are over-conscientious, anxious or highly strung. Singers of this type are often to be seen in amateur operatic performances, glueing their eyes on the conductor, concentrating on their lines, and striving to be heard in the last row of the gallery.

EXERCISE 39

Put up a theatre or concert placard or a popular newspaper with large headlines and stand near enough to be able to see the big letters easily without glasses.

Pick out an A, mentally pronouncing it as if it were an Italian vowel *A*. You see the letters on either side, and above and below it, but A is the central part of your vision. If you feel yourself beginning to stare, blink, and go on blinking at short intervals.

[96]

Movement I

As you take breath, your eyes are studying the large A, moving round and across it from point to point.

Movement II

Close the eyes. Bring the mental image of the A right up to the apex of the chest, where you simultaneously establish a breath compression and emotional condition. Be careful throughout the exercise to keep the neck long. As a result of the compression the neck should feel as if it is climbing away out of the body.

Movement III

The sacro-spinalis muscles contract. The emotional condition is strengthened simultaneously with the compression, and the vocal cords start to vibrate spontaneously.

Movement IV

Launch the *A* in the usual way, opening the eyes simultaneously, but continue to associate the *A* at the apex of the chest. If you visualized the *A* correctly, the eyes will seem to have been brought to an extremely near-sighted focus from which they will be unwilling to shift until the act of singing is completed. The same thing happens immediately prior to and during the act of kissing.

Repeat on the Italian vowel *E*.

The exercise can be practised equally well by identifying the *A* (or *E*) with an object in a picture or an ornament. The important thing is that it should be small and have a concrete position in space.

f. The tongue muscles: II

It is important that this section should not be studied until Section c has been thoroughly absorbed and put into practice; otherwise there is a danger that the instructions contained here will be applied superficially.

In contracting the tongue muscles the reader's attention up to now has been concentrated on bringing the root and the back part of the tongue upwards, and not bothering about the front part. This was the only practical means of achieving a condition which is absolutely essential to good voice production. At the same time the front part of the tongue may have been carried farther backwards than is desirable. Any such tendency must be eliminated as soon as possible.

In this connection the analogy of the begging dog is of enormous help. There are two symptoms—out of the lengthy list on page 80—which should be kept in mind; these are the lifted cheeks and wide nostrils. Much the best means of securing their co-operation is to imagine that your begging dog is manipulating a puppet which takes in the cheeks, nostrils and upper lip. These parts of the face will now seem to be lifted from above, and not pushed from below. Moreover you will avoid making any of those distressing grimaces which ruin so many performances.

EXERCISE 40

Practise the following jingles daily:

  i. speaking.
 ii. on a monotone.
iii. down the scale.
 iv. up the scale.

(a) Wide nose and cheeks up
     Raised high by begging pup
(b) Begging dog makes wide nose
     And cheeks high as climbing rose
(c) Wide nose and cheeks on dizzy height
     With begging dog make voices bright
(d) Wide nose with cheeks and dog in attic
     Make the voice more operatic
(e) Begging dog with feel of sneeze
     Lifts the cheeks and lip with ease

In repeating these couplets the reader must not think of the sense of the words, nor make any conscious attempt to obey their instructions; he will remember that in the last section it was shown that the more one stares at an object, the less well one is likely to sing. Concentrated will-power not only obstructs the imagination, but plays havoc with physical co-ordination. In a skilled athletic activity the conscious will has to be jettisoned; one becomes an instrument of art, and ceases to be a mere technician. The runner becomes a pair of legs, moving not only as fast, but as gracefully and beautifully as possible; the tennis player becomes a racquet, and the archer a bow and arrow.

There is no sense of rivalry or striving for achievement. Likewise, in the unusual double condition of a particular breath compression and specially prepared resonator, a kind of trance-like state is built up. The singer becomes a voice; he does not sing a note any longer; with an almost alarming intensity the note comes out of him as if it alone had any reality, and he was a mere inanimate shell. Quite literally the note sings him. The same feeling of violent possession occurs when one is desperately unhappy. Sighs and groans are no longer just heaved; they seem to heave you, overrunning the whole body as if it was their private playground. This sense of possession is experienced by almost all creative artists, though naturally the physical symptoms take many different forms. Luckily they constitute one of the major pleasures of life.

The whole art of singing, in its technical aspect, may now be summed up as the management and control of breath, and the tuning of the resonator; or—if you prefer the homelier analogies—the baby and the begging dog. When we have mastered these two arts we can sing; until we have mastered them we are not singers at all. And in attaining our ends, nothing will serve but hard and methodical work; and let me hammer it home that practice which is unmethodical is not only a waste of time but definitely harmful. You are starting out to cultivate a voice of which the beginner has no previous experience whatever, and which will develop gradually. The very worst kind of practice consists of an anxious search for perfection before there has been time for the true singing voice to develop, and indeed before you have gleaned the least idea of what it should sound and feel like. The great majority of students come to their first lessons with the idea that good voice production is a kind of conjuring trick, involving no physical effort, and that once they have learned this trick they will be singers. Like bluebottles on a window pane they bump hopefully around in quest of a magical escape route into a world of bel canto. Singing demands hard physical effort, as does the playing of any musical instrument. The oboist, for example, takes it for granted that effort will be thrown on to his lungs, because he can see with his own eyes the effect which the very small aperture of the reed will have upon the outflow of his breath. The singer's instrument is tucked away inside his body, but that does not give him the right to look upon singing as a conjuring trick, nor to behave like a bluebottle!

g. The singer and his instrument

We have now covered the main aspects of technique in launching a pitched note on *A* or *E*. They may conveniently be boiled down into the following private code of the points to keep in mind when preparing to sing:

Before you begin	Spanish dancer (page 9).
Movement I	Begging dog (page 88).
	Expression of laughter (page 83).
	Blinking eyes (page 95).
Movement II	High centre of gravity (page 52).
	Emotion of weeping (page 91).
Movement III	Bow and arrow (page 54).
Movement IV	Baby (page 91).

Above all it is vital to keep in mind that singing, from the technical point of view, is a dual process. There is the resonator and there is the compressor-vibrator; each have completely different functions, and if you try to absorb them into one unity it will be disastrous. A master violin-maker and a fine violinist are seldom or never united in the same person. This is what the singer has to be, building his own instrument as a master craftsman and playing on it as skilfully as any virtuoso performer, but never confusing the two functions. Compared with the singer an orchestral player has a very easy task. His instrument, having been already prepared for action, will remain, apart from occasional minor adjustments, a reliable apparatus for making music. Admittedly the voice, without any kind of preparation, will emit the requisite sounds, but these will be merely pitched notes coming out of a speech-producing instrument. To make beautiful sounds, the singer must first transform his throat from a speaking into a musical instrument; in other words, like the violinist who must provide himself with a tuned fiddle, the singer must first of all provide himself with a music-making throat, and no amount of aesthetic sensitivity can compensate for this elementary need.

Of the many unfamiliar points of view which good singing demands of us, the problem of concentrating not upon a sound, but upon the shaping of a resonance cavity is perhaps the most difficult. Somehow or other the singer must learn to maintain a predominantly feminine, indeed a maternal attitude towards his tone. Like a pregnant woman whose sole responsibility is to see that her body provides the requisite conditions for the birth of a healthy child, the singer must look primarily to the careful shaping of his throat in order to create a beautiful tone.

You may bring about this attitude of mind with the help of any imaginative concept which appeals to you, but be careful not to be taken in by loose catchwords. For instance we hear so much about the virtues of an open throat that it is only natural to associate it with a wide throat, and to take practical steps to induce this condition. In fact it is about the worst thing you could do. The throat should be considered as a mould out of which a cunningly shaped object is created. The only difference in this context between a jelly mould and a throat shaped for an *E* sound on a particular note is that in the first case the cunningly shaped object is jelly, and in the second it is energized air. If you try to widen the throat as if it was a sack which had to be held open to receive a load of sand, the swallowing muscles stiffen, and the root of the tongue moves towards the back wall of the throat; as a result the throat becomes constricted and inflexible, and the tone will sound white and shallow. This is more or less the same condition as in yawning which, in contrast to the moment immediately before starting to yawn, is entirely detrimental to the act of singing. If, on the other hand, you think of narrowing the throat as if to shape both itself and the vowel which it contains, the tone will be deeper and darker. These qualities are as desirable in voices as in all musical instruments, whatever the pitch. No pianist in his senses would prefer a shallow-toned minipiano to a concert grand; the reader should show the same common sense in his choice of instrument.

THE CHIEF RESONATOR
AND VOWELS

Vowel sounds are heard whenever the air inside the throat and mouth is disturbed either by breath or by sound waves. So long as the mouth cavity is not stopped up by closing the lips or teeth, as in humming, or by damming the flow of tone as a result of humping the tongue against the hard palate (when singing on *n*) or the soft palate (as on *ng*), we cannot help producing a vowel. Whether whispering, speaking or singing, some kind of vowel must occur. In whispering the vocal cords remain apart; both throat and mouth cavities are energized wholly by air pressed upwards by the abdominal muscles; a great deal of breath needs to be expended, and the resulting volume of sound is very small. In normal conversation the vocal cords are approximated, but unless we are trained singers, the one thing we never do is to energize the throat and mouth cavities wholly by means of sound waves; when we do so, the vowel sound is vastly different from that of normal speech. It is deeper, though not necessarily lower, and gives an impression of dignity, authority and sincerity.

a. Vowel and tonal resonance

In contrast to vowel resonance, tonal resonance means the sounds given off by the various vocal resonators in sympathy with the pitched notes created by the vibrating vocal cords. It is a little hard for the beginner to understand the difference between vowel and tonal resonance because, except on high notes or in sustaining notes on *ng*, *n* or *m*, good tonal resonance is invariably accompanied by clearly defined vowel sounds. Nevertheless he must do so, otherwise he will find himself in an unholy muddle!

As regards tonal resonance, the throat is the important resonator, whereas the mouth is little more than a passageway connecting the throat to the lips. Thus we have a throat cavity whose tonal resonance is all-important, but whose vowel resonance is unidentifiable, and a mouth cavity whose tonal resonance is insignificant but whose vowel resonance is predominant. In these conditions the beginner need only bother about producing a clear vowel in the mouth cavity, and a deep resonance in the throat cavity. He can do neither properly unless the appropriate tongue muscles are contracted. In ordinary conversation the tongue flattens and tends to block the upper part of the throat, causing a bottleneck which is bound to have a disastrous effect on the tonal resonance. This is why the contraction of the tongue muscles is so important in voice production, and why the Italian *E* which can be easily articulated with the back of the tongue against the rear upper teeth is preferable to the Italian *A*. Pronounced in good technique the vowel *E*, which in the mouth of the average Englishman is a light superficial affair, suddenly becomes much more significant. It should in fact be considered the basic vowel sound in the sense that all the other vowels are modifications of *E*, just as a green, red or yellow spotlight is a modification of the basic white bulb which provides the illumination. This conception will impart a feeling of depth to all the vowels; so much so that in the mind's eye they will resemble tall fir trees rather than sprawling willows. The feeling of depth however must be combined with the inward and upward tendency already described in the sections dealing with breath compression and the management of the tongue muscles. Only in this way is it possible to suggest the dignity and underlying seriousness which is characteristic of good singing, no matter how trifling the words.

b. The Italian vowel sounds

The Italian vowel sounds consist of the five vowels *A*, *E*, *I*, *O* and *U*. Unless you are completely familiar with them, it would be wise, before embarking on this section, to re-read page 71 in which their respective sounds are described.

Compared to his Italian colleague the Englishman with his thirteen vowels and innumerable diphthongs of everyday speech starts with a formidable handicap. His first priority is to make every vowel as narrow as possible and to keep the tongue muscles habitually contracted. When he has learned to do this, the beginner will probably prefer to sing the Italian open *E* rather than *A*, in which the back of the tongue recedes and flattens itself. It is therefore common sense to regard the open *E* as the basic vowel, *provided it is sung or spoken in the manner indicated in this book* (Fig. 14(*a*)).

The Italian closed *E* is pronounced in exactly the same way as the open *E*. The corners of the lips are pulled inward towards each other so as to bring the centre of the upper lip a little farther forward. Both movements are hardly noticeable. The sound corresponds roughly to the English AY, but without the slightest suspicion of the characteristic *E*-ĭ (as in 'it') diphthong. The superficial resemblance between the two vowel sounds makes the clean pronunciation of the closed *E* a matter of considerable difficulty for English and American singers; for this reason, when practising on *E* they are advised to use the open vowel.

In pronouncing the Italian *A* the back of the tongue is flattened, but this should be a very temporary affair; in other words you shift the tongue just far enough from the *E* position to enable you to pronounce *A*. The tongue seems to be drawn backward into the *A* position somewhat as if it were on a spring which pulled it up and forward into the *E* position as soon as the vowel was completed. It need hardly be said that this temporary retraction must not seem to affect the tension of the tongue muscles. You sing *A* but go on thinking *E*; and so long as good posture is maintained, this is not nearly so difficult as it sounds (Fig. 14(*b*)).

Like *E* the Italian vowel *O* has two distinct sounds, open and closed. The closed sound resembles more or less the English 'oh', but without the characteristic diphthong (oh-uh). For this reason it is wise, as in the case of the Italian *E*, to prefer the open *O* when practising on pure vowel sounds. Whether open or closed the vowel *O* is not altogether easy, owing to the misdemeanours of ordinary speech habits. The danger will be evident if you pronounce the Italian *A*, and then, without altering the shape of the mouth or the position of the lips, pronounce *O*; this cannot be done by the average beginner except by retracting the tongue, as in Fig. 17(*b*), thereby ensuring a throaty production. As with every vowel the back of the tongue should be against the rear upper teeth. To turn the Italian *E* into *O* you must superimpose the lips much as the operator of a theatre spotlight superimposes a coloured slide to bathe the fairies in a blue haze, or the villain in a ruddy glow. The upper lip (the singer's, not the villain's) is folded forward and over the entrance of the mouth, while the lower lip moves in sympathy. This forward movement is one which English lips are

Fig. 21 The Lip
Vowels
(*a*) Italian open *O*

(*b*) Italian closed *O*

(*c*) Italian *U*

Fig. 22   Lip and Teeth
Vowels
(*a*) Italian *I*

(*b*) French *U* and
German *Ü*

(*c*) French *EU* and
German *Ö*

peculiarly reluctant to make, even though it is the same as for kissing. Simultaneously the cheeks move upward and inward towards the nose, and the nostrils splay outwards (Fig. 21). The sensation in pronouncing O should be of a pulling movement towards the back of the head, somewhat similar to the act of rowing.

The Italian closed vowel O is pronounced in the same way as the open O, except that the upper lip is folded farther forward and over the entrance to the mouth. For the Italian vowel U, the upper lip is folded still farther forward, and the sensation of backward pull is even stronger than on O. Pronounced in this way U will possess a joyful emotional quality, rather as if you had just received an unexpected gift of a mink coat or a box of cigars!

As in every other vowel except the Italian I there should be at least a finger's breadth between the teeth; Scottish readers should be careful about this; many of them tend to close the teeth as well as the lips, making a thin reedy sound like an indeterminate German Ü.

In learning to articulate the Italian O and U vowels, the conception of the superimposed slide is of great value. Once the technique has been mastered, both vowels must be pronounced with the feeling that they spring, not merely from the throat, but from deep in the chest. On U in particular there must be no cooing like a dove or hooting like an owl. You may sing with a perfect legato but every time you let your U slip up into the mouth the effect will be similar to an organist pushing in a stop in the middle of a phrase. The remedy is first, to make sure that the lips are moving forward into their rightful position; secondly, in feeling the tongue high in the mouth, to imagine that the vowel is being pulled over the teeth towards the back of the head.

In pronouncing the Italian vowel I the teeth are brought closer together, so that there is much less than a finger's breadth between them (Fig. 22(a)). As in O and U the cheeks tend inwards and upwards, and simultaneously the nostrils splay outwards. In this way the vowel will sound narrower and more dignified, with none of the spreading, catty quality which, in tenors particularly, is so distressing. It will in fact, without disturbing the authenticity of the vowel, take on some of the quality of the German Ü. The back of the tongue remains against the rear upper teeth, and the middle is humped a little higher, so as to turn the Italian sound of E into I. The humping movement should not be consciously induced; with the teeth half closed and the desire to make an *I* sound, it will happen automatically.

The old Italian teachers were well aware of the special difficulties of *I* and *U*, though not all of them can have been as drastic as Pellegrini Celoni who, in his *Grammar of Rules for Beautiful Singing* published in 1810, wrote: 'The vowels *I* and *U* one ought to avoid, and leave to those who have the madness to imitate horses and wolves.' To English speakers and singers his reasons will be sufficiently evident. The near closing of the mouth sets up an instinctive compensatory impulse to project the tone forward; this must be overcome by a directly contrary induced impulse.

Very probably you will feel that, although the tone on *O* and *U* sounds all right, it must to some extent be stifled by the position of the lips. Admittedly the movement of the lips causes a certain loss of power, but you have to remember that the listener is not a machine into which sound is fed. Sounds are received by the ear and communicated to the brain, which selects whatever seems good and jettisons the remainder. Any receptive listener's brain accepts the obvious fact that *O*, *U* and *I* will not realize quite as much tone as *A* and *E*; the implicit variations in dynamics do not however disturb him, so long as each vowel is correctly pronounced. Subconsciously he allows for their unavoidable discrepancies.

EXERCISE 41

Sing the following, using Italian vowels:

c. First brush with consonants

The problems of articulation will be discussed in Chapter 10, but there is no reason why a few consonants should not be introduced at this point in order to allow the long-suffering reader the much overdue pleasure of actually singing a few words! Needless to say we are confining ourselves to the fewest and easiest consonants possible.

In good speech it is desirable, and in singing it is essential, to make the pronunciation of consonants a split-second affair. They are the lines between the squares on the pavements, the cracks between the piano keys, the bar-lines in written music. Consonants play a vital part in transmuting words into poetry but from the point of view of production they must be kept severely to their single duty of dividing one vowel clearly from another. Any departure from this rule causes an interruption in the legato of the vocal line; and legato is an essential element of bel canto singing. There are of course many occasions in performance when consonants should be emphasized for dramatic effect at the expense of the legato line. This is a matter of individual interpretation. Here we are concerned, so to speak, with the roast beef of singing.

As regards the articulation of consonants the reader at this stage need only remember that with contracted tongue muscles the jaw will be slightly retracted from its habitual position of ordinary speech. Consequently all the consonants involving the lips or the tongue will be articulated a little farther back. The new positions will feel unnatural at first, and the reader may protest that the clarity of his speech is affected. But not for long. After a very little practice he will find himself pronouncing the most complicated sentences with absolute ease and far more fluency than in his accustomed way of speaking.

Whatever the consonant, it should be regarded as part and parcel of the vowel. In other words you do not consciously pronounce the consonant at the place where it is articulated, any more than you switch on most electric lights at the place where the bulb is situated. You have to identify the consonant so intimately with the vowel which it precedes, that both seem to spring simultaneously from the apices of the lungs. The consonant, as it were, has no independent existence. It appears as an adornment of the vowel, like a hat on the head of a lady which, for a mere male at any rate, is only significant inasmuch as it enhances the beauty of the wearer.

This conception of the relationship of consonants to vowels is by no means characteristic of most contemporary singing. Indoctrinated with the theories of forward production, the average student tries to bring the vowel sound forward to the place where he articulates consonants, enunciating his words with the tip of the tongue, the teeth and lips in the manner of ladies' seminaries. Thereby he ensures a notably scooped attack, a minimum of vowel tone and exceedingly efficient, if somewhat spitty consonants. His diction is so obtrusive that it seems to swamp everything else. After the first song the average listener will clap. He will not say, 'What a lovely song!' nor, 'What a beautiful voice!'; more probably he will say, 'What good style!' or, 'How clear his diction is!' After the second song he will say, 'Of course you can hear every word!' By the end of the third song the cataract of syllables will have piled up on him to such an extent that he could not care less, so long as he does not have to unravel any meaning from them.

In working on the following exercise and indeed all the other exercises in later sections, be particularly careful in pronouncing O vowels; this applies not only to the open and closed Italian O, but also to the English O as in 'know', 'ought' and 'of'. If these vowels are properly articulated, the chances are that the singer, whatever his faults, will be pronouncing the remaining vowels properly. Furthermore, O vowels which are beautifully articulated provide, to a far greater extent than the other vowels, the groundwork of an expressive interpretation.

EXERCISE 42

Say the following, keeping a sustained legato with absolutely no gaps:

i. (a) *A U O*
   (b) Far to go
ii. (a) *O U O*
   (b) Go to Rome
iii. (a) *E I O*
   (b) May we go

iv. (a) *O U E*
   (b) Go today
v. (a) *I E I*
   (b) We may see
vi. (a) *I A O*
   (b) Iago

EXERCISE 43

Sing the same on a monotone; on a downward three-note scale; on an upward three-note scale.

d. The French U and EU and the German Ü and Ö

Not so long ago singers were expected to be perfect linguists. Recitals by aspiring vocalists consisted of groups of Italian, French, German and

English songs; since these were chosen from the same handful of composers, one programme was almost indistinguishable from the next. So were the languages!

In these days of jet-transported artists, and of readily accessible music on tape, record and radio, the vogue of the multilingual singer is mercifully dying out. One wonders how it came about in the first place, for with a few honourable exceptions hardly any great artist has made a habit of singing in more than two languages; many indeed have refused to sing in anything except their own mother tongue. This is not a plea for all vocal music to be sung in translation, but for singers to stop behaving like versatile parrots. Superficial polyglotticism is an offence to the art of music.

What exactly young singers should do depends of course on themselves, their opportunities, their musical tastes and their personal inclinations. One can at least be certain that an intimate acquaintance with one foreign language is enormously beneficial to the singing of English. With this end in view the reader should at an early stage adopt a foreign country, just as some teenagers adopt film stars. He should not be content merely to learn its language; he should steep himself in its music, its literature, its pictures and meet and talk to its people, eat its food, watch its films and if possible spend holidays there. In this way he will be contributing to his education, his culture and his worth as an artist. Best of all he will find himself singing his native language with far more depth and discrimination; his vowels will be more beautiful, his sense of poetry keener, his instinct for rhythm and intonation securer. When the time comes for him to sing in his second language, listeners will feel that he is still on his home ground, and able to convey an emotional message with none of that dreadful missionary atmosphere which the polylingual singers are so apt to exude.

Mercifully questions of pronunciation are in this book limited to Italian and English vowel sounds. But since many readers will be making French or German their second language, a word may be said about the pronunciation of the French U and EU and the German Ü and Ö. English students often seem to take for granted that their nationality prevents them from pronouncing these vowels effectively. So far from that being so, there is no difficulty whatever. To pronounce U (French) or Ü (German) one simply combines the Italian vowels *I* and *U*; the teeth are brought nearer together as a result of a stronger contraction of the tongue muscles, while the upper lip is simultaneously folded forward and over the teeth to form the Italian *U*. An *U* vowel is superimposed on an *I* so to speak (Fig. 22(*b*)). To pronounce EU (French) or Ö (German) *I* is combined with UH (as in *wood*); the teeth are brought nearer together, and the upper lip is folded forward and over them (Fig. 22(*c*)). On all four vowels the tongue remains in the same place. Naturally these instructions provide only a rough and ready means of acquiring a correct pronunciation. Both must be assimilated by attentive listening.

e. The English primary vowels

The English language contains thirteen recognized vowel sounds as well as a number of diphthongs. Moreover, of the five English vowels which very loosely correspond with the Italian *A, E, I, O* and *U*, the two counterparts of the Italian closed *E* and *O*, namely AY and OH, though listed as vowels, are invariably pronounced as diphthongs. This is in no sense a disparagement of contemporary pronunciation; in fact it would be a distortion of the English language to attempt to pronounce them as pure vowels. The English AY does not correspond to the Italian closed *E*, but consists of two vowel sounds approximating to *E-I* or *E-ĭ* (as in 'it'). Similarly the English OH is more or less like the Italian closed *O* followed by the English UH, viz: O-UH (as in 'wood'); the latter may be taken as the correct pronunciation, but variants resulting from local dialects and slovenly voice production are innumerable.

In themselves diphthongs do not inhibit good production so long as you are aware of the identity of the vowels involved, and of the technique to be employed in producing them. In every case one of the two vowels which make up the diphthong is quickly touched, while the other is sustained in the ordinary way. The quickly touched vowel should be treated as a species of consonant, being pronounced clearly but given no part in sustaining the tone. An enormous amount of bad singing is caused by attempts to share out the burden of sustaining the tone between the two vowels.

In this section only the two English vowels AY and OH are under consideration, the remaining vowels being discussed in Section f. In pronouncing the diphthong AY, make the first vowel a closed Italian *E*, and to all intents and purposes take the second vowel for granted; assuming that English is your native tongue, the second vowel cannot fail to appear. Similarly on OH, the first vowel must be a closed Italian O, while the second vowel is taken for granted.

EXERCISE 44

Say or sing on a monotone the following:

i. Eugene O'Neill.
ii. Joe Barlow may go gay.
iii. We may be lame.
iv. You owe me no boon.
v. Maybe Romeo may roam.
vi. Joe made you obey me.
vii. Joe gave you no dues.

f. The English secondary vowels

The following sentence is a convenient means of tabulating the thirteen pure English vowels in their order of pitch:

Who would know aught of art must work and then pay his fees

In ordinary speech or song the pitch variations of the vowel sounds are swamped by the sound resonance of the throat cavity, but if you whisper this wise aphorism their rising scale can be immediately distinguished. Incidentally the reader is warned never in any circumstances to practise whispering. It is invariably deleterious to good voice production, since the tone is brought forward on to the mouth and lips, the larynx rises, the tongue muscles are slack and the feeling of compression is lost. Furthermore the vocal cords assume a loose bowlegged attitude which they should not be allowed ever to experience.

There is no excuse for slurring over or mispronouncing any of the short vowels such as in 'in' or 'and'. Fifty years ago singers habitually referred to the 'sick cat' as the 'seek cart'. Today such misuse of the English language is rightly deplored. Short vowels are just as easy to sustain as the five Italian vowels, provided the tongue muscles are contracted and a proper use is made of the lips. Naturally the position of the tongue, lips and teeth varies according to the pitch of the note, the vowel sound, the volume of tone, the character of the song, the emotional implications and the singer's physical idiosyncrasies; nevertheless the following classification may be considered a reliable guide:

Who would know: 'Would' must be associated with the Italian closed O (Fig. 21(*b*)). In ordinary conversation the lips are hardly used at all; consequently the vowels included in the half sentence 'Who would know aught of', if clearly pronounced, are invariably throaty. There are no effective exercises to awaken recalcitrant lips to their responsibilities, nor need be since there is a direct relationship between their flexibility and the degree of contraction in the tongue muscles. If the tongue muscles are properly contracted, the upper lip will be brought forward and a little upward, and in this condition will be prepared on the instant to move into the O or U position. Remember also that the folding of the lips over the teeth cannot be overdone. You may easily feel that you are putting the lips in an U position in order to pronounce 'aught' and an O position to pronounce 'of', but the articulation of the vowel sounds will almost certainly be cleaner and more accurate than if you were to use the lips in what you considered to be an adequate fashion.

The tendency of almost all English-speaking singers is to spread their O ('know') sounds. To some extent everybody says nā-o, nă-o, né-o or nŭ-o. All these variations can be eliminated by keeping the vowel sounds very close to U. There will be no danger of its actually being mistaken for U.

Aught of should be associated with the Italian open O (Fig. 21(*a*)). The English AW (as in 'aught') is traditionally associated with certain comic English types including peers, colonels and horsy people. In the mouths of most Anglo-Saxons the vowel sounds throaty and bottled, as if a lid were obscuring half the tone quality. To rectify these defects be careful to keep the tongue in the E position, and bring the lips farther forward.

Art is pronounced as in Fig. 14. Be careful to keep the tongue high and narrow, approximating as nearly as possible to the position for 'must'. In this way the vowel will sound deep and serious, but not throaty.

Must is pronounced as in Fig. 14, and should be associated with the Italian E. Although the tongue has to flatten, it must not be allowed to recede. Many singers do not know, or tend to forget, that this position of the tongue causes the shaping of the vowel Ŭ; even worse, they try to form the vowel by shaping the lips into a vague approximation of O. Visual association of Ŭ with the Italian U makes this understandable, but the consequent throatiness and distortion should prove a salutary reminder of the virtues of the tongue muscles. The vowel in any case needs particular care because it is so easy to pronounce in slapdash fashion.

The correct pronunciation of Ŭ with contracted tongue muscles produces a deep and serious tone quality. To a great extent this tone quality is what the singer should aim for in pronouncing *A*. If there is any tendency to throatiness, it is a great help actually to sing Ŭ instead of *A* in order to bring the back of the tongue forward. So long as the vowel is pronounced with conviction, it will appear to the audience a perfectly true *A*.

Work is pronounced as in Fig. 22(*c*). The actual sound should be as the German Ö, the teeth being brought comparatively close together as in the *I* position, and the upper lip folded forward and over as in the UH ('wood') position.

And then are pronounced like the Italian open *E*. Notice the extremely high position of the whole tongue.

Pay is pronounced like the Italian closed *E*. The slightly stronger contraction of the tongue muscles brings the corners of the lips a little nearer towards each other, making the upper lip protrude a little more than in the illustration.

His: The tongue remains in the *E* position; the teeth close sufficiently to pronounce the short I. Be careful in closing not to allow the tongue muscles to relax and the jaw to come forward. The vowel must be kept narrow, and both in appearance and sensation it should bear a certain resemblance to the French U (Fig. 22(*b*)).

Fees: The teeth are half closed, the cheeks tend inwards and upwards, and the middle of the tongue is humped (Fig. 22(*a*)).

However helpful these directions may be, it must be understood that they are no more than a useful rough and ready guide. The shape of the resonance cavity needs to be modified, albeit imperceptibly, to accord with each and every vowel and each of the thirty-odd pitched notes of the average singer's voice. That is to say there are something like four hundred different shapes which the throat and mouth of a good singer is liable to adopt. Naturally these modifications are subconscious and minute, but they have to be continually made in order to achieve an effective vibrato. The resulting vowel will vary in tone quality, according to the pitch, but should sound completely authentic on all notes up to E flat. Above this level the vowel will vary markedly as will be explained in Chapter 9. The process of modification may be compared to the way field-glasses have to be continually and instinctively focused in order to suit not only every variation of distance but every variation of eyesight in order to secure a clear image. Alternatively it resembles the continuous adjustments of sheet and rudder which the yachtsman makes in order to keep a way on his boat.

The reader should now write down at the back of his pocket diary the following summary of vowels, and his technique of pronunciation:

Lips and tongue: Who would know aught of
Tongue: art must work and then pay
Teeth and tongue: his fees.

One of the chief differences between singing and speaking lies in the relative accentuation given to different syllables. In English speech we almost always accent one particular syllable in a word, slurring over the remaining syllables and dropping the voice to a degree unsurpassed in any language. In song each syllable must be clearly pronounced, and given its proper musical time value. This is a rule which applies not only to grand opera and oratorio, but to operetta of all kinds and in fact every combination of words and music in which the words are neither crooned nor spoken. There is no question of bringing out the music to the detriment of the words, or vice versa. If a correct relationship between the two elements is established, the one will help the other, assuming that the composer knows his business and writes in terms of the human voice.

The modern manner of speaking on and off the stage makes the pronunciation of every syllable sound like an imitation of an old-fashioned Shakespearian actor, but it is significant that the few remaining stalwarts of a past era can be heard far more easily than the actors of today. Some of them may have carried over techniques which nowadays seem artificial and mannered, but this is no reason for emptying the baby out with the bath water. Good singing in any case does partake of the characteristics of the old stage technique, inasmuch as every syllable must be given its due value. This brings a distinction and an expressiveness to the whole word, and therefore to the whole sentence, which cannot emerge when unimportant syllables are swallowed.

This is perhaps the place to reassure certain readers who are understandably anxious to put the results of their training to practical use. The methods described in this book are designed to make the singing and speaking voice deeper, stronger, more expressive and considerably wider in range. If you find, as a result of your progress, that you are speaking like an old-fashioned actor, for goodness' sake use a little common sense. The new method of voice production is a highly important tool of your particular trade; it is an enormous improvement on the old method just as a new set of plugs or valves will enormously improve the performance of your car or your television set. But that does not mean that you have to drive all the time at eighty miles an hour and deafen the neighbours, or alternatively that you need to jettison the new plugs and valves because of the added power they give. You learn to drive your car or tune the television to give a performance that is appropriate. In the same way you stick to the vocal methods you have learned, but contrive to moderate the sounds you make to consort with the mood you wish to convey. Unfortunately it is not all that easy. On soft tones everything suggests that you should relax the compression, the begging dog and the whole body posture. Soft high-pitched singing or speech which remains absolutely distinct and pleasing is in fact the greatest challenge that an artist has to face. But to lose hope just because, at a moment when you are barely half-way through this book, you cannot achieve what you want is childish. Take for granted that you will in due course be given all possible help in mastering an uncommonly difficult art.

And finally do not be led astray by gadgetry, fribble and claptrap. 'If it sounds right it is right' is the most dangerous of all slogans. If it sounds right to whom? To the singer? But what the singer hears is quite different from what the listener hears. The singer in fact is the last person in the world to be able to assess the beauty of his own voice. Caruso himself, for all the records he made, could never understand why people raved about the beauty of his voice; and my own experience of tape-recording friends and pupils has been that a fair performance plunges them into a deep depression, and that not even an excellent performance gives them the slightest pleasure.

The proper and far safer slogan for the singer is, 'If it feels right it is right'. But he must understand the nature of the feelings he hopes to experience. Feeling right does not mean feeling easy or natural; after all this is what we feel when whispering or sighing, and both conditions are in direct antithesis to good singing. To know what feeling right means, to be able to induce the feeling at will, to recognize and keep it, all these demand time, thought and concentration. And time above all, to assimilate what you have learned. In this most personal form of music-making, the highest rewards seldom go to the most sharp-witted. And if your mind works slowly, do not forget the old motto of the great Italian singing schools: *Chi dura vince*—'*who sticks it out will conquer*'.

The sentences in the following exercise contain the thirteen pure vowel sounds but no diphthongs other than 'AY' and 'OH'. As in the preceding exercise, consonants are reduced to a minimum.

EXERCISE 45

Say or sing the following on a monotone, sustaining each vowel for an appreciable period, and allowing no breaks in the legato line.

  i. Did you dig over the bed in the alley?
 ii. Jane will be forty minutes overdue.
iii. The lowly Dane is in a gay mood.
 iv. The dog is in a bog.
  v. The bogey man is a dud.
 vi. The moon is over the river.
vii. The bud is on a bush.
viii. Bob Wood is in a bad way.
 ix. The loganberry bush is not in season.

N.B. (*a*) 'The' should be pronounced to rhyme with 'ER' before a consonant, and with the Italian *I* before a vowel.

     (*b*) 'You', 'Due'; the Y should be regarded as a consonantal sound to be abandoned as instantaneously as possible.

     (*c*) The English indefinite pronoun 'A' should be pronounced as 'ER'.

g. English diphthongs and indeterminate vowels

Diphthongs can be divided into two classes according to whether the first vowel is sustained and the second touched off, or vice versa. The vowels themselves are not always easily identifiable, and vary according to the native dialect of the speaker or singer, and the degree of solem-

nity which the occasion requires. For instance, the personal pronoun
'I' should be pronounced as the Italian *A-I* in a classical aria, as if you
were making a grave announcement before a large gathering. In
ordinary conversation not many people other than fully-blown
contraltos would use such a pronunciation. They would be more likely
to say '*A-Ĭ*' (as in 'fit'), '*O* (as in 'hot') -Ĭ', '*U*' (as in 'shut') -Ĭ', or something approximating. Singing however demands the best quality
vowels and these are the long primary vowels of classical pronunciation. The group in which the first vowel is sustained and the second
vowel touched off includes, in addition to 'AY' and 'OH', such words
as the following:

Eye   =   *A-I*;
Now   =   *A-U*;
Toy   =   *O-I* (as in 'fit')
Fair   =   *E*-'ER'
Fear   =   I (as in 'fit')- 'ER'; or *I*- 'ER.' Do not attempt to pro-
            nounce it as a single *I* vowel.
Moor   =   'UH'-'ER'
Flower =   *A-U*-'ER', a triphthong in which the first vowel is sus-
            tained and the remaining two are lightly touched off.

Each vowel must be clearly pronounced, but only the important
vowel in each diphthong is given any part in sustaining the tone.

EXERCISE 46

i. Say the following, being careful to sustain the tone exclusively on
the first vowel of each diphthong, the second being touched off as you
complete the word.

(*a*) Now bow down.
(*b*) My nine eyes.
(*c*) Eyebrows.
(*d*) Nine owls.
(*e*) Noisy boys.
(*f*) A noisy noise annoys an oyster.
(*g*) Nine in my bower.
(*h*) My bear is in a lair.
(*i*) You poor bare boy.
(*j*) Mice are out.

(*k*) My wife and child.
(*l*) Buy me flowers.
(*m*) Drear, drowsy night.

ii. Sing these on a monotone.

In the other group of diphthongs the first vowel is touched off and the tone sustained exclusively on the second vowel. The following belong to this group:

Words beginning with 'W' are pronounced 'UH' (as in 'stood') plus whatever vowel or diphthong follows, e.g. 'word' = UH-ER.

Words beginning with Y are pronounced Ĭ (as in 'Fit') plus whatever vowel or diphthong follows, e.g. 'yard' = Ĭ-*A*.

Words beginning with QU are pronounced 'KUH' plus whatever vowel or diphthong follows, e.g. 'Quite' = KUH-*A-I*.

Words ending with the letters 'EW', e.g. 'few', 'mew', are pronounced Ĭ (as in 'fit')-*U*.

EXERCISE 47

Say the following, sustaining the tone exclusively on one vowel of each diphthong:

 i. Quite a wide world.
 ii. I arrive in due time.
 iii. Yards and yards of white and yellow.
 iv. A few guys are right.
 v. Quite a pile of woolly toys.
 vi. Where is your night attire?

Many English syllables seem to have no true vowel at all; yet a vowel of some kind must be found from the key sentence on page 111. When in doubt 'ER' will almost invariably be found most appropriate to the syllable. The indefinite pronoun 'a' is a case in point; so also is 'the' when it precedes a consonant.

All words ending in -tion, such as 'station', should be given an open O vowel for their final syllable.

The second syllable of words like 'treasure' should be pronounced 'ER', as also the second syllable of words like 'harden', 'strengthen'. They must never be sustained on the nasal N.

Similarly, words like 'syllable' and 'kettle' must be equipped with a vowel of some sort on the final syllable, even though no one may have heard it in ordinary speech. Here again we fall back on our old friend 'ER', though we may rightly feel entitled to curse any composer or translator who invites us to sustain a long note on such an elusive second syllable. Admittedly we are doing damage to correct pronunciation, if indeed there is such a thing. But in choosing between good pronunciation and the claims of bel canto, there can be no question which must yield. As serious artists with a pride in our technique, we have no business to compromise with the principle that pure vowels are the conduit for beautiful tone, and that beautiful tone must be the invariable aim of the singer. Accordingly we equip our kettle with a tactfully fitted 'ER' vowel, singing it with all technical sails set. The audience, moved by the beauty of the song, will neither notice nor care whether the words are an exact replica of spoken English. Do not however make this an excuse for mauling the English language to suit your idiosyncrasies. There are only a few occasions when the best English pronunciation has to be tactfully violated. In all other instances the vowels are there to bring the words to life. If you ask the newsagent for a *New Statesman and Nation*, the chances are that you only sound one of the last four syllables, the remaining three being sustained on *m*'s and *n*'s. This is all very well in speech, but not if you make your request in song; and it is no use putting up a plea of nasal resonance. A note sustained on *m* or *n* is a note sung in the nose with a low soft palate and a high tongue and larynx. It may feel and sound magnificent to yourself, but the audience will not agree.

One further point should be mentioned. The ear hates monotony and all of us are prone to sluggishness. Consequently, when two similar vowels or diphthongs follow each other, the second of the two tends to be a little worse than the first. Like a carbon copy the definition will be satisfactory perhaps, but of a lower standard. This is a universal phenomenon and the only way to ensure a constant level of excellence is to concentrate on making the second of the two vowels or diphthongs as defined as possible.

The examples in Exercises 44 to 48 have two characteristics which make them a suitable choice. In the first place, consonants are strictly segregated, so that two hardly ever meet at the beginnings and ends of words. Secondly, in order to avoid unnecessary difficulties, heavy consonants such as B, D, G and V are used in preference to their light counterparts, P, T, K and F. There is no reason however why you should not consolidate your command of vowels and diphthongs by taking the words of any song, even though you may find them a little harder than the present examples.

EXERCISE 48

i. Say the following in slow motion, giving every syllable its due vowel or vowels:

(a) Bow down beside your bride.
(b) Will you wait about?
(c) Do you bow low on a dewy day?
(d) Where e'er you walk.
(e) The ninth issue is now out.
(f) Women of every shape and size.
(g) I ride over the moor.
(h) The quotient of the equation.

ii. Sing these on a monotone.

THE ACT OF SINGING

For the experienced artist who has learned to keep the sacro-spinalis contracted, the technique of singing has no resemblance to the act of accelerating a car or blowing any musical instrument. By building up a compression he turns his lungs into a kind of power unit capable of providing as much breath as is requisite for any note within his compass. An electric light plug can supply sufficient power to activate a 40 watt bulb, a 150 watt bulb, a radio or an electric blanket. Electricity is forthcoming; it is not doled out according to the needs of the various appliances. In the same way breath compression is made available to to the singer; he need not and must not consciously vary it according to the pitch and volume of the note he wishes to produce. In fact the compression is being varied all the time, but unconsciously. If it becomes a conscious voluntary act, his singing will be in every way a disaster.

If you are confident of treating your compression mechanism as a power unit, and not as a hand operated bellows, it is fairly certain that your reading up to this point has been both intelligent and profitable. If you are less confident, it would be wise to do some drastic revision, otherwise you will find yourself right out of your depth in the next few sections.

a. The consonantal sound NG

There is a simple means of discovering whether you are putting excessive breath-pressure on a note. All you need do is to hum the note on *ng* (as in 'hang') with an open mouth, and then sing on the vowel with an equivalent amount of breath pressure. More than likely you will find that on the hum you employ considerably less pressure than on the vowel, and that the amount used cannot be comfortably increased. The same amount of pressure—and no more—is all that is needed to sing any vowel sound on that particular note. If you find that you have been in the habit of using appreciably more breath pressure on vowel sounds than on the hum—and ninety-five out of a hundred singers have been guilty of this—you were doing so to the detriment of your voice production. Once again *ng*, in the following exercise, proves a valuable stand-by. It should be practised intensively until you are able subconsciously to gauge exactly the right amount of breath pressure needed for each sung note.

EXERCISE 49

Sing the following in a comfortable mezzo-forte:

If there is a temptation to increase breath pressure on a rising scale, the temptation to relax concentration on a descending passage is even greater, particularly at the end of a phrase. The composer will have set the melodic line to match the spirit of the words as they would normally be spoken. Consequently the end of the sung phrase will probably drop in pitch, just as a speaking voice tends to drop at the end of a sentence. This constitutes an almost overwhelming temptation to relax body posture and to lower the intensity of the compression by allowing the cords to lose some of their approximation. Even with the best singers the tongue muscles tend to relax on a descending scale. On all notes they will relax if emotion is superseded by thinking, shouting or crooning.

As far as possible dynamics must be guided by emotional impulse rather than conscious decisions of musical taste. Naturally attention has to be paid to the composer's markings, but they should be considered not as irrevocable commands so much as suggestions to keep you on your emotional toes. The moment you allow dynamics to be controlled mainly by intellectual considerations, technique will be impaired and you will be cut off from the true source of inspiration.

The heart will go out of your singing, and only the head will remain. I am not suggesting that a singer should be all emotion and no brain. Both are needed in a high degree; but if the head starts to encroach on the heart's preserves, all chance of maintaining a true production is gone.

The reader, involved perhaps in choral activities, may feel inclined to dismiss this as moonshine, or at least as grotesque exaggeration, but the emotions are far more at the service of the solo singer than any layman can conceive. There is no question of artificially stimulating feelings that are practically non-existent. The double condition of contracted tongue and sacro-spinalis muscles seems to release a flow of emotional adrenalin which causes the music to spring into a life of its own with no outside prompting.

EXERCISE 50

Sing the following on all vowels, beginning mezzo-forte, and making a steady crescendo to the end. Diminuendo must not at present be attempted.

The value of *ng* is by no means confined to rescuing us from the temptation of excessive breath pressure. It also provides the singer with a clearly defined sensation of the apparent backward track which a well produced voice seems to pursue from the top of the throat to its outlet a little below the crown of the head. Fig. 20 page 94 shows this apparent track, but the reader must understand that the sensation of frontal resonance which *ng* gives, has in this diagram been deliberately ignored; it will be discussed in the appropriate section. At present the reader should simply bear in mind that a sound track seems to lead back to the singer's apparent mouth at the back of the head, that he must be intensely aware of this track and keep his voice inside it. As an actor has to remain inside a spotlight if his performance is to be in any way effective, so the singing voice must remain inside its sound track if it is to have any beauty or vibrancy. This is where *ng* is of enormous value. On vowel sounds the average singer may feel he is keeping inside his track but he will probably be way off his mark; the tone may be strong, but it will not be vibrant. On *ng* he will almost certainly be correct, because to stay off the track is positively uncomfortable. All singers except those happy few with natural voices visualize their vocal track too far forward. I am not talking here about people with forward production, but about singers with the kind of production described in this book. They may be singing correctly, but almost invariably they are not quite in the centre of their sound track; they are just out of the spotlight; they have not struck the ball with the middle of the bat. Their vocal 'mouths' are too high up in the head and too far forward. Once they have found their authentic track they must concentrate on keeping the voice ruthlessly inside it, and think of nothing else until it becomes part of their being. Only in this way can they hope to discover the gold for which they are prospecting.

b. Intonation

In his first attempts to sing in correct production the reader will probably pass through a distressing phase of which he should be fore-warned. It is not an invariable, but it is a common experience to find oneself singing notes considerably higher than were intended, the discrepancy being anything from a semitone up to a perfect fifth. This is naturally disconcerting, but the beginner must realize that, just as a new grip on a tennis racquet deprives him temporarily of a proper control of the ball, so a new vocal technique plays temporary havoc with intonation.

Women suffer even greater turmoils than men. In many cases their first attempts at pitching notes in the new production will result in loud baritone sounds, as unfamiliar as they are embarrassing. They may console themselves with the thought that they are the proud possessors of a subsidiary mechanism of which far too little use is made by most English singers. It is however subsidiary, and should not be used until the singer has become mistress of her normal mechanism. The woman who finds herself apparently unable to produce anything which is not loud and deep should utter several high-pitched cries on Ŭ (as in 'but') with retracted jaw and raised cheeks. She should then sing a note on the pitch approximating to the cry, and preferably in the neighbourhood of high E flat. Once this is established she should gradually attempt lower notes, or else sing down the scale from the

E flat with the same breath compression as on the top note. As a rule women do not have much trouble in getting out of this phase, but some voices can be particularly obstinate. If yours is one of them, take heart; I have never heard of any that did not come into line.

Apart from this, faulty intonation is generally due to the singer's natural tendency to concentrate on the note. It is understandable, since no one likes to sing sharp, but it is about the worst thing he could do. If he wants to sing in tune, he must concentrate not on the note, but on the vowel. A keen ear for vowel quality, combined with the vocal technique outlined in Chapter 7, will ensure a well produced vowel and a reasonably good chance of correct intonation. Concentration on the note builds up a condition something like staring. The greater the concentration, the more likely the singer is to press on the note and cause it to be sharp. In short he must take for granted that he is going to hit the right note. If despite careful preparation he is consistently inaccurate, he would be wise to give up serious singing.

As one might expect, sharpened intonation occurs most often on descending scales or arpeggio passages. Having more or less successfully negotiated the heights, the singer loses concentration on the way down, allowing the tongue muscles to relax, so that he is unable to tune the resonating cavity to the pitch of the lower notes. The remedy is simply to retain a lively consciousness of a sympathetic relationship between the cords and the throat. With the tongue muscles contracted the rear part of the tongue must remain against the upper back teeth, while the forward part is allowed to move into whatever position is comfortable.

Needless to say, intonation must depend on the individual ear. The qualification will be readily endorsed, but speaking personally I believe that there are very few people whose ears are really defective. Persistent offenders are nearly always aware when other people sing out of tune, and to a great extent when they themselves are at fault. Furthermore they are as sensitive as anyone else to the nuances of a spoken voice. In short they are perfectly normal people, but their reactions to intonation are either sluggish or psychologically inhibited.

There are three reasons other than congenital defects for singing out of tune. The singer in his early formative years up to the age of twelve may not have been given the chance to hear sufficient music whose predominant characteristic was melodic. To folk songs, popular ballads or classical quartets a child's ear will respond and grow sensitive, whereas a diet of Bartók, Berg and blues may develop a sensitivity in other directions, but not the feeling for pure intonation which is the very life-blood of singing, and which must be acquired in early years.

A second reason for singing out of tune is a psychological one. A person may long to sing well, but being naturally quiet, insecure in some way, afraid of making too much noise, or uneasily aware that he may not measure up to the standard he is striving for, he will subconsciously inhibit his technique in some way. This is very likely to happen in the case of quiet people with big voices, particularly if in their early childhood they have been told not to make so much noise, or if they have been active in choral or madrigal work.

A third reason, and one which to some extent affects nearly every-body, is the discrepancy between musical and speaking pitch. The musical pitch of voices extends over two octaves. Speech pitch of most people does not normally extend beyond the interval of a fourth, and as a rule occurs in a low part of the voice. Unless they have been trained, students will almost inevitably sing as they speak, associating the initial word with the pitch of ordinary speech. This accounts for the scooped attack so characteristic of every class of singing today. The more the inexperienced singer tries to put expression into the word, the more likely he is to start on spoken rather than sung pitch; consequently the initial vowel may easily journey through three or four semitones before landing on the correct note.

The choral tradition in which most English singers have been brought up with its emphasis on careful blending, has helped to foster the national custom of never launching a note cleanly and with full tone. The first note of every phrase starts flat, and then is made to swell out in a crescendo. This deplorable habit is enthusiastically bolstered by the exhortations of teachers and choirmasters to 'listen to the tone'. Apart from being a direct invitation to the novice to listen to himself by means of bone conduction, it is an idiotic idea. One might just as well be told that to become a fine golfer it is essential to watch the direction and trajectory of one's drive. No one denies that the impor-tant element in singing is what is heard, just as the important element in golf is for the ball to arrive on the green, but to make a method out of a truism can only result in a half-hearted attack. How could it be anything else? Until the singer has started there is nothing for him to listen to. He then has to combine the functions of performer and critic simultaneously. Anybody who has acted in both capacities knows that this is impossible. In practice it would be like a person gingerly stepping on to a frozen pond, uncertain whether the ice will bear his weight. Singing must never be tentative, negative or compromising. Right or wrong the singer must launch his note with all the panache of a scratch golfer or a bugler at dawn. Afterwards there can be post-mortems galore, but in the act of singing he is a performer pure and simple.

In early stages almost all singers find difficulty in making a firm clean attack on a sung vowel. They can speak an *A* and sing *ng* with no trouble, but a pitched vowel seems to spell disaster. If you are one of this company:

(*a*) Feel that the shoulder blades are attached to some sort of strut running between them, and holding them firmly with the points facing squarely backwards. This will prevent you either swaying backwards or hunching the shoulders forward.

(*b*) Keep a clear vowel quality in mind, but do not consciously think of the pitched note. Your subconscious will do this for you.

(*c*) The emotional condition created by a breath compression reacting on a resonating cavity should make the launching of the note comparable to the release, in a backward direction, of an arrow from a bow. If the emotional bowstring is allowed to go slack, the attack, so far from being the result of a release from tension, becomes a feeble flabby push, like shoving a rowing boat away from the bank. The condition of tension must remain until the moment after the note is completed.

(*d*) See that the tongue muscles are properly contracted, the back of the tongue touching the rear upper teeth, with the cheeks lifted.

(*e*) Feel that you are skating or skiing, and that a relaxation of the sacro-spinalis would inevitably land you on your bottom.

(*f*) Make sure that the neck is all the time climbing up and out of the body.

(*g*) Feel that the vocal cords are already vibrating before they come into contact with the compressed breath. (See page 25.)

c. The platform of resistance

It has already been shown that instruments of the double-reed type, such as oboes and voices, give their best results only when the two reeds are approximated so that all the air which passes between them is transformed into sound. The act of approximating the vocal cords is involuntary. We know what the cords should do in order to produce an effective sound, and we are able to make them obey us more or less; yet we have no more idea how it is brought about than we know how we get out of a chair and walk across the room. But despite our ignorance of anatomy and mechanics, at least we are aware that the chances of reaching the door depend on our knowing how the legs should behave! It is equally important to be aware of how the vocal cords should behave in order to achieve a tolerably good standard of speaking and singing. Contemporary teaching does not stress this point, and many singers are ineffective because the very existence of the vocal cords never enters their consciousness. For their benefit let me repeat that, for a well-produced note to be launched, the vocal cords must be drawn together until the edges are approximated along their complete vibrating length, and at the proper tension to deliver a note at the correct pitch. In this condition they form a barrier or platform of resistance, against which a compression of breath is built up. As the note is launched the vocal cords vibrate at very high speed, but to ensure a good production the singer must think of them as remaining approximated, so as to form a permanent and deliberate closure. In this way the vocal cords will seem like a solid vibrating diaphragm such as an eardrum or the soundbox of a gramophone. Probably a diaphragm of this sort would be considerably more efficient than our present equipment—always provided that breathing was supererogatory!

Whenever a singer sings with a perfect approximation of the vocal cords, he no longer feels that he is moving breath out of the lungs. He seems to be bringing the compressed breath to a state of immobilization against the undersides of the vocal cords, and maintaining it in that state throughout each phrase. Here is the true meaning of the old aphorism that 'the Italian school of singing is a school of the voice upon the breath'. It has been interpreted by many teachers as a stream of breath on which the voice is projected like a ping-pong ball supported on a jet of water, but this is a misleading analogy. A fountain's energizing force and its means of supporting a ping-pong ball in mid-air are one and the same thing, namely hydraulic pressure; its water is not converted into a power element as breath is converted into sound waves. If you think of the power element of the voice as mere breath, you will quite certainly allow some of it to escape through the glottis like water through a valve. The singer should never feel that he is emitting breath; he feels that he is retaining it, and the softer and higher the note, the more pronounced is the feeling of retention.

Singing, in effect, is the process of converting breath pressure into sound waves capable of filling a large hall. It may be compared to the working of a power dam cutting across a great river such as the Rhône or Danube. Above the barrier is a pressure of millions of tons of water. This constitutes a source of power which can be converted into electricity sufficient to provide for the needs of a vast population. The success of the project depends upon two conditions. In the first place, a high potential pressure of water must be available. Similarly it is impossible to achieve the lung tension which is to be discussed in the next section unless the obstacles likely to intercept a free, upward flowing breath stream against the glottis have been removed; a correct posture must be maintained, the sacro-spinalis and the tongue muscles must be contracted, and the eyes must co-operate in keeping the tone buoyant. In the second place, the dam must constitute a sufficiently formidable barrier to prevent any water passing through it except as much as is required to feed the pipes connecting the reservoir above with the power station below.

In the effort to overcome wrong habits and to create a platform of resistance, it is important never to push downward on the larynx. Naturally it shifts upward and downward on every change of vowel and pitched note, but this movement must never be interfered with; it is a subconscious process. Misguided and entirely ineffective attempts are often made to induce the larynx to remain in a low position, and the consequences have often been literally disastrous.

d. Compression and suppression

The very first thing to do in order to make voice, whether for speech or song, is to inflate the lungs. We then, unless we are trained singers, disperse the air pressure by trying to emit the voice. The tendency is conditioned by habits of speech, but is primarily caused by our very human instinct for remaining alive. The respiratory cycle makes it natural for us to inhale and exhale, but to suppress the breath instead of expelling it contravenes all our natural habits. This is what the singer must learn to do, making a continuous act of suppression at the point where his breath meets the resistant platform of vibrating vocal cords. Obviously suppression cannot be induced without compression, but it is only when both components are more or less equally matched that good singing materializes. Almost all students go through a period when they overdo their compression on middle and low notes; as a result they either sing sharp, or else the tone is stuffy, gravelly and unvibrant. This is hardly surprising considering how much of their attention in early days is taken up in acquiring a body posture and a technique which stresses the need for an upward tendency and a consistent breath compression, but it is a condition that must be dealt with before it becomes a habit. The remedy is comparatively simple. After all, the singer's predominant feeling can be one of two things; either that he is compressing or that he is suppressing, and he has the freedom and the power to choose whichever of the two is most likely to benefit his singing. He does not act differently, but merely thinks differently according to the pitch of the note. On high notes which demand of the vocal cords a considerable degree of tension and a shortened vibrating length he should feel primarily the need for compression; on medium and low notes, in which the tension of the cords is comparatively slack and their full vibrating length engaged, suppression should be the chief consideration. In this way he will keep an even balance between compression and suppression, avoiding the Scylla of throaty and the Charybdis of breathy production.

Since the normal tendency is to project the voice, the act of suppression always makes the beginner feel that he must be suppressing the voice along with the breath. It is a very natural reaction, particularly when one has been trained on contemporary methods; but provided you are fully aware of the mechanics of voice production, there is nothing to be afraid of. You have to suppress the breath, but allow the voice to go; it is as if the compressed air in the windpipe squirts the voice into the back and top of the head. A rather inexact but very helpful analogy is to recall your technique of squirting schoolfellows by placing the thumb over the nozzle of a running tap. In order to drench a colleague, you suppress the main stream of water, but take care to leave a small crack out of which a powerful jet may issue. Voice production is rather more complex, but essentially similar. Your primary objective is to make beautiful sound, and with this in mind you would no more stifle the breath completely than you would be likely to suppress the entire water stream in the middle of a squirting contest.

Assuming that the compass of the average voice is two octaves, the range of the six commonly recognized voices is as follows:

Naturally these double octaves are no more than a rough and ready guide, for singers come in all shapes and sizes. As a rule the range of good voices is considerably wider than that of poor ones, but by no means invariably. The voices of the pupils of one contemporary singing teacher are said to extend over seven octaves, but it is unlikely that their quality is necessarily superior to that of a world-famous singer of German *Lieder* who, according to her devoted accompanist, possessed an effective range of no more than nine notes. Nevertheless we may assume that the description, compass and range of most voices approximates with the above list.

If you take a perfect fifth above the central note of your voice this interval may be said to constitute its middle range. On any of the notes contained inside it you should think in terms of suppression, except in upward leaps of a sixth or more; in that case you may give yourself a choice of either suppressing or compressing. Below the middle range you think exclusively in terms of suppression. All notes above the middle range should be sung in terms of compression, though even on the highest notes it is wise to keep suppression in mind, feeling in fact that you are making a compression in terms of suppression.

The matter of deciding between compression and suppression may seem to introduce a tiresome complication, but in a very short time it can become as instinctive a habit as the tennis player's habit of deciding between backhand or forehand. With very little practice on his slower pieces, the reader will quickly acquire the same aptitude; high notes will be adequately prepared, low notes will lose their gravelly growl, and all notes will be launched with far greater accuracy, vibrancy and clarity. Moreover the complication of high notes and of the registers will be much more easily negotiated.

For most singers this section is one of the most important in the book. For actors and speakers also, but as in many other respects their problem is a relatively simple one. Scarcely ever do they need to exercise anything like the degree of compression needed for sung high notes, and in at least ninety-nine per cent of their work the predominant feeling must be of suppression. Only in the most dramatic moments of blistering agony or wild desperation need they allow compression to dominate. Simple though this may seem, speakers of every kind should, with the memory of their early training, take my warnings to heart.

EXERCISE 51

Take a breath. Place the edge of a card against the lips, which are pressed fairly tightly together, as if to blow a trumpet. Push the breath out between the lips, trying all the time to maintain a perfectly steady breath pressure. The sound of the breath passing the edge of the card will register the degree of your success. Using only a gentle force so as to press the breath out very slowly, you will feel a considerable tension in the lungs. If you use a heavier pressure, so as to push the breath out more quickly, the sensation will hardly be noticed, because the more rapid expenditure of breath causes a correspondingly rapid decrease in the degree of suppression.

EXERCISE 52

With a lighted candle in front of the mouth repeat Exercise 48 (page 120), making every effort to prevent the flame from flickering.

e. The elastic-sided collar

In good singing there is always a sensation of upward tension. It is as if there were two moving staircases running like the two arms of an inverted V from the front hip-bones up to the bridge of the nose. On their way they seem to pull the sides of the abdomen and the sides of the neck inward towards a common centre. In the case of the neck it is as if one was wearing a kind of elastic-sided collar which pulled the sides of the neck inward but left the back and front perfectly free. Paradoxically, if the reader holds his hands against each side of the neck while singing, he will find that, so far from contracting, it swells perceptibly, collapsing like a concertina at the end of a phrase or if his pronunciation is vitiated by an awkward consonant or vowel. For this reason it is a sound instinct to wear roomy shirt collars, and to loosen them while singing. Indeed tight necklaces on chubby sopranos have on occasion aroused expectations wholly unconnected with matters of tone quality.

The hoary old instructions about singing with an open throat and being completely relaxed have made it extraordinarily difficult to keep the tongue muscles contracted. Even harder is the conception of a consistently elastic collar. Like elastic stockings throats can be visualized as being either broad or long, but not both at once. In good singing throats are always long. They must be stretched upwards, and they can be made to feel as if they were being squashed inwards. Simultaneously the corners of the lips seem to be pulled inward and upward towards the centre of the face.

The strength of the sensation of the elastic collar depends first on the contraction of the tongue muscles and secondly on the quality of the sung vowel. You may protest that open vowels, closed vowels, wide, narrow, forward and covered vowels have all been at different times recommended or condemned by well-meaning colleagues, who did not explain very clearly what they meant. Your confusion may have been aggravated by their almost unanimous championship of the five Italian vowels. It is perfectly true that to the listener Italian vowels sound more or less open and seem to be forward, but this does not necessarily mean that they feel either open or forward to the person who sings them. The degree to which they feel open has nothing whatever to do with nationality, musical taste or pronunciation; it depends entirely on the amount of air circulating in or passing through the mouth cavity. Since the vowel sound that engenders the maximum feeling of openness is the whispered vowel, you will understand that the blind advocacy of open vowels needs considerable qualification.

So far from even wanting to produce a whispered vowel, the technique which you have already acquired will ensure that the vocal cords are approximated, and that the air flow between them is very small. This makes the vowel feel closed and concentrated, and will seem to anchor it near the bottom of the throat. But the moment you begin to talk, all this will be lost, for in everyday English speech the vocal cords are very loosely approximated and the vowels feel close to the front of the mouth. And not only in English! However accurate your vowel sounds, your Italian accent will be comparatively poor, for the thing which makes Italian a vocal language is not its open vowels but the native manner of articulating it. You cannot in fact acquire a correct Italian accent unless you learn, like an Italian, to articulate at the throat.

EXERCISE 53

Say or sing the following words first without and then with the feeling of the elastic-sided collar, and notice the startling increase in depth and dignity.

Wide; Deep; Great; Large; Broad; Tall; Long; Lone; Far.

f. The sensation of lung tension

The technique of establishing a compression is easy, and the sensation of squeeze at the top of the lungs immediately recognizable. Suppression is a little more difficult to make an integral part of voice production, but no one who has ever indulged in a bath-time squirting contest could possibly be unaware of the technical implications involved.

Compression and suppression together set up a condition inside the chest which, for lack of a better word, I shall call lung tension. The condition differs radically from compression. To begin with the sensation is not, as in compression, at the apex of the lungs, but in the middle of the chest on a level approximately with the nipples. Secondly, it is an emotional sensation; it seems to come outwards from inside, and is just as real as a small child's distress after falling down, and immediately before starting to yell. We can remember the feeling very vividly, and the physical and emotional condition is easily induced, especially on *ng*. Thirdly, lung tension is intimately connected with musical pitch. It is in fact impossible to induce lung tension as an independent sensation, in the same way as you induce compression; it has to be identified with a definite pitched note in the singer's mind, which will demand and, as it were, summon forth an appropriate

[134]

degree of lung tension. The higher the note the greater the degree required, in exactly the same way as the tension on a string increases according to the finger's position on the neck of the instrument. It should be noted however that there is no question of a change in the locality of the sensation of lung tension. You do not move up and down the chest as if it was the fingerboard of a cello; whatever the pitch, lung tension seems to issue out of one and only one place, i.e. the very middle of the chest, but the effort of bringing it to birth becomes more strenuous the higher you go.

One very effective method of inducing lung tension is in fact to imagine that you are about to give birth to a vociferating baby, not in the usual place, but out of the middle of the chest. There is no question of your shooting it out of yourself, or even actively helping it on its way. The baby must have grown to full maturity inside you, and you have to restrain its overmastering impulse to burst out of the chest, just as an archer restrains an arrow from flying away from the bent bow. Feel that the energy you put into your singing has all gone into making this lusty infant, and that you yourself are simply the framework out of which it springs. The first experience of launching the note in this way is as if the whole of the area between collarbone and nipples was opening outwards; it is not in the least painful, but the feeling can be overwhelming.

An induced sensation of tension occurs on the lips of the players of brass instruments; a trumpet player for instance is able to feel with great accuracy the degree of firmness with which he approximates his lips. But suppose the player for some reason was deprived of all feeling at the lips; he would then be forced to rely on the nearest part of his anatomy which could accurately gauge the tension needed; this part would presumably be the cheeks. It is precisely this hypothetical situation with which the singer has to deal. He cannot recognize the degree of closeness with which he approximates the vocal cords, since the singer's cords, unlike the trumpeter's lips, cannot be felt at all. The nearest part where he can gauge the proper tension is inside the chest, and it is here that the singer must develop a keen and unremitting sensitivity. He plays his instrument exactly as if it were a trumpet; but whereas the trumpeter consciously varies the tension of his vibrating lips, the singer is forced to use a method of remote control, varying the tension of the vocal cords by means of the sensation of lung tension.

There can be hardly any doubt that the technique of inducing and maintaining lung tension is the singer's most valuable acquisition. Once it has been mastered, he may forget about posture and about contracting the sacro-spinalis because, if lung tension is to materialize, these things will have been already attended to. In particular the struggle to achieve and maintain a sturdy compression with a bulging chest can, and indeed must, be shelved. Lung tension is a sturdy spontaneous growth from deep inside, and must remain the all-important technical factor until the day you retire. It is the gateway to the singer's paradise. Without it, the most serious and hard-working student will give performances which may be artistic, but which can never be good.

The degree of lung tension needed in any particular context is conditioned by five components, namely:

1. The pitch of the note.
2. The vowel sound.
3. The volume of tone.
4. The emotional tension contained in the singer's reaction to the words and music.
5. The aesthetic context of the music.

1. *The pitch of the note.* Lung tension is governed by the degree of tension of the vocal cords, the firmness of their approximation, and the breath compression. Of these, the firmness of approximation of the cords is the most important and the most neglected. A casual reader would take for granted that, just as he increases lung tension when singing an ascending passage, so he relaxes the tension when singing a descending one. But this is what he must never do. As he descends the scale a good singer does his utmost to maintain the tension of the highest note:

This is the only way of ensuring good production; the pitch tension relaxes automatically on a descending scale, but the tension of the approximated cords will simultaneously relax into the habitual condition of ordinary speech, unless the singer takes steps to prevent this happening. Admittedly he will not be able to maintain the approximation achieved on the highest note, but the mere fact of trying will ensure an approximation firm enough on each note to stop the intrusion of unphonated breath into the throat cavity. As the notes descend the vowel will seem to narrow increasingly and the tone will not be capable of being increased beyond a rather small dynamic range. This is something that will be discussed in the chapter dealing with registers. At present, singers—and especially women—must be content with the assurance first, that in nineteen cases out of twenty this method of technique will form the basis for an artistic interpretation of whatever they may be singing; secondly, that any relaxation tends to make the vowel spread and encourages pressing on the note with all the concomitants of gravelly and sharpened tone; thirdly, that while the technique of dealing with exceptional cases is comparatively simple, the maintenance of a consistent lung tension throughout a series of descending notes is an absolute necessity for every kind of voice.

EXERCISE 53(*a*)

Sing on the Italian *A*:

On upward scale passages or leaps, secure lung tension is not nearly so easy. To start with a degree of lung tension appropriate to the highest note in the phrase would seem to be the obvious move; unfortunately this cannot be done. One launches the first note with the lung tension needed for that particular pitch, but with a very conscious awareness that on the following note the tension will need to be increased.

Sing the following on *A*:

 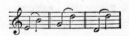

On successive notes within a phrase the singer must strive to maintain the same lung tension as on the highest notes so far arrived at.

Sing on *A*:

2. *The vowel sound*. Different vowels demand a varying degree of lung tension. The central vowel, the Italian *E*, may be said to demand an average degree; this same amount should be induced on *Ŭ* and *A*, even though not quite so much is in fact needed. The half-closing of the lips on *O* seems to demand an increased lung tension, and this can be induced by associating the vowel with the act of rowing. The Italian vowels *I* and *U* are particularly difficult sounds, and demand an even greater degree of lung tension.

EXERCISE 53(*b*)

Repeat Exercise 53(*a*) on *A, E, I, O* and *U*.

3. *The volume of tone*. The majority of singers, in making a diminuendo, relax the lung tension, very often to a point where nothing whatever is felt. In reality a diminuendo causes a heightened sense of tension whenever the vocal cords are maintained in perfect approximation, owing to their shortened vibrational length and the reduced size of the air aperture, which together cause a high degree of resistance to the breath flow. The reader must make an effort to understand the scientific reason for this; otherwise, to the end of his days, one of the paradoxes of good voice production will be that despite the heavy pressure needed for loud notes there is a sensation of decreased lung tension. If you are unable to corroborate the sensation inside the chest on high soft notes, it can only mean that you are not producing them correctly. Probably you are still associating breath pressure with volume of tone; accordingly when you wish to sing softly, you unconsciously relax your compression or the approximation of the vocal cords, or both together. From your own point of view the result may sound charming, but it will not possess the characteristic 'ping' which gives the impression that the softest note has started close up against the ear of the most distant listener.

Lung tension is the secret of all piano singing and, by implication, of the messa di voce. This is the act of swelling or diminishing the tone by imperceptible gradation from a soft piano to full volume and back to piano: that is to say: ————— ————— . It would perhaps be an exaggeration to say that soft singing without lung tension is the same as crooning; yet as a snap definition it is by no means inaccurate. Soft notes and diminuendos cannot be sung without a sensation of increased tension, but it must not be consciously induced. As an automatic pitch control lung tension is absolutely indispensable, but it cannot be used as a volume control as well. Dynamics are governed primarily by emotional considerations, in other words you feel loud or soft and in some miraculous way the voice will obey you; but on those alarming occasions when you are in danger of running out of breath you can, by pushing forward and outward with the chest, as when swimming breast stroke, make certain of reaching the end of the final note with no kind of fade-out. The tone may of course be so soft as to make the interpretation of the particular passage seem unconventional, if not daring. Critics have even been known to expatiate on an artist's subtlety and imaginative interpretation of passages when he was concerned solely with the problem of breath! If he is a wise man he will take full credit for these compliments, since they form a deserved tribute to his methods of production.

EXERCISE 54

i. Sing a medium note on the Italian *A*, starting *mf* and feeling a steady crescendo to the end. Hold the note as long as possible.

Owing to the exigencies of breath, the note will finish in a perfect *piano*. Repeat on the Italian *E*. When you feel that you can reproduce the same sensation of lung tension at will:

ii. Sing the same note piano. Repeat on Italian *E*.

iii. Make a messa di voce on the same note. Repeat on *E*.

4. *The emotional tension*. The lung tension felt by a singer is not merely a mechanical tension; it is an emotional tension as well, which he graduates according to the mood which he happens to be expressing. For the aria 'Eri tu', in which the mood is one of heartbroken despair, he will need a greater emotional tension than when singing a tender and caressing song like 'Where e'er you walk'. In a role like Verdi's Otello, the emotional strain is almost overwhelming, and only an unusually strong man can sustain it throughout four acts. Emotional tension is in fact a physical tension, centred on the lungs, in

[139]

which the body participates. As Jenny Lind so truly said: 'A good singer sings with the whole body, including the legs.'

5. *The aesthetic context of the music.* Instinctively a singer varies his technique and his style according to the music he is interpreting. Musical comedy, operetta, romantic opera, classical opera and church music are all treated in different ways. The main technical distinction is that classical opera and oratorio demand a higher degree of lung tension than operetta and the lighter branches of music. Tone quality will be purer and the pitch waver of vibrato considerably narrower. This is one reason why all students should be encouraged to sing operatic and classical arias, however modest their talents and aspirations. Operetta and musical comedy may be their eventual stock-in-trade, but on such flimsy diets it would be very difficult to build up any reliable degree of lung tension.

All readers, whether sopranos or bass-baritones, should follow up the reading of this section by listening carefully and critically to any available recordings of high sopranos. Artists like Galli-Curci and Toti dal Monte display such vivid certainty of lung tension that one can almost visualize the perfect functioning of these exquisite organs. But there is no need to limit your investigations to celebrities. In any budding Gilda or Queen of the Night you will quite certainly recognize the same characteristics. The heavier voices do not reveal the secrets of their technique nearly so obviously.

g. Vowels and ventriloquism

Vowels are formed not by an orifice of a certain shape, but by the shape of the cavity behind the orifice. Anyone can, for instance, put his lips into an O shape, and then sing A or I. The lips themselves are comparatively unimportant. It is the cavity behind the lips that evokes the vowel sound.

In the previous chapter we were concerned mainly with the shaping of the lips, the condition of the middle part of the tongue and the changes of facial expression in forming different vowels; with the mouth cavity, in fact. But this is only half of the actual vowel cavity which extends all the way from the lips down to the upper part of the larynx. The vowel sound in the throat cavity may be unidentifiable, but that gives us no right to ignore its potential for imparting a richness and nobility to what would otherwise be a commonplace light-weight vocal tone. In fact as a moulding agent of the vowel the posterior part of the tongue changes shape just as much as the front part, and is probably even more responsible for the ultimate impression which the listener receives.

Now it is impossible to use the anterior half of the tongue for the formation of vowels without shifting the position of the tongue root, which forms the front wall of the throat; and this in turn causes alterations in the shape of the throat cavity. Practical experience shows that the less the lips are used in the moulding of vowel forms, the more vigorous the movements of the root become, and it is these movements which the singer needs to recognize and cultivate. The sensation is of the bottom of the tongue root tilting slightly forwards and upwards. It is an entirely pleasant feeling, and gives the singer an impression of his throat being free, open and energetic. The movement is very visible on the front wall of the throat of a ventriloquist who, in animating his dummy, has to rely on the tongue root exclusively.

I am not suggesting that speakers or singers should revolutionize their present technique and start behaving like ventriloquists. But there is a lesson to be learned here. After all there is nothing magical or supernormal about a good ventriloquist. He just uses a different method of making voice; and anyone who can remember how, before the invention of microphones and loudspeakers, performers like Arthur Prince and Coram could make every word easily audible at the back of the gallery of the huge London Coliseum, will agree that it is a highly efficient method.

Basically the technique of the ventriloquist is almost exactly the same as that described in earlier chapters. Like a good singer he does not allow breath to flow out as he speaks. Instead he squeezes voice out of the body as paint is squeezed out of a tube, and he uses a similar respiratory technique. If no illusion was needed, the ventriloquist could sing on all pitches in a tone quality to rival the best of us! As it is he has to deny himself all freedom of the jaw and lips, and this prevents him from giving the dummy a beautiful tone quality on high notes.

The extraordinary skill of a good ventriloquist derives from his power of energizing the whole vowel cavity from the top of the larynx to the front of the mouth. In ordinary conversation we use a mixture of breath energy and sound energy, varying the proportions according to whether we wish to murmur sweet nothings or to lay down the law. But unless we are well-trained singers or ventriloquists, the one thing we never do is to energize the vowel cavity wholly by means of sound waves. The reader will have to take my word for it that whenever we do so energize it, we produce sounds vastly superior to those of normal speech. The vowel is far more concentrated, and the tongue root is brought into the vowel moulding process so that one feels as if the mouth has slipped back into the throat and the throat is now saying the vowels.

When singing or speaking in this way the vowel seems to be drawn inwards in two directions—downwards towards the lungs and upwards into the back of the skull. The depth towards which the vowel is drawn depends partly upon the particular vowel—for instance the Italian *I* always seems to be drawn both deeper and higher up than any other; and partly on the pitch. As might be expected, the higher the note, the deeper into the lungs and the higher into the head the vowel seems to be drawn. The highest note in any voice seems to extend all the way between the very base of the lungs and the back of the head.

A well-produced vowel sound is in fact an amalgam of two characteristics: brightness and depth of tone. Neither of these is satisfactory by itself. Without the depth, the bright quality sounds brittle, catty and thin; without the brightness the deep quality sounds dull and muffled. It is the combination of both qualities that makes the perfect whole.

To achieve this desirable condition the reader should continue to use his lips on the '*who would know aught of*' vowels, but should set out to acquire a much more vigorous movement of the tongue root. In achieving this he will at the same time experience a feeling of added length and freedom in the neck.

EXERCISE 55

The begging dog must beg as usual, the upper lip is raised and mobile, but by putting two fingers of each hand at the corners of the lips, so as to prevent them from folding over the teeth, the singer learns to produce a vigorous ventriloquial movement of the whole tongue root.

Speak the following:

i. No boats go to Boulogne tomorrow from Folkestone or from Dover.

ii. You know Hugh to be due.

Once the reader has acquired a truly professional skill in apparently manipulating his tongue root there is nothing to prevent him singing or speaking his '*who would know aught of*' vowels without folding the lips over the teeth. At all times he should rely on the movement of the tongue root, and use the 'folding-over' routine according to the particular shading that he wishes to give to his words. So long as he remains aware of the movement of the tongue root, he need have no qualms about the back of the tongue blocking the top of the throat. A good ventriloquist never sounds the least bit 'throaty'. Even so, it is wise to remember that you are a singer; and that lips are intended for active use!

h. Vibrato and tremolo

Vibrato is part and parcel of the characteristic quality of a well-produced voice. Naturally it varies from person to person, depending not only on the size and quality of the voice, but on the temperament and musical taste of its owner, who in turn reflects the tastes of his time, his nationality and background. Unfortunately there is a tendency today to confuse vibrato with tremolo. *Grove's Dictionary* (third edition) for example says that 'vibrato, more commonly called tremolo, seems to be a natural property of some voices and has been cultivated, often with deplorable results, by others'. Admittedly both are conditions in which there is a wavering of the pitch. In vibrato this wavering is part and parcel of the various muscular movements contained in the act of singing. If the tongue muscles are properly employed, the wavering is consistent and conditioned by the quantity of tone which the singer uses. Tremolo, on the other hand, except in the case of ill-health, fatigue or senility, is invariably the result of bad production; it may be due to a poor or excessive breath compression, a flaccidity of the tongue, a rigidity of the jaw, or a totally wrong idea of the principles of production. If the reader is still not entirely clear about the difference, let him put on a record of any good singer and play it at a slowed-down speed.

Vocal tone without vibrato is no more singing than a photograph of a kitchen chair is a Van Gogh. Vibrato transmutes the raw material; but it will not do so without some degree of encouragement. This is one reason why it is so desirable for beginners to seize every chance of hearing examples of really good singing. Anyone who thinks that no more is required of him but a certain degree of tone on a particular pitch will be left with just this and nothing more; he may be a useful member of a choral society, but no one will ever want to hear him in a solo, because what he does is simply not singing. Such a voice will be without vibrancy, charm or significance; to a greater or lesser extent it will be unfocused, pushed and shouted.

Vibrato only becomes perceptible when it rises above a certain dynamic. In soft singing it is present but not perceptible. In mezzo-forte vibrato causes the tone to waver to the extent of about a semi-tone; yet so long as the waver remains regular, there is no suggestion of the note being anything but consistently steady and in tune. Out of tune singing is far more likely to be associated with a lack of vibrato, particularly in the case of big voices.

The old acoustic method of recording does not give an accurate idea of the vibrato in the old singers' voices. To ensure good reproduction they had to move nearer the microphone in soft passages and away from it in loud ones. Their soft notes are proportionately louder on the record than in actuality, and the amplitude of their vibrato sounds inadequate for the amount of tone which they appear to be using. Inversely, on loud notes, when the singer had to move away from the microphone, the intensity of tone was reduced but the amplitude of the vibrato remained. In fact there is an imbalance on the loud and soft notes of all the older recordings, which accounts for much of our disappointment or dissatisfaction when listening carefully to them. I need hardly say that in other respects the old recordings are admirable, and provide an object lesson in bel canto, intonation, clean and gentle attack, and musical phrasing.

i. A summing-up

The true singing voice is controlled by the tongue muscles, but springs from the lung tension in the chest, and seems to be squirted up the back of the throat and head. On their way up into the head the vowels are concentrated and moulded by the throat, which seems to narrow from side to side. Finally the lung tension has not merely a mechanical basis, but an emotional basis as well, and the reader must always keep this in mind. His first objective in learning to sing is to make a vibrant and beautiful sound; he acquires an efficient technique to help him make these beautiful sounds, but without the primary objective the most perfect technique is meaningless. However obvious this may seem it is something about which every student must be warned occasionally during his strenuous period of probation. The keener and more conscientious he is, the more apt is he to go for the tightest possible approximation of the vocal cords. Vowel and tone have to be shot or squirted up into the back of the head, and if the cords are approximated too tightly the sung note cannot get off the ground; the rocket platform may be firm enough, but the rocket itself must be allowed to become airborne.

The mistake of nearly all beginners is that, no matter how clearly they understand the basic structure of their instrument, in the act of singing they endanger their technique by not discriminating sufficiently between resonator and compressor. Both components tend to be regarded as a single entity and in attempting to fuse two completely contrasting elements they spoil what might have been a perfectly sung note. The different functions of resonator and compressor are as clearly defined and distinct as those of husband and wife, and to try to fuse them is as disastrous in the one case as in the other. There is only one way to go about your singing, and that is to follow the example of the violinist. You build yourself the most Stradivarius-like resonator possible and make sure that it does not fall to pieces until the vocal phrase is completed. Then, with the loving concentration of a fine artist, you devote all your attention to the act of bowing; and in vocal parlance that is called lung tension.

In learning the technique of launching the note it is most helpful to think of the vocal cords already vibrating before they come in contact with the compressed breath. The condition may be compared to the moments of silence between turning on the radio in the middle of a well-known symphony and hearing the first sounds. There is the feeling that the music, though still inaudible, is already there. We have all experienced this, and provided the radio is properly tuned the first impact on our ear drums gives a peculiar aesthetic delight. Our mental image of the symphony takes concrete shape; in the humblest possible sense we have taken part in an act of creation. In the same way the singer feels that his vocal cords are already vibrating, and that the whole phrase he is about to sing is already both physically and mentally in the air.

A characteristic of almost all beginners who have been trained by the methods of this book is that when singing they tend to look downwards. It is not altogether surprising when you remember the various injunctions in Chapter 2, but the tendency must be avoided. If you have been thinking of a long spine stretching up to the crown of the head, think instead of the ears going away from the shoulders. Practise also Exercise 11 (page 20) while singing. Make a habit of looking along a line just above the pictures and bookcases, and as you make your attack turn the head very slightly. In performance looking downwards suggests that the singer is concentrating so hard on his technique or on remembering his words that he could not possibly be any good. Technically there is nothing inherently wrong, but almost certainly it will lead to some of the symptoms described on page 96. There I suggested that the singer should turn himself into a giant magnet, drawing the audience towards him. If he looks down on the floor, he becomes more like a vacuum cleaner. This is not only a dusty answer to his problems, but discourages the eyes from moving or the head from turning. As a result the eye muscles stiffen, the diaphragm becomes heavy and the neck shortens. The general condition is very similar to that of those earnest people who fix their eyes on the butter dish while developing some cogent line of argument.

HIGH NOTES AND WIDE JAWS

Every musical sound resonating in the throat consists of a pitched note and a vowel, and is germinated by a contraction of the tongue muscles and a particular degree of lung tension. On high notes it is impossible to maintain these conditions, and at the same time to sing certain vowels with an absolutely accurate vowel quality; and here let me say categorically that any method of singing in which vowels are deliberately and consciously changed is utterly wrong, and destroys any feeling of spontaneity which the performance might otherwise possess. The vowel is never changed, but in the interests of making beautiful sounds on high notes is modified. The process, which is called covering, is not as drastic as might appear. It is as if the vowel starts to grow narrower from about D at the top of the treble clef in the case of women, and one octave lower in the case of men. The higher the note, the more it narrows into a ribbon of sound until to all intents and purposes it disappears. Yet all the time, like the grin of the Cheshire Cat in *Alice in Wonderland*, the essence of the vowel remains.

In every part of the voice, and especially on higher notes, lung tension and contracted tongue muscles are the singer's first priority, but good covered tone will not be forthcoming unless at the same time the singer is prepared to allow the jaw to swing open. The reason for this will be clear if you take the lightest of all the vowels, the Italian *I*, and sing it on C in the middle of the treble clef. To pronounce *I* in good production the teeth must be partially closed so that the larynx is pulled up by the tongue, while the soft palate, moving in a contrary direction, sinks. In consequence, the tongue will be very close to the soft palate. If you sing up the scale without modifying the *I*, the larynx will continue to rise and the soft palate to sink. Sooner or later the tongue and soft palate will meet and block the entrance to the mouth, so that the sound is diverted into the nose, with the expected change in tone quality. It can be convincingly verified by pinching the nostrils while singing a full-blooded *I* up the scale. The Italian vowels *E* and *A* can be sung almost to the top of your compass with no fear of this happening; but the higher the pitch, the more the tone seems to be directed forward into the mouth, the quality becoming increasingly nasal, catty and superficial, and the tongue muscles less and less contracted.

There is an obvious means of ensuring good covered tone on high notes if you remember that the soft palate is part of the upper jaw and the tongue part of the lower jaw. Therefore, the farther you remove the upper jaw from the lower one, the more distant will the soft palate be from the tongue. Bring the lower jaw down and back to its fullest stretch, and you will find not only that the mouth is wide open but that the tongue and soft palate are so far away from each other that it is physically impossible to articulate an uncovered tone. A helpful dodge is to feel that, by raising the cheeks, you are lifting the upper jaw rather than dropping the lower one.

The technique of opening the jaw has already been described in Chapter 6. Its importance can hardly be exaggerated. Unless you have conscientiously practised Exercise 36 (page 82) you will never be able to sing high notes without a sense of strain and discomfort; furthermore you will quite certainly be depriving yourself of several notes at the top of your compass. For some not very obvious reason, students are extraordinarily unwilling to devote a few odd moments to breaking down the stiffness characteristic of any joint which in ordinary life is hardly ever moved through its complete field of manipulation. Let me assure them, and you in particular, that it is not an ordeal, and is neither painful nor burdensome. If you were acting in a play in which you had to open and shut a window several times, you would take very good care to see that the window moved easily up and down without sticking. The track along which a good singer's jaw must learn to move is not used for any other habitual activity, and quite naturally is for the beginner hardly identifiable. In contrast the old familiar track has been worn smooth by years of talking and eating. Not surprisingly the old familiar one is preferred by any jaw which has not been subjected to systematic training. In good production the jaw, as it moves back and up, seems to slide backwards into the throat; if this sensation is not present the position is still too far forward, and you will find talking with a fully opened jaw absolutely impossible. In the right position it is quite easy to talk with a fully opened jaw provided you avoid using the lip consonants *p*, *b*, *m*, *f*, *v* and *w*; the remaining consonants will be perfectly intelligible, but inevitably the vowel sounds will be without

[148]

their normally distinctive quality. A few sessions of purposeful yawning will quickly accustom you to the correct swing of the jaw. In other respects the movement will confirm the symptoms already mentioned. The cheeks will feel chubby and there will be no temptation either for them or for the lips to spread sideways. Furthermore the jaw will not seem to have been opened nearly so wide nor so uncomfortably.

In learning the technique of opening the jaw, the following analogy is immensely helpful. Imagine a giant pair of geometrical compasses with the upper jointed ends located between the eyebrows, and the lower end with the pin point at the spot where you associate the lung tension—or, if you like, the baby. The arm holding the pencil moves backward towards the back of the neck as the jaw opens (Fig. 23).

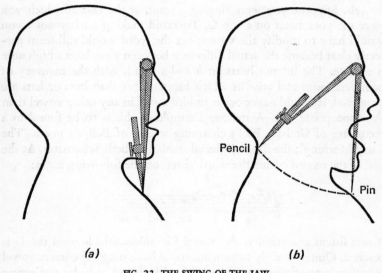

(a)   *(b)*

FIG. 23. THE SWING OF THE JAW

But high notes must not be regarded simply as a cue for opening the jaw. A singer who deliberately opens his mouth when he reaches E or F is as much an abomination of preciosity as the singer who deliberately changes the vowel sounds. So long as the tongue muscles remain contracted, the jaw will automatically open wide enough to prevent the vowels sounding nasty. Open vowels on high notes are invariably symptomatic of uncontracted tongue muscles and an equally inelastic-sided collar. But do not think that closed vowels will automatically guarantee good technique. With uncontracted tongue muscles closed vowels mean throaty or plummy tone. There can be no true voice production unless the tongue muscles are doing their job. They and only they are the brains behind the movement of the jaw.

Most young English and American singers have a far keener sense of words than of tone quality, and dislike the idea of having to sacrifice the clarity of their words for the sake of better production. You may be one such. Nevertheless there is no doubt that you are already to some extent covering the tone as you go up the scale. Nobody reading this book could be so insensitive to nasty noises and physical discomfort as to take their high notes on completely open vowels. Suppose you were singing a song, at the end of which you gave me your heart on a top G. To avoid making a nasty noise you would have to modify the vowel; yet the word would still seem perfectly clear because the actual difference between vowels on a high note is minute. The listener hears an *h* and a *t* and, with the memory of countless songs and arias in which hearts rather than huts or hats are presented, it would never occur to him to fill in any other vowel than the appropriate one. A striking example of this is to be found in a recording of Graham Peel's charming setting of Belloc's poem 'The Early Morning'; the singer is the adorable Elisabeth Schumann. At the end of the record occurs the word 'sister' on the following notes:

My Si - - - ster, good - night!

If one listens analytically, the vowel ĭ is unidentifiable until the D is reached. Quite certainly Schumann could have sung the correct vowel on every one of these notes had she wished, but only by neglecting to open her jaw, and incidentally relaxing her tongue muscles; it is equally certain that she would not have dreamed of doing so, because the tone would have sounded thin, squeaky and laboured. No doubt she was thinking 'sister' all the time but the opening of the jaw would not allow the required vowel to come. In fact she would hardly know what vowel she was singing on these notes; probably it would be something like the German Ö. But if Schumann had deliberately aimed at 'serster', that is what the listener would hear. It is because she aimed at 'sister', and merely permitted the alteration caused by the opening of the jaw, that one apparently hears 'sister'. It is a curious phenomenon and cannot really be explained. For me at any rate it contains a refreshing element of magic.

But magic notwithstanding it is only common sense that the singer should know the direction in which each vowel tends on high notes. No hard and fast rule can be given, but the following may be taken as a fairly accurate indicator of what happens:

WHO	tends towards the Italian open O
WOULD	tends towards the Italian open O
KNOW	tends towards the Italian open O
AUGHT	tends towards the Italian open O
OF	remains the same
ART	tends towards Ŭ (as in 'must')
MUST	remains the same
WORK	remains the same on soft notes, and tends towards Ŭ on loud notes.
AND	tends towards Ŭ.
THEN	tends towards the German Ö on soft notes, and Ŭ on loud notes.
PAY	tends towards the German Ö on soft notes and loud notes.
HIS	remains the same.
FEES	tends towards the French U (tu) or German Ü.

This table must be regarded, not as a guide to good singing, but merely as corroborative evidence of what the contracted tongue muscles make of high-pitched vowel sounds. In other words, read it through once or twice and then forget about it.

Finally it is well to remember that the prime reason for the opening of the jaw is not vowel articulation or contracted tongue muscles, but a definite degree of lung tension above which a jaw movement is automatically induced.

EXERCISE 56

i. Looking and feeling very like an angry tiger, open the jaw as wide as possible and close it several times in quick succession.

[151]

ii. Do the same thing with appropriate animal snarls.

iii. Make the same sounds on a pitched note.

EXERCISE 57

With the jaw wide open;

(a) Speak some lines.

(b) Sing the same lines on a monotone.

(c) Sing them on a descending scale.

EXERCISE 58

Sing the following on the Italian vowels *A, E, I, O* and *U*.

Notes with upturned tails will probably be sung with an open jaw.

10
THE ARTICULATOR

All singing is governed by mental association and the sensations of voice depend entirely on the nature of these associations. If the launching of the note is associated with the mouth or the front of the face, there will be one set of associations; if it is associated with the windpipe and lungs, a totally different set. The greatest source of weakness of nearly all modern methods of voice-training is the insistence of teachers that the tone shall be forward. 'Well spoken the English language invariably brings the tone forward into the mouth. Let singers do likewise' seems to be their argument. The falsity of this has been already explained in Chapters 3 and 6, and will be further discussed in the section on nasal resonance. If the vocal passage is not obstructed by a stiff tongue or a constricted throat, the voice could not fail to sound forward, even if it had to travel the length of a giraffe's neck.

In spoken English, in which consonants are invariably emphasized at the expense of vowels, lung tension is practically eliminated. Even in good voice production it is bound to be momentarily dissipated at frequent intervals. The singer's job is to see that the breaks are as transitory and temporary as possible. Consonants in fact might be compared to the cracks between the floorboards of a room inasmuch as their most important function is to provide a clean line of demarcation between one vowel and another. The cleaner and more momentary this is, the more defined both vowels and consonants are likely to be, and the more sustained and musical the completed phrase.

a. Light and heavy consonants

Most consonants can be grouped in pairs, of which one is the heavy edition of the other; for instance, *b* has a heavy quality compared with the light lip consonant *p*. The following is a list of these pairs of consonants:

b (heavy)	*p* (light)	*gw* (heavy)	*qu* (light)
d	*t*	*z*	*s*
v	*f*	*j*	*ch*
g	*k*		

Articulation of the heavy consonants is, generally speaking, favourable to good singing. If you provide the heavy consonant B with an Italian *A* vowel fore and aft (*ABA*) you will have no difficulty in maintaining a correct production. So far from the consonant coming forward, you will have a strong sensation of it moving inwards and backwards. This is not nearly so easy to induce in the corresponding light consonant, (*APA*), which tends to create the opposite sensation of moving in an outward direction. Obviously the singer should make the light consonant resemble the corresponding heavy consonant as nearly as possible, without actually distorting the pronunciation. It is important however to realize that not only the light but also the heavy consonants have to be articulated in a way somewhat foreign to the speech habits of the average Englishman, who cheerfully allows gusts of wind to blow through his lips as he talks. The light consonant *p* suggests the act of spitting something out of the mouth, and the consonant *b* in the exclamation 'Bah' suggests much the same thing, albeit of a more ponderous variety. But this is by no means the only way of pronouncing the monosyllable B*A*; a person might easily convey the idea of being in desperate need of a drink, and in this emotional context would almost certainly use correct voice production, with tongue muscles contracted, the back part of the tongue near to or against the rear upper teeth, and the vowel seeming to be drawn backwards from the front of the mouth.

Light consonants in fact should emulate as far as possible the imbibing habits of their heavy-weight colleagues. In other words you mentally turn every light-weight consonant into a heavy one, and jettison aspirates at the beginning of words. Thus, if you wrote down the first four lines of Handel's 'Where e'er you walk', with the light consonants changed into the corresponding heavy ones, the poem would read as follows:

> Where e'er you walg
> Gool gales zhall van the glade;
> Drees where you zid
> Zhall growd indo a zhade.

Notwithstanding the glorious oddity of this spelling—and singers of Vaughan Williams' 'Linden Lea' will notice a family resemblance to the original Dorset version of William Barnes's poem—the actual pronunciation of the light-weight consonants must not be noticeably disturbed. All that is permissible is the feeling that each light consonant is as close to its heavy counterpart as it can safely get without actually losing its identity. The effect on the voice will be a noticeable increase in depth, suggesting that you have lived some years in Central Europe.

The better the contraction of the tongue muscles, the better will be your consonants. If you have studied Chapter 6, Section c, which concerns the jaw and Chapter 7 which concerns the different vowels, you should have absolutely no problems. Most books on singing and speech devote a huge proportion of their space to the pronunciation of consonants. In my opinion none of it is needed. All apparent failures of articulation are due to wrongly positioned jaws and slovenly vowel pronunciation. The same holds good in the multitudinous problems of regional dialects. Train the tongue muscles, and you will be able to eliminate your Cockney or your Glasgow accent, and by the same token you will, with the help of careful listening, be able to acquire an acceptable French, German or Italian accent.

As regards Cockney, at any rate, the reverse holds good. It is quite impossible to sing a Cockney song or play a Cockney role in good voice production. In professional life one has to resort to a good many compromises, but if students make a habit of singing Cockney songs, their whole technique will be in danger. You can sing in most Irish, Scottish, Welsh, Somerset, Yorkshire and Northumbrian dialects without coming to any harm, but Cockney and the various dialects to be heard in and around London and other huge urban agglomerations cannot be managed without spreading the vowels, relaxing the tongue muscles and eliminating lung tension. In other words you have the choice of learning a difficult technique which will enable you to speak musically, expressively and distinctly in your native tongue; to cope with the various dialects and languages in which vowel sounds are purer and narrower; and, if you possess a singing voice, to use it as nature intended. Or else you can learn to speak and sing in a Cockney, Glasgow, Liverpool or Brooklyn dialect. But you must choose one or the other.

You may think that an occasional holiday from good voice production does not matter much; but the situation is not in the least like getting a bit drunk on a birthday spree. For the great majority of students it is more like a partially cured alcoholic being allowed to indulge himself. With the best will in the world he will not be able to help reverting to his old habits, because this is how he has been mentally and physically conditioned. In the same way the singer or speaker, who has only lately mastered the new methods, cannot help reverting to the habits of years unless he takes care to keep himself on the right track.

b. Soft palate consonants: NG, G, K

In the next few sections dealing with the pronunciation of different consonants I would like to make it clear that the advice comes out of the practical experience of one who was born and brought up in south-eastern England. Consonants are pronounced in such a variety of ways that it would be foolish to lay down one law for the many different types of tongue and jaw structure, language and climate.

Modern forward technique demands that, in pronouncing any consonants, the tongue, teeth and lips should move in the same manner as in everyday speech but with a nice precision in contrast to the slovenly habits of the average speaker. The true technique of singing can admit of no compromise. Except in special cases when some interpretative effect is desired, all consonants must be articulated so as to cause the least possible interruption to the vowel line. Particular care should be taken, when similar vowels follow each other, to make the second vowel equally clear. Similar consonants following each other, e.g. *a baby boy*, demand the same attention. Examples will be found in all the following exercises. As far as possible the back of the tongue should always be against or close to the upper back teeth.

The consonants involving the soft palate are far and away the easiest for the beginner. Being pronounced as a result of the back of the tongue coming up to meet the soft palate, they do not involve the jaw or lips.

NG. It has been already explained how helpful this consonant can be in securing contracted tongue muscles and clear vowels. Although the ringing nasal tone is favourable to good production, the singer should only in exceptional circumstances allow himself to linger on it.

EXERCISE 59

Sing on a monotone:
  i. Sing a song.
 ii. Ring the gong.
iii. Bring along anything.

G, K. The back of the tongue comes up to meet the soft palate, but it is wise to think of the sound materializing as a result of their parting company. The cheeks must be raised prior to the attack, otherwise the soft palate will come down to meet the tongue, instead of the tongue going up to meet the soft palate. '*ng*' is the only positively helpful consonantal sound in learning good voice production; of the other consonants one may safely say that *g* is the least unhelpful. Therefore the beginner should make extensive use of *g* until he has acquired a serviceable legato technique.

EXERCISE 60

Sing:

    i. Can you kick a goat?
   ii. I go to catch a cock.
  iii. A cat is comic at cricket.
   iv. The coat is caught in a gate.
    v. I am all agog.

c. Tongue consonants: Th, S, Z, L, J, Ch, T, D, N, R

The tongue tip is placed higher up and rather farther back than is customary (Fig. 24). As with the lip consonants, the actual sound takes place as the tip of the tongue is drawn backwards. Note that on heavy *th* sounds, such as 'This', the tip of the tongue is against, but not pressed against the upper teeth.

EXERCISE 61

Sing:

    i. Thirty for Ethel.
   ii. Either thin or thick.
  iii. The thief is a thug.
   iv. A thorny thoroughfare to the theatre.
    v. The thought of a theme.

It is important to acquire the utmost clarity in pronouncing the various light and heavy consonantal sounds which involve *th, thr, s, ch* and *z*; e.g. *though, through, sat, shock, zebra, vision*. Many people find them difficult, but this is hardly ever due to any physical disability.

As a rule they accept their habitual sounds in a spirit of resignation, or even self-satisfaction. Let all such offenders read in their Bible what befell the Ephraimites after the Gileadites had captured the forts of Jordan.

And it was so, that when those Ephraimites which were escaped said, Let me go over; that the men of Gilead said unto him, Art thou an Ephraimite? If he said Nay; then said they unto him, Say now Shibboleth: and he said Sibboleth: for he could not frame to pronounce it right. Then they took him, and slew him at the passages of Jordan: and there fell at that time of the Ephraimites forty and two thousand.

EXERCISE 62

Sing:

    i. Such a saucy shirt.
   ii. Sister Susie sews.
  iii. Six or seven asses.
  iv. Surely it was a silly shot.

On *l* the tip and a tiny part of the underside of the tongue are drawn backward from the front of the hard palate. If, in the act of articulation, the tongue is against or close to the front teeth, it is difficult to avoid making an involuntary *h*, especially on high notes when there is little time for preparation. In 'Dalla sua pace' for instance, the tenor would

Dal-la sua pa - ce La mia di

be liable at the third bar to sing h'la if he placed the tongue too close to the teeth.

The backward movement of the tongue is by no means the complete solution to the technique of pronouncing the tongue consonants. Unless pronounced right, they have a peculiar tendency to send the back of the tongue backwards and downwards, so as to block the throat cavity. The upper back teeth are of considerable help in preventing this; otherwise one can do no more than bring the whole body into a condition of such readiness, erectness and vitality that the tongue will

In articulating all tongue consonants the underside of the tongue should be clearly visible.

(a) TH is the only sound in which the tongue actually touches the upper front teeth.

(b) S and Z: the tip of the tongue touches the hard palate immediately behind the front teeth.

(c) L; the tip touches a point a little behind S and Z.

(d) J and CH: the tip is farther back.

(e) T and D: the tip is still farther back.

(f) N: the tip is even farther.

(g) R: the tip is curled right back so that the underside of the tongue strokes the hard palate.

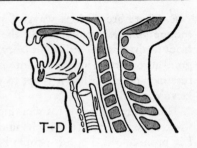

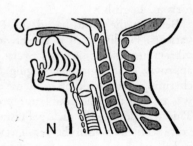

FIG. 24. CONSONANTS AND THE TIP OF THE TONGUE

be persuaded to follow suit. As regards those consonants with which the tongue is particularly concerned, imagine that, immediately they are articulated, they are swept backwards and up through an air-shaft situated a little behind the centre of the hard palate; as if pulled by a powerful vacuum the consonants disappear up the shaft, and into the back of the skull. All consonants can be disposed of in this way, but it is especially desirable in the case of the tongue consonants, and *l* in particular.

EXERCISE 63

Sing:

    i. Lily is all alone.
    ii. Willie is a lucky lad.
    iii. I love a lass on the level.
    iv. A lullaby for Lola.

R. There are various ways of pronouncing *r*. In the trilled *r* the tongue vibrates rapidly against the roof of the mouth just behind the front teeth; it is a Scottish speciality, but most English people are pretty good at it. For beginners it is not very desirable because the tone, being sustained on the trilled *r,* is apt to come forward and away from the larynx and throat.

Then there is the *r* of Russian singers in which the tip of the tongue strokes the hard palate, with its underside at about the place where the *l* is pronounced. English people have no difficulty in managing this, and for true production it is undoubtedly far more satisfactory than the forward English *r*.

Between the Scottish and the Russian *r*'s there are all manner of variants. Finally there is the French method of making the tongue vibrate in a trill against the uvula. Even in France it is not altogether approved of in legitimate singing. Nevertheless, in its place it is quite charming, and should be made use of. I once had a pupil whose tongue was tied so that she could not pronounce *r* except with the uvula. This was done with such exquisite virtuosity that her clear soprano voice seemed to distil the very essence of the French spirit. It was hard to believe that her name was Macintosh and that she had lived all her life in Perthshire.

EXERCISE 64

Using the Russian-style *r*, sing:

    i. Ring-a-ring-a-roses.
    ii. Radio round up.
    iii. Ready to write.
    iv. A rhinoceros in a river.

J (as in Judge); *Ch* (as in Church). The tip of the tongue is pressed against the hard palate and springs back to produce the sound.

EXERCISE 65

Sing:

    i. A Jew and a Gentile.
    ii. China or Japan.
    iii. Jack enjoys a jelly.

iv. Church or Chapel.

v. Charlie challenges a judge.

T, D. The tongue should be pressed not against the upper teeth but against the roof of the mouth. In this position the muscles beneath the tongue are plainly visible.

EXERCISE 66

Sing:

i. Topper took a trip.

ii. Dad adored Edward.

iii. Take a bite out of a teapot.

iv. Double or quits.

v. The tiny tot ate a potato.

N. The tongue is in the same place. As with *m*, the temptation to exploit the nasal humming element must be avoided.

EXERCISE 67

Sing:

i. I never knew Ned.

ii. Nobody knows anything.

iii. Anonymous or inanimate.

iv. Noon in the nunnery.

d. Lip consonants: B, P, W, M, F, V

B, P. The lips are not immediately opposite each other. The underlip meets the upper one more or less where the latter begins to be smooth and pink.

EXERCISE 68

Sing:

i. A baby boy.

ii. Bite a piece of apple.

iii. Bob imbibes beer in a pub.

iv. Billy pays a pound apiece.

v. The purpose of a porpoise.
vi. Poppy buys a puppy.

W is of course equivalent to the Italian vowel *U*, but since the *U* must be vigorously articulated and quickly abandoned, it is easier to think of *w* as a consonant rather than a vowel. In pronouncing *w* the lips have a strong tendency to move outwards, particularly when it precedes a diphthong, e.g. 'white'. To avoid this, feel that the corners of the lips are pulled inwards, and that the word or syllable is both serious and dignified.

EXERCISE 69
Sing:
  i. We were with Will.
  ii. What words!
  iii. Always wet weather.
  iv. Wee Willie went a-walking.
  v. The water is wide.

M. The temptation to exploit the nasal humming element must be avoided. As with *b* and *p* the underlip meets the upper lip farther back than in ordinary speech.

EXERCISE 70
Sing:
  i. May we meet William or Maud?
  ii. The mummy of a mammal is in a museum.
  iii. Many men are merry.
  iv. May be a man and a maid.

V, F. These consonants are formed by the lower lip pressing against the upper teeth. Production is much the same as in ordinary speech, but the reader should think of the consonant being drawn backwards, and the sound materializing as a result not of their meeting, but of their disengagement.

EXERCISE 71
Sing:
  i. Fee, Fie, Fo, Fum!
  ii. Follow the vicar to the font.

[162]

iii. Wave over the fort.

iv. Violet and Ivy are favourites.

e. The glottis consonant: H

The glottis consonant is the aspirate *h*. In order to articulate it the vocal cords have to open momentarily to allow some breath to escape. This is bound to cause a break in the legato line. To make it as unobtrusive as possible, you need to pronounce the aspirate as if you were literally gulping it inwards. Take particular care to establish a very firm lung tension before the attack.

The technique of the inward gulp is essential in singing examples such as those in Exercise 72. It need not produce an audible aspirate, and its chief value is by no means confined to this elegant consonant. Every note and vowel is clearly detached from its neighbour, yet the overall effect need not be in the least superficial. The vocal line will be neither legato, marcato nor staccato; it will be non legato, and comparable to the legato of a good pianist who does not have recourse to the loud pedal. The aspirate can be quite inaudible, and there is not the slightest risk of your being found guilty of intrusive aitches. There are moments naturally when the intrusive *h* is not only forgivable but positively desirable, in lending dramatic emphasis; an obvious example occurs in the refrain of Dame Carruthers's bloodthirsty aria in *The Yeomen of the Guard*:

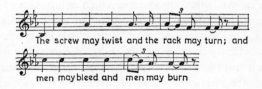

The screw may twist and the rack may turn; and
men may bleed and men may burn

On occasions like this the vocal line on the note preceding, and on the notes containing the intrusive *h* should be visualized as a highly buoyant, forward bouncing ball. Such passages call for a high degree of nasal resonance, suggestive of melodrama, piracy and derring-do. In ordinary passages, such as we encounter in Bach and Handel, the same technique is employed but with no thought of anything beyond the achievement of a consistent legato.

[163]

EXERCISE 72

i. Sing the following on all five Italian vowels.

Ah -ha -ha -ha - ha

Ah -ha -ha -ha - ha

Ah -ha -ha -ha - ha

ii. Sing the following on a monotone:

(*a*) He who hates horses.
(*b*) He hopes to hear from Helen.
(*c*) Happily he holed with a hell of a hit.
(*d*) The hill to Heaven is hard and high.
(*e*) Hallo young Harry! Harness Helen's horse.
And hie thee hence to Hastings.

f. Consonants in crowds

When consonants come in crowds, the singer looks to his lung tension. In this way he will offset those crises when consonants at the ends of words seem to pile up against consonants at the beginnings of other words, and hapless vowels, like henpecked husbands at charity matinees, practically disappear from sight. Yet even the most insignificant vowels must maintain their pride of place. They are the cocks round which the hens cluster, and on which the hens depend for their very existence. Without a vowel to cling to, a consonant, however sublimely dressed, is ridiculous.

The examples in the next exercise are all instances of consonantal charity matinees. In every case the vowel must be given priority, and the consonants dismissed as quickly as they appear. One need have no qualms about joining the end of one word to another beginning with a vowel. 'And I' for instance, should sound precisely similar to 'And die'. Nor is there the slightest reason for separating 'And' from 'die'.

To do so would sound absurdly pedantic and guarantee the unwelcome intrusion of that horrible little upstart '*er*', so beloved of the hesitant speaker. '*Er*'s' are particularly insidious when two consonants of a kind meet, one at the end of a word and one at the beginning of the next. 'Female's strength', 'Captain Naylor', 'distinct tone', and such-like, are wonderful breeding grounds for '*er*'. Do not attempt to sound the two consonants separately; they should always merge and be considered as one, except on the rare occasions when misunderstanding might arise. Conceivably Mister Raven and Mister Avon might find themselves in the same opera and it would be most important to distinguish between them; but such coincidences would be rare even in opera.

Consonants should be sounded quickly and departed from immediately, but all rules have their exceptions. In this case an exception occurs when two consonants, both of which can be sustained on a pitched note, come together either in the middle of a word, or at the end of one word and the beginning of the next, e.g. 'Mister Raven'. These consonants include *r*, *l*, *m*, *n* and *ng*, *z*, and *s* when pronounced like *z*, e.g. 'boys'. If it seems dramatically appropriate, the singer may at his own discretion sustain the first of the two consonants; he must however be sure that the increased expressiveness of his interpretation will more than compensate for the momentary deterioration in production. On no account must he attempt, for the sake of expression, to apply this to other consonants. For instance the first of the two middle consonants of 'arrow', 'follow', 'common' and 'penny', of 'armour', 'elm' and 'umbrage' may be legitimately sustained, but any lingering on the corresponding consonant of such words as 'massive', 'hidden' or 'hobby', can only result in a cessation of musical tone. Examples in Exercise 73 can be found in i, iii, iv, vi, ix, xi, xii, xiii and xv.

In England there is a curious prejudice against the pronunciation of the final *r* in words which precede a vowel. It probably stems from the justifiable disapproval of the insertion of *r*'s between two words with no connecting consonant. Thus 'the idear of a vanillar ice' would be most offensive, but if you 'hear about Miss Fortescue, a singer of talent', it is pure pedantry to deprive 'hear' and 'singer' of their final *r*'s for fear of the two words colliding; they should collide both in speech and song.

EXERCISE 73

Sing the following on a monotone:

    i. Brown drinks strong beer.
    ii. Brave British lads.
    iii. Friends throng round.
    iv. Plunge straight down.
    v. Drinking six pink gins.
    vi. Round rocks and against points.
    vii. Crowned heads toppled down.
    viii. A blot on the escutcheon.
    ix. That female's strength thrills me.
    x. Plantation medley.
    xi. Its distinct function.
    xii. That madman's drumming.
    xiii. He munched his thistles.
    xiv. Twelve dangerous stragglers.
    xv. Fragrant reminiscence.

g. Words in action

Now let us cut our teeth on the words of a song. Perhaps the most familiar to every sort and species of singer is Handel's 'Where e'er you walk'. Simple though they look, the beginner will discover that the very first lines are laden with problems. The main one is to keep an absolutely smooth legato. The only way to achieve this is to have continually in mind the very end of the last vowel of each phrase. Similarly in a race the mind's eye is on the tape at the finish, though the physical eye may be coping with the intervening obstacles. Otherwise you will quite naturally relax either your mental or physical concentration immediately after negotiating a difficult midway obstacle, as anybody knows who has done any skiing.

Where e'er: Mercifully the first line presents very little difficulty owing to the comparative scarcity of consonants. There is no necessity to sound the *h* in 'where', and both the *y* of 'you' and the *w* of 'walk' are pronounced as vowels. Consonants are therefore limited to the two *r*'s and a *k*. The vowels are not such plain sailing, since all four are in fact

[166]

diphthongs. In ordinary conversation these diphthongs are subject to all manner of variegated regional distortions. When singing them it is wise to choose a pronunciation which sounds natural, but which is sustained if possible on one of the five Italian vowels. On this basis the first two diphthongs will be pronounced *E-'er'*, giving a darkish quality to what is normally a rather light, catty sound. Admittedly Ă (as in 'fat')-'er' would be perfectly correct, but it is far more difficult to sing properly. In this case, when similar diphthongs follow each other it is particularly desirable to choose a dark Italianate sound. Similar vowels or diphthongs following each other can be a trap for the unwary; but properly pronounced, the words in which they are contained can be made to sound curiously moving, e.g. 'Go home', 'May-day', 'Forlorn'.

If the *r* at the end of 'where e'er' is sounded, you will find it much easier to pronounce the two short vowels on either side. Without the sounded *r*, both vowels become light indefinite noises which will certainly interfere with the legato line.

You: The *U* is formed exclusively by the lips, the tongue remaining in the Italian *E* position.

You walk: Must be joined firmly together. If they are half separated, as they probably would be in ordinary conversation, the legato line will be broken.

Cool: The tongue remains in the *E* position and the lips form the vowel. The *c* partakes of the quality of its heavy counterpart.

Cool gales: Under no circumstances must they sound like 'cooler gales'; this will happen if you allow the *l* of 'cool' to drop forward against or between the front teeth, instead of drawing it backwards.

Gales shall: . . . should be elided and sound precisely like 'gale shall'.

Shall fan: Pronounce both vowels exactly as in everyday speech, taking care to keep the tongue muscles adequately contracted. Another instance of similar vowels.

Fan the: Make *th* a heavy backward sound to avoid risk of an intrusive *'er'*.

11
THE MODES OF MUSICAL EXPRESSION

According to the old Italian singing schools there are three accepted modes of musical expression, namely:

1. continuous unbroken sounds—legato.
2. pulsed or accented sounds—marcato.
3. detached sounds—staccato.

Other modes of expression are variants of one or other of these three.

a. Legato

The greatest and most expressive of the three modes is the legato. This word is the past participle of the Italian verb *legare*—to bind. Such stress was laid on its importance that all singing was held to be legato unless the composer expressly indicated one of the other modes of expression. For this reason a popular saying among the old Italian teachers was *chi non lega non canta*—'he who does not bind (note to note) does not sing'. In other words, notes must be bound together into an unbroken and tonally homogeneous melodic line.

A serious stumbling-block to the legato line is the beginner's awareness that almost all other musical instruments are able to move cleanly and instantaneously from one note to another with no upward or downward slur. For the singer this is impossible; the voice can no more jump straight from A to E without travelling through B, C and D, than a car can accelerate from 30 m.p.h. to 60 without the speedometer registering momentary speeds of 35, 40, 45, 50 and 55. Yet so accustomed is he to the sound of the piano's clean intervals that he subconsciously attempts to do the very same thing with the voice. With an interval of several notes to be spanned, he diminishes the tone at the end of one note and accents the beginning of the next, so as to create the impression that he is not sliding up or down the scale.

It is no exaggeration to say that singers who behave thus are betraying the whole art of music. The human voice's most glorious jewel is the power of projecting words on an unbroken legato line. To pervert such a unique faculty in order to create a false impression of being able to do the one thing practicable on man-made instruments but impossible on the voice is nothing short of criminal. Vocal music was founded on the assumption that voices must slur their intervals, and that the wider the interval, the more conspicuous must be the slide. For this reason intervals of more than a sixth are rare in vocal music, and intervals of over an octave practically non-existent. Mercifully the transition between notes can be executed with such swiftness and accuracy that there is no excuse for allowing the slur to obtrude.

Our old friend the pianoforte has been a poisonous influence on many students' ideas of tone colour. In accepting its percussive quality as a desirable and natural sound, you may have grown up content for the voice to blend with it rather than to contrast. In later years you realized that such an idea is nonsensical. The pianist cannot bind notes together; all he can do is to give an impression of legato by using the sustaining pedal and playing 'molto cantabile'. The singer, if he knows his job, sings every note legato, except for purposes of contrast or when it is otherwise indicated. The music may be anything from the most melting 'lacrimoso con dolore' to the most vigorous declamato, but for him legato does not indicate any particular emotional mood. It is a mode of expression associated above all other instruments with the human voice, and consists of an unbroken and homogeneous stream of sound.

Another difficulty for the singer is that, in playing his tune, he is also beset by the many ingrained habits of speech which conflict with the basic principles of legato. In conversation the importance of a syllable is indicated partly by a momentary rise in pitch, and partly by a spasmodic increase in tone. If the singer talked his tune in such a way as to give the same speech emphasis, his phrasing would be syllabic rather than musical. The effect would be something like this:

Shall crowd in-to a shade

Admittedly this looks quite ludicrous. No decent instrumentalist would indulge in such concertina-like tricks. If there were any dynamic variation, the swell would be evenly graded, because the player would be thinking only in terms of musical emphasis, and not at all in terms of syllabic emphasis. The singer must learn to talk his phrases as musical sentences, and not as a collection of syllables with notes added to them; but he can have no hope of doing so unless the contraction of the tongue muscles is maintained as unremittingly as the tension on a violin string. If it fails, he is no longer a singer; he is a mere crooner, and the voice will be spasmodic, strong on the strong syllables and weak on the weak ones. Any reader who is not entirely clear about this should practise phrases out of songs on *ng*; if he is a male, let him think of himself as a horn or cello; and let the female think of herself as an oboe or violin. Both should supplement this work by doing something they have hardly ever done in their lives; they should go to an orchestral or chamber concert of classical music, and listen attentively to the way in which the music is phrased. Most singers allow their interpretation to be vitiated by a tendency to speech emphasis, because they have never really listened to non-vocal music, and because they are ignorant of the very existence of any singing technique worth mentioning. In fact it is fair to say that, while the forward production singer fights a losing battle against the undesirable habits of speech emphasis, the traditionally trained singer becomes a willing victim of the habits of instrumental phrasing. But both kinds must do some serious listening.

All singers know that legato is an indispensable part of singing. Many of them however do not realize that an unremitting tension and pure vowels are essential properties of this mode of expression. They behave as if the only thing needed was to link the last consonant of each syllable mentally with the syllable that followed it. Thus the second line of 'Where e'er you walk' would be sung in this manner:

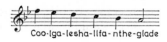
Coo-lga-lesha-llfa-nthe-glade

It is true that this is the effect of a well sung legato phrase; but if you aim simply at producing the effect without attending to the means whereby it is achieved, you will not come within miles of your objective. This kind of pseudo legato always begets inaccuracy of pitch. From concentrating upon the consonants rather than upon the vowels,

[170]

upon the words rather than upon the maintenance of a bow-and-arrow tension, the vocal cords adopt a looser approximation, so that the tone becomes shallow and white.

EXERCISE 74

Sing the following on all vowels:

EXERCISE 75

Sing the following: (i) as written; (ii) without the grace notes and in perfect legato. Watch that the tongue muscles, elastic collar and lung tension remain firm at the end of one note and the beginning of the next.

It is of course inevitable that the slur on intervals of a fifth and more should take long enough to be noticeable. In cases when the note preceding the slur is sung on a diphthong in which the first vowel is the strong one, e.g. 'Crowd into'; or alternatively when the note following the slur is sung on a diphthong in which the second vowel is the strong one, e.g. 'Will you walk', the weak vowel may be sustained during the period for the slur. This makes the scoop much less obvious; moreover the whole phrase can sound curiously expressive.

EXERCISE 76

Sing the following:

[171]

The same thing can be done when the consonant connecting the two vowels, between which the slur is made, is one which can be sustained on a pitched note. These consonants are *r, l, m, n, ng, z,* and *s* when pronounced like *z*, e.g. 'boys'. In both cases be careful not to linger on the slur; it should be made as swiftly as possible, except when you wish to delay it for the sake of expression.

EXERCISE 77

Sing the following:

a) The dull – eyed night
b) My Ju – lia close
c) A pen – ny piece
d) A com – mon man
e) And fol – low me
f) The sun – lit strand
g) A lone – ly shore
h) An ar — row head

i) The morning light
j) A – dorn-ing me
k) The flowrs shall rise
l) A sol — emn feast

m) Hel — lo there! Hel — lo there!
n) Bring you home, Bring you home.
o) Mon – day morn, Mon – day morn.
p) On — ly you, On — ly you.
q) Man and boy, Man and boy.
r) Some-thing more, Some-thing more.

But for the practical singer legato means much more than 'bound together'. Bel canto should carry with it a sense of movement from one point towards another point. Without this the most beautiful sustained singing will sound monotonous and half dead. Perhaps the most vivid comparison is between the same note sustained by an organ and by the bow of a violinist. The organ will sustain the note quite perfectly for as long as the player chooses but cannot inspire the sympathetic response which one gives to a skilled violinist. It is not possible for the organist to suggest that the note has a life of its own; that it comes from a particular place and is on its way to somewhere else. This is what the violinist with the limited length of his bow and the singer with his limited breath capacity can suggest. Even so, the singer will not be able to convey this impression unless he makes a conscious effort; more particularly if, like yourself, he is still absorbed with technical problems. The feeling of movement depends both on technique and on musicianship; each of these aspects must be taken into consideration. From the point of view of musicianship think, as far as possible, of each musical phrase as a dance with an individual shape; help this image by relating it to your associations with other forms of mobile activity such as skiing, sailing, cycling, swimming and dancing; in all of these there is a sense of journeying from one point to another, and no suggestion of violent jerks, or of being temporarily stuck in the mud. The famous singers, whose voices and artistry you revere, were of many different sorts; yet they all displayed the characteristic of sustained mobility most strikingly. Even if they did not all sing legato, they had the power of keeping their words mobile. How else could they have joined the immortals?

b. Marcato

Marcato is used occasionally in vocal music as a purely instrumental effect, as in the baritone aria 'My heart now is merry' from the cantata 'Phoebus and Pan' by J. S. Bach.

Here the marcato is used instrumentally to give the effect of laughing. The singer momentarily increases the weight of breath pressure at the top of the chest in response to an emotional impulse, as in sobbing. It is not difficult, but the impulse must be based on an emotional and not a merely mental stimulus. Often the marcato consists of a slight sforzando, or series of sforzandi, each on a separate syllable to emphasize some dramatic point. Innumerable instances of this can be found in the operas of Verdi. Here again the stimulus must be emotional, otherwise the increase in breath pressure will be overdone. Very occasionally the emotion may express a mood of violence; as a rule it expresses tenderness, yearning or nostalgia. In any case, whatever the context, the sforzando must be rooted in emotion. It is not merely a momentary increase of sound.

EXERCISE 78

Sing the following on all vowels. The slight variations in pitch are a natural result of singing this passage in good production. It was this characteristic which caused composers to use the appoggiatura.

EXERCISE 79

Sing on all vowels, making sure that none of the notes in each phrase is detached.

The marcato is also employed to emphasize a rhythm; in many such cases the effect depends on the ability of the singer to contrast the marcato passage with the legato which precedes or follows it, as in the Seguidilla from the first act of *Carmen*:

If the marcato effect of bars 8–12 is to come off, the legato of bars 1–7 must be as smooth as possible. If the entire passage is sung marcato the rhythm will clump along heavy-footed with no feeling of dancing.

c. Staccato

In making a staccato the singer halts the upward thrust of the diaphragm the very moment the note is started. This is done by contracting the upper abdominal muscles in the triangle below the breastbone into a tight clench, and immediately relaxing them. The singing lady can imagine that she is tightly lacing herself up in that region. The notes should feel like a resilient ball rebounding off a hard surface.

EXERCISE 80

Sing on all vowels:

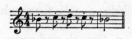

EXERCISE 81

Sing on all vowels:

12

WORDS

The most useful thing a singing student can do is to learn to speak well. It is not merely a question of shedding his regional accent and being able to tackle dialogue in musical plays. He will have to make announcements in concerts, introduce himself at auditions, argue with producers, agree with conductors and impress agents and managers. On all such occasions, to say nothing of day to day social contacts, a good speaking voice is indispensable. It can only be acquired by applying the lessons of this book all day long in his casual conversation. With sixteen hours a day of perpetuating bad vocal habits, half an hour's singing practice is not likely to make for much improvement.

a. Speech and song

It might be thought that the speaking voice would automatically change its manner of use as soon as the reader learned to sing correctly. In the majority of cases this is not so. The singer after all is generally adult before he receives proper vocal instruction. Furthermore the speaking voice is such an intimate part of his personality that, however dissatisfied he may be with its present manner of use, he will be subconsciously unwilling to make any drastic change. For better or worse his speaking voice seems as much part of himself as his own face. Yet it is not a natural characteristic. It has been acquired over the years, and can be transformed in a very few weeks. But he must really desire the transformation, applying to his speaking voice consistently and diligently what he has already acquired in learning to sing, lung tension in particular.

EXERCISE 82

Sing a note on *ng* in the lower middle of the voice, e.g. middle G for sopranos and tenors, and E for lower voices, making yourself keenly aware of the degree of lung tension required.

With the same degree of lung tension make a spoken, i.e. a non-pitched *ng* sound.

Take a line of poetry, e.g. 'To be or not to be', and speak it with exactly the same degree of lung tension. Be careful not to drift into a pitched sing-song.

Take the next note, one tone higher, and go through exactly the same procedure, using the same line of poetry. Do not visualize the pitch or quality of your speaking voice, but concentrate solely on keeping the same degree of lung tension which you had in singing the pitched *ng*.

Do the same thing on higher pitches, but not beyond D.

Now come back to the original note and work downwards in the same way as far as you can comfortably manage.

Do this daily, using a fresh line of verse at each session, and be careful always to speak the words and not chant them.

This exercise enables the actor to speak his words so that they sound like natural speech, but with an enormously increased range, expressiveness and carrying power. The average speaking voice relies mainly on emphasis and variation of pace, but very little on change of pitch and the beauty of sustained tone. It is like a piano with three notes missing and no sustaining pedal; whereas a properly trained speaking voice possesses all the advantages of an octave range, a natural sostenuto and a wide variety of dynamic expression. After working on this exercise for some time the reader will experience a noticeable degree of discomfort when speaking on stage without lung tension. Even though he may be able to make himself heard, he will feel like a person with astigmatic vision who has mislaid his spectacles. Forbes Robertson, who from a vocal standpoint was the greatest Hamlet within living memory, attributed his superb technique to this exercise.

There are two traps into which the reader may easily fall when working on his speaking voice. Either, in his anxiety to maintain consistent lung tension, he becomes a victim of his own technique, holding in the tone as if to enclose it in a bottle at the bottom of the throat. He will get over this the moment he realizes that a much lower degree of lung tension is needed in speech than in singing, and that in any case, a beautiful tone quality is his first priority. Alternatively he may allow his voice to degenerate into a sing-song. Obviously this will happen if he has not first mastered the basic principle of lung tension, or if he loses concentration. Many actors in earlier days have lapsed in this way; my memory of Sir John Martin Harvey in *The Only Way* was of one huge musical recitative. Nowadays such performances would be ruthlessly and quite justifiably dismissed as examples of that heinous contemporary misdemeanour known as 'the voice beautiful'.

The very mention of this phrase throws many young actors into a state of nerveless panic. Whether it is a relic of English puritanism, a reaction from the slovenly habits of many actors of yesterday, or one more example of the tendencies of much contemporary art I will leave you to decide. Admittedly there may be some justification in the case of certain creative artists; a modern painter may appropriately use dirty drab colours in his picture, and an author may write in a style so ungrammatical as to be nearly incomprehensible. For an interpretative artist there is no excuse at all. A violinist may be called upon to perform Bach, Offenbach, Bartók or Schoenberg, but he would never dream of playing any of these composers with scratchy scrannel tone. Yet for some obscure reason actors who try to bring as much beauty and expressiveness as possible into their lines are frequently accused of not 'striving after truth', or some such vague catchword; and this in roles which cry aloud for nobility of speech. No doubt there are many actors who do not trouble to understand the significance of their words, or to concentrate on what they are doing, just as there are lots of violinists with meltingly beautiful tone who cheapen and vulgarize anything they touch, but this is no reason why Shakespeare should be interpreted prosaically with thin dry tone. As an example of throwing the baby out with the bath water such logic could hardly be bettered.

An actor has to meet a challenge from every person in the audience who says in effect: 'I am tired, cold and jaded. I have eaten quickly and badly and paid too much for a seat which is too far away and rather uncomfortable. Moreover I am missing my favourite television programme, and am not particularly interested in this play.' Such a challenge cannot possibly be met by anyone who does not know how to make an instinctive emotional response to the words with which he is entrusted. Only in these circumstances is there any hope of our man in the audience experiencing, as he should, a double delight: in the beauty of great poetry, and in watching an actor who delights in revealing it to his listeners.

[178]

All singers have suffered, and will go on suffering, from not being able to practise when and where they like. Speech technique can be cultivated at almost any time without fear of disturbing the neighbours. Furthermore, whereas the whole mind and body has to be concentrated on singing, speech is not nearly so demanding. The management of the breath need not be anything like so exact or delicate, and you may safely work on it at odd moments while you are washing the dishes, having a bath or driving a car. You might even find out in the process what the words of your songs are about!

b. Words and music

Assuming that your technique is on a firm basis, it is now possible to make an important adjustment in the handling of consonants. On page 172 it was shown that the slur on an interval between two differently pitched vowels can be sustained on the intervening consonant, provided the consonant was one capable of sustaining a pitched note, i.e. *r*, *l*, *m*, *n*, *ng*, *z*, and *s* when pronounced like *z*. You may now extend this rule to all consonants provided you do not allow yourself to linger on the non-sustaining ones. In practice you need not and should not make a conscious differentiation in your treatment of the two classes of consonant; you merely keep an awareness of the glory of a smooth legato line, and the dignity of the English language. Despite the momentary plunges into an apparently forward production the basic technique will not be affected, whereas the legato line will be much steadier and more spontaneous. In fact you will be able to make each new sentence or musical phrase spring like a phoenix out of what has gone before, and out of your inner feeling. You do not sing a melody. You sing a poem; a poem which is born anew in all the splendour and loveliness of a composer's inspiration.

To realize this goal you must soak yourself in the words and the music. Most singers tend to favour either one or the other, but not both together. Generally speaking those whose technique is poor or non-existent, and those with a strong dramatic or imaginative sense, go for the words and take the music for granted. On the other hand those whose main interest is musical, or who have been engrossed in technical problems tend to take the words for granted. Neither can be more important than the other. Words came first and gave inspiration for music; but before words and music can become a song, your interpretation has to breathe life into both, welding word and tone into a single whole so that the poet sings and the composer becomes a poet.

Too often words are treated as if they were unimportant passengers riding on a musical bus which had to reach its garage on time and intact. Admittedly they may be poor or quite shockingly translated. Even so they were the inspiration of music, and it is part of your job to discover the ideas and feelings they express, and the mood or situation out of which they were born. As a rule they can be crystallized into a single word or short phrase such as 'remorse', 'joyous surprise', 'regrets for lost youth'. This will provide a springboard from which you may imagine the circumstances which brought the poem to life, what happened to the poet before he was moved to write as he did, and what was likely to happen to him in the days to come. Each song can be made into a tiny drama, and in setting the imagination to work you can bring colour and life into what may otherwise be merely a beautiful voice.

By themselves words possess a music which is waiting to be drawn out of them. A song in fact remains a mere *vocalise* until you have learned to mould each verbal phrase, so that the meaning is absolutely clear, not just to yourself and your accompanist, but to the lonely person at the back of the hall. Here is the challenge which the singer accepts every time he opens his mouth. And that is not all. The message which our man in the back row receives is primarily a piece of intelligible information, but out of it comes far more than just the literal meaning. Like ripples on a lake, the words must carry with them an emotional undercurrent which kindles the listener's awareness and sharpens his sensitivity.

Finally words by themselves must fall like a gentle chime on ears jaded by traffic and television. The world of today cares precious little for sheer beauty of tone; but the singer must be its doughtiest defender, aiming continually to move his listeners, so that unconsciously they echo the words of Robert Herrick:

> So smooth, so sweet, so silvery is thy voice
> As, could they hear, the damned would make no noise,
> But listen to thee (walking in thy chamber)
> Melting melodious words to lutes of amber.

c. Musical and rhetorical eloquence

Nowadays interpretation is too frequently discussed and taught as though it had no relationship to the singer's fundamental technique. Admittedly technique is no more than the tool of the interpreter, yet a painter gives a very different impression of a landscape according to whether he uses oils, water colours or pen and ink. Every artist in fact is limited by the nature of his medium and the tools which he uses.

The fundamental tools of the singer are the tongue muscles and the tension which he builds up against the chest wall. The tension is both physical and emotional, and it is very largely by means of this tool that the singer derives his powers of interpretation, channelling the emotional tension into what may be called two separate eloquences, musical and rhetorical. The proportionate relationship of these two eloquences depends on the style in which the song is written.

According to the old Italian singing schools vocal music was divided into three kinds, viz:

1. *Canto fiorito*, or florid song.
2. *Canto spianato*, or smooth song.
3. *Canto declamato*, or declamatory song.

It is hundreds of years since these three styles were first classified; but despite the claims of *Sprechgesang* there is every reason for assuming that all vocal music, ancient and modern, falls into one or more of these categories. Their different characteristics are almost self-evident. In *canto fiorito*, where a single syllable may be sustained for anything up to a dozen or more bars of constantly changing note patterns, musical eloquence must predominate; the singer expresses the significance of the words almost wholly through his phrasing of the music. In *canto spianato* the proportions of the two eloquences are much more evenly balanced, and for this reason *canto spianato* has always been considered the noblest vocal style; most *Lieder* and art songs are written in this style, though of course there are many exceptions, e.g. Schubert's *Prometheus* and *Der Doppelgänger*. In *canto declamato* rhetorical eloquence predominates over purely musical eloquence; it is the drive of the words that carries the music along.

In all three styles of singing the decisive factor is not just one of running passages, or melodic line, or words that are solemn or silly; it is a question of the predominating mood of the piece, and the way in which the singer channels the springs of his emotion. In *canto fiorito* his emotional interest is mainly on the melody. In *canto declamato* it is mainly on the words. The note in this context has no meaning at all; it is merely an ink blot on the printed page. The singer thinks, not of playing notes, but of saying words on predetermined pitches with the utmost eloquence at his command. He takes hold of the words in the same way as you shake hands for the first time with someone you have longed to meet, putting your hand in his, and allowing the friendly pressure of fingers, thumb and palm to suggest that here is a nice sensible person with a voice to match.

As might be expected there are comparatively few works written wholly in a single style. Quite often there are elements of all three, and in studying a song you have first to determine which is the predominating style, and then to identify those passages where it departs from that style and enters another. This is by no means a simple matter. Few singers would be unanimous in every instance, but as a would-be interpreter it is of enormous help if, when tackling a new song, you can decide on both these points. Next year perhaps you will have changed your mind; this year your interpretation, though perhaps wrongheaded, will at least be positive and alive.

Whatever the style, the basic mode of expression is invariably the legato. Even the rhetorical eloquence demanded by *canto declamato* is far closer to legato than to the spasmodic and syllabic accentuation of everyday speech. The words may seem to drive the music along, but the singer must never forget that the musical phrase is the foundation on which he builds his interpretation, and the legato the mortar which binds the words together. Even in the most thunderous bursts of Wagnerian indignation the vocal cords must not be subjected to hammer blows of compressed air, because such blows are inevitably followed by a relaxation of the muscular tension. Singers who indulge in this sort of thing soon cease to be singers and become barkers; and this has been the downfall of many operatic artists who, in concentrating overmuch on the dramatic side of their work, have done a notable disservice to music.

In determining the style of a composition, a further important aspect is the language in which the words are sung. We have all at some time listened to a familiar song or opera in translation. Sometimes the effect has been charming, sometimes unexpected, and occasionally ludicrous, as when *Götterdämmerung* becomes *Le Crépuscule des Dieux*. However good the translation, the best performances can never be more than an approximation of the original composition, owing to an unavoidable change in the relationship of the musical and rhetorical eloquences.

Generally speaking, while the Italian language seems to favour *canto fiorito* and the German language *canto declamato*, French and English both favour *canto spianato*. This explains why a singer needs to have a much deeper understanding of the German language than of Italian, and why he finds Italian such a grateful language in which to sing. It is not just a matter of easy vowel sounds and comparatively few consonants. The Italian language, even in slow solemn arias, invariably favours *canto fiorito*.

Nothing can be done about this. The artist simply adapts his interpretation and especially his choice of tempo to suit the language in which he sings. He must realize that a song with translations into three languages becomes, and should be regarded as, four completely different compositions. Schubert's 'Wohin', for example, would probably—but not necessarily—suggest a rather quicker tempo in a good French or English translation than the usual speed adopted by most German *Lieder* singers. I have never heard it in Italian, but I can imagine it moving even faster and sounding right and wholly delightful—except to the upholders of the fine old traditions of the German *Lied*!

No matter in what style a vocal composition is written, the words and music together call for a rhythmical sweeping flow which builds up into a succession of phrases; these phrases build up into a melody, and a succession or repetition of melodies builds up into a song. Every phrase contains a verbal high spot which as a rule coincides with a musical high spot. If you feel that in certain instances the two do not coincide, you must choose either the verbal or the musical high spot. In *canto fiorito* the words yield to the music; in *canto declamato* the music yields to the words; in *canto spianato* you must follow your own instincts, but do not simply compromise. Either the verbal or the musical high spot has to be paramount, and remember that in every phrase there is one such. Similarly there is a high spot in every complete song. I am not suggesting that you should make a fetish of consciously determining all these high spots in everything you learn; even so it is a good exercise to take one or two songs, and find out whether in performance you are realizing these spots subconsciously, and whether they seem to come invariably in the right place.

d. Figure in a landscape

In good singing every note must be properly produced, and take its rightful place in the procession of notes. It is only the exceptional artist who approaches his work in this way. The remainder, however they may protest, think of the shape of the phrase, but of the individual vowel hardly at all except on difficult notes. The consequence is that, however beautiful the quality of the voice, it always tends to get a little worse. The phrase may gain in expression or significance, but more and more unimportant syllables will be skated over. Consonants will be suspiciously in evidence—and note that I say 'in evidence'; there is no reason to believe that they will be clearer or more expressive. Bel canto alas will be doomed.

No doubt the reader is well aware of this, and will have found that in the early stages of acquiring a reliable technique he could cope with one, two or three notes, but no phrase of any length, let alone a song. His tone may be satisfactory, but the overall impression he gives will not be of music so much as a succession of notes. He will readily agree with such a verdict, explaining that the turmoil of concentration, in which the act of singing at present involves him, does not allow a moment to spare for the demands of musical expression.

It is important to get through and out of this stage, otherwise you will be written off as unmusical. Every phrase, every scale and every arpeggio must be visualized as a whole, just as in painting a picture one has to make each section alive and interesting, without allowing it to overbalance the composition of the whole. It is not a matter of keeping a complete song in the mind's eye, or even a complete verse. At present it is enough if you are able to visualize each musical phrase. An extremely short-sighted person might, with his nose almost touching the canvas of a lady's portrait, be able to give a highly accurate description of her chin or her parasol, but one would not trust him to give a balanced description of the whole picture and its emotional impact. The beginner who has just mastered the foundations of his technique is in much the same state. He pokes along from one note to the next with no sense of the rhythmical flow or shape of the phrase. It is a sorry condition and he must take steps to get out of it as quickly as possible.

[184]

He will have every encouragement to do so because breath will escape, and continue to escape through the vocal cords at the end of each note, until he learns to think of music as a succession of phrases. Then the shortage of breath will miraculously disappear.

A sentence consists of a succession of words, which have to be written or spoken or sung one after the other, but that does not mean that the artist's mind follows any such laborious pattern. 'The cat sat on the mat' demands the articulation of six separate words, but the single visual image, in this case a gay evocative picture out of a child's book, should run like a steel thread throughout the spoken or sung phrase. So obvious is this that the reader will perhaps wonder why I trouble to mention it. Yet there are many performers whose interpretation seems to be influenced by the physical conditions of the written or spoken language. Their visual memory feeds them with a long procession of words, and despite beautiful production and a good legato the final result becomes as laborious as trudging across a ploughed field on a November evening.

As a rule singers who are deficient in this respect have a poorly developed rhythmical sense. Faced with a tune in 4/4 time they mentally beat out 1 2 3 4 instead of recognizing two strong beats on 1 and 3, or perhaps just the single beat at the beginning of a bar. In their world every quaver in 2/4 time is given its beat, and in 3/4 time every crotchet. These people—and many of them will protest they have an excellent sense of rhythm and are devoted to jazz—must be taught to think of their music purely and simply in terms of one remorseless beat to the bar, and of one instantaneous pictorial image to each musical phrase. Otherwise their performances, whether in music or in straight drama, will be lacking vitality, and their future careers will be in jeopardy.

13

BREATHING

a. Relaxation and breathing

Both in the act of inhalation and in the act of compression, two antagonistic sets of muscles are involved. In each case the muscles of one set relax in order to allow the muscles of the other set to contract. During inhalation the diaphragm contracts automatically, provided the abdominal muscles have previously relaxed. Unfortunately these muscles do not relax automatically in the act of taking a quick breath, particularly when the new technique of breath compression is being mastered; in fact, the more efficiently the student maintains a relaxation of the diaphragm, the more reluctant he will be to relax the abdominal muscles at the end of a sung phrase. The only way of overcoming this tendency is to make a habit of looking and thinking ahead at the end of every phrase. If this does not help, he must consciously relax the whole of the upper abdomen, making it as soft and yielding as a blancmange. Needless to say, the spine must remain long.

Despite the most solemn warnings, almost all students habitually take in too much breath. In a position of readiness the relaxation of the abdominal muscles will automatically cause the lower ribs to expand, almost as if they were attached to a powerful spring which pulled them apart. Inhalation must be an entirely unconscious process.

EXERCISE 83

Go through Handel's 'Where e'er you walk', taking two lines at a time, i.e. 1 and 2, 2 and 3, 3 and 4, and similarly in the other two verses. Breathe at the end of each line, without breaking the rhythmic flow.

b. The two techniques of breathing

It has been already shown that the diaphragm, being a muscle of considerable size, needs a certain amount of time in which to contract. Whenever an over-rapid breath is taken, you risk a poor attack on the next note, in addition to submitting the body to a physical strain that very quickly makes itself felt. Diaphragms can be trained to work at an efficient speed, but even so every student finds that singing his first song in proper technique leaves him surprisingly exhausted. Slow and simple it may be, yet he comes to the end with a new feeling of reverence for the interpreters of Tristan and Salome. His exhaustion stems partly from a combination of mental and physical concentration, but much of it is due to the quick energetic series of contractions to which he has been submitting his diaphragm. He learns in time to make these contractions smoother and easier. Nevertheless no diaphragm can be trained to move into contraction more quickly than its size allows.

Singers are curiously slapdash about the technique of breathing. They all agree that it is one of the most important elements of voice-production, and many take pride in displaying the strength of their diaphragms; yet they never seem to be aware of the limitations of this muscle. It is a symptom of the vocal myopia which is discussed on page 184, but it is due in a greater degree to their insensitivity. The diaphragm is a willing cart-horse and not the piston of a modern combustion engine. If it were able to move at the speed which some singers expect, runners would be doing the mile in well under three minutes. As things are, both runners and singers have to be content with their present imperfect bodies and allow the diaphragm to move into contraction at a reasonable pace. The singer can only manage this by supplementing the ordinary diaphragmatic breaths with what are known as catch breaths.

Smooth inhalation, as I explained in Chapter 4, depends absolutely on the singer's body posture. To enable the lower ribs to move, a position of readiness is essential. This is equally true in taking catch breaths, but in other respects the two methods of breathing are wholly different. Diaphragmatic breathing must be confined to the lower ribs; if expansion is felt anywhere above the level of the bottom of the breastbone, it means either that you have taken in too much breath or that your method of breathing is wrong. Catch breaths on the other hand have to be confined to the upper ribs; there must be no sensation of the lower ribs being involved. A partial contraction of the diaphragm enables you, as a result of the diminished breath pressure, to increase the size of the upper chest by means of an upward thrust of the ribs immediately under the armpits. So long as the body is in a position of readiness, it is a perfectly simple movement but, like so many specialized techniques, not very easy to describe. Imagine that you have air pockets in the armpits which can be inflated like balloons, and that additional air can be piped through these balloons and stored under the shoulders. Many people find it helpful to bring the shoulders very slightly forward.

Catch breaths should always carry an emotional implication. In other words, feel that it was not lack of oxygen, but a genuine emotion, sparked off by the words and music, which made you take breath at that particular moment. In turn the act of taking a catch breath should intensify your existing emotional state, and also reinforce the physical conditions embraced by the 'Spanish dancer', the 'bow and arrow' and the contracted tongue muscles. A listener can sense both these aspects most vividly in the records of Caruso and Gigli.

In taking catch breaths the reader will find the conception of the spontaneous vibration of the vocal cords an invaluable help. Feel that the cords are continuing to vibrate throughout the period needed for inhalation; in exactly the same way a car engine remains running when in neutral or when the clutch pedal is depressed. This analogy is most helpful in the launching of all notes, and particularly in the case of catch breaths.

Diaphragmatic breaths should only be taken when there is adequate time; when there is, so to speak, a musical full stop. Musical commas as a rule only allow time for catch breaths, but since he can take them so quickly and easily a wise singer should not scruple to indulge himself with an extra helping of breath whenever he feels so inclined. If you begin worrying about your breath supply, it means that you cannot be concentrating on your production and interpretation. Moreover there is nothing which audiences notice so quickly. They stop listening and start speculating, and the performance crashes in ruins. Not only is that particular song a dud, but the atmosphere of friendly concentration is irretrievably dissipated. Having been made uneasy once, an audience never again feels completely confident. Anyone may forget his words; but breath management is the singer's business, and you have no right to let the public down. The importance of this can hardly be overstressed because, although the breath supply in good production lasts longer, it gives out much more suddenly than in forward production and without any warning. The tone just stops and you are left gasping and embarrassed.

As soon as you have become familiar with the two techniques of breathing, you should make a habit in your songs of mapping out breaths as if they were stops on a bus route, the diaphragmatic breaths being the regular stops marked with a V, and the clavicular breaths the request or emergency stops marked with a '. The famous old song 'Drink to me only with thine eyes' provides an excellent illustration of the two techniques. The first verse is as follows:

> Drink to me only with thine eyes,
>   And I will pledge with mine;
> Or leave a kiss but in the cup,
>   And I'll not look for wine.
> The thirst that from the soul doth rise,
>   Doth ask a drink divine;
> But might I of Jove's nectar sup,
>   I would not change for thine.*

A very few singers can manage with only three interruptions of the legato line. They take breath at 'mine', 'wine', and 'divine', but such bravura is not for ordinary mortals, and savours more of a circus act than an artistic interpretation. In company with most singers you will certainly decide to take the normal amount of breaths, and in this case there is no doubt where they should come. After 'mine', 'wine' and 'divine' you take a diaphragmatic breath, and since help is needed to bring each of these long phrases to a conclusion, you take catch breaths at half-way points. Both music and poetry make it inevitable that these breaths occur at the end of each line after 'eyes', 'cup', 'rise' and 'sup'. The audience will be hardly aware of a breath being taken, but it will sense a new feeling of confidence and steadiness as the singer announces his determination first to pledge, then not to look. In other contexts catch breaths can convey heartfelt love, overwhelming impulse, a particular emphasis, a hesitancy and a dozen other things which are the very stuff of song interpretation, and of which the exclusively diaphragmatic breather deprives himself.

* 'but in the cup' and 'look for wine' are the correct words. Why must editors presume to improve on Ben Jonson!

[189]

In a song like this, with huge legato phrases, the quickest of catch-breaths causes an interruption to the vocal line. The singer's art is not so much to conceal this interruption, as to contrive that it escapes notice, and does not break the march of the song. The final syllable before the breath must be cut as short as possible, but this will not be noticed provided you retain the same degree of tone right to the end, making as it were an implied crescendo; in other words provided you think louder without actually increasing the tone. Not only is the final vowel securely produced in this way, but a feeling of carry-on is given to the following phrase which banishes any suspicion that your interest in the words or the music is waning. The first catch-breath follows two quavers on which the word 'eyes' is sustained, and to give yourself time to take breath you turn the second quaver into a short semiquaver. The quaver on 'and' can now be given its full value without the march of the song being disturbed. If you make an implied crescendo on the short second quaver of 'eyes' and are careful to give sufficient weight to the s, the audience will not notice the break in the vocal line; their attention will be carried onwards; they will say to themselves: 'yes, and what then?' and can hardly wait to be informed of your intention to pledge. The same thing occurs at the words 'cup', 'rise' and 'sup'.

The rule of cutting short the final syllable, so as to have comfortable time to breathe without interrupting the march of the song, applies equally to diaphragmatic breathing. However long the note on 'mine' in your copy, you should sing it as a dotted crotchet tied over to a semiquaver. Thus you have nearly three quavers in which to go through Movements I and II with an imperceptible pause between each. On the word 'divine' you give the same time value as on the word 'mine', making an implied crescendo on the short second note. 'Wine' is followed by the word 'the' on the last quaver beat of the bar. With that much less time for breath you should abbreviate 'wine' to a crotchet tied over to a semiquaver. In all such cases be careful to take off the note on a strong rather than a weak beat, otherwise you build up an impression of lackadaisical uncertainty.

The reader must not expect to be able to rid himself immediately of the tendency to remain on the final note of a phrase longer than is advisable. The better the voice and the more careful his production, the stronger the tendency will be. To a great extent this failing encourages him to avoid taking breath in the middle of phrases; and indeed it is surprising what can be done as soon as one learns a proper control of the vocal mechanism. Nevertheless it is better to err on the side of caution, and under no circumstances allow the audience to suspect that breath is running short. On page 139 it is shown how the singer can avoid running out of breath by inducing a strong pressure against the front of the chest. Naturally this is only a partial remedy. In the end we come back to the same piece of advice as that great financier Mr Micawber once gave to David Copperfield:

> Annual income twenty pounds, annual expenditure nineteen nineteen six, result happiness. Annual income twenty pounds, annual expenditure twenty pounds ought and six, result misery. The blossom is blighted, the leaf is withered, the God of day goes down on the dreary scene, and—in short—you are for ever floored.

It goes without saying that inhalation of either sort should be as unobtrusive as possible. The technique of taking diaphragmatic breaths or catch breaths has been fully explained, and if you feel that breathing is slow, noisy or tiring, the first thing to check up on is your posture. But over and above technical defects, quick breaths become unpleasantly noticeable unless the dynamic on the words immediately following the breath is precisely the same as on the preceding words. If 'thine eyes' is sung *piano*, 'and I' must also be sung *piano*; if 'the cup' is sung even softer, 'and I'll' must also be sung with the same quiet intensity. Sometimes there is a tendency to start the new phrase with a burst of rather breathy tone. It can be avoided by making sure that lung tension is inspired by a genuinely emotional impulse.

As a rule singers tend to put in far too much expression, most of it rather meaningless and lamentably reminiscent of an accordion. This can be avoided by a strict attention to the fundamentals of technique and a particular care to sustain an emotional attitude. Crescendos and diminuendos must arise gradually and naturally out of the context of the music or the words, and not just for their own sake. Sudden changes of tone should only be made when there is an excellent reason. An actor who was guilty of meaningless gestures and false emphasis in his lines would rightly be dismissed as a 'ham'. At present there are far too many 'ham' vocalists. There is no fear of your becoming one of them, so long as you treat the voice as an instrument with all its peculiar qualities and frailties, and play it as it would wish to be played.

c. The resources of breath

All students habitually take in too much breath, and nothing is more destructive of good tone. In other sections I have compared inhalation to the backward swing of a tennis racquet which is merely a preparation for hitting the ball correctly; I have also compared it to the meal an athlete consumes before running a mile. Both analogies are sufficiently vivid—and they need to be—for the extravagant emphasis conductors place on singing a long phrase without taking breath upsets the beginner's sense of relative values far more seriously than is generally realized.

But what about the huge runs of Bach and Handel and their long sustained notes? Do you simply break them up, even at places where the most efficient catch breath is only too obvious? No, you do not! You tackle your problem from a sensible, practical, but not necessarily the most obvious point of view. In other words you provide yourself, not with an outsize air-container, but with an extra special squeezing apparatus; and this is a matter, not of better body building, but of simple resolution. Like many bullies, the bogey of breathlessness can be put to flight if you take your courage in both hands and *go on*. A runner has to be nagged by his trainer or his conscience into pulling out physical resources which he hardly realized he possessed. The singer can do likewise. The abdominal muscles are not, and never have been conditioned to meet the fearsome demands of the St. Matthew Passion. But they can and will do so provided they are—quite literally—forced to. Instead of surrendering to the defeatist fear that breath will be used up long before the end of the phrase, you must constantly ask yourself: 'Can my tummy go in a bit farther?' If the answer is 'yes'—and in ninety-nine cases out of a hundred it will be—then you must flog yourself for that much longer. The discomfort, though real enough, will gradually disappear after regular practice, but only if you work seriously and consistently to overcome it.

EXERCISE 84

i. Without taking any bigger breath than usual, repeat Exercise 51 (page 132). See how long you can last out. You should be able to manage 15 seconds without too much difficulty.

ii. Sing the last scale in Exercise 106 (iv) (page 236) three times round, then four times.

iii. Sing the last two arpeggio figures in Exercise 107 (page 237) three times round, then four times.

iv. Sing 'Drink to me only' (page 189), breathing only at the end of every other line, i.e. after 'mine', 'wine' and 'divine'.

14
NASAL RESONANCE

a. Humming and nasal resonance

Almost all singers indulge in humming, some because it is an integral part of their training, some because it feels pleasant, and others as a substitute for singing. One such was Samuel Pepys who, in his diary for 30 June, 1661, wrote: 'After dinner to Graye's Inn Walk, all alone, and with great pleasure seeing the fine ladies walk there. Myself humming to myself (which nowadays is my constant practice, since I began to learn to sing) the trillo, and found by use that it do come upon me.'

Humming as an exercise may be beneficial or harmful according to the way you go about it. It can certainly do a great deal of harm if wrongly applied. For instance, if you hum on *m* you will find it difficult to keep the tongue muscles braced or the jaw retracted; consequently the tone quality on the ensuing vowel will be comparatively poor.

Humming on *n* is not nearly so pernicious. The cheeks can be raised, and the jaw feels loose. On the other hand, the tip of the tongue is against the hard palate and feels stiff. This is hardly to be wondered at, for the tongue forms itself into a barrier which stretches right across the hard palate, and is every bit as effective in excluding sound waves as are the lips in articulating *m*. Thus on *m* the jaw feels stiff, the tongue is relaxed and the tone is centred in the nose, while on *n* the jaw feels relaxed and the tongue stiff. In neither case is any contraction of the tongue muscles possible.

On *ng* there are no technical dangers. The back part of the tongue is against the rear upper teeth, and so long as the mouth is opened the tongue muscles remain contracted. There are strong sensations of vibration round the nose and eyebrows and all over the skull. As for the ringing noises in the neighbourhood of the ears, they are merely a sympathetic vibration, as irrelevant to the tone as the ornament on the mantelpiece which starts tinging in the middle of a piano solo. During the hum the back of the tongue lies up against the palate so as to block

[194]

the entrance to the mouth. If you finish a phrase on *ng*, as for instance when the last word is 'hung', you may hear a rather alarmingly audible kind of click as the tongue and the soft palate part company, causing the word to sound like 'hung'er'. To avoid this, take care to end all *ng* words smartly and neatly.

EXERCISE 85

On an *ng* sound, with the jaw open throughout the exercise, make a rapid sirenlike portamento. The jaw should be open to its fullest extent on the top notes.

In learning nasal resonance almost all students are terrified that they are going to sound nasal in the wrong sense of the word. It is a very natural anxiety, but it can be resolved by a simple test. If you pinch the nostrils together and the voice is brought to an abrupt standstill, you will have been singing with the wrong kind of nasality, and almost certainly in forward production. If the voice continues unabashed, the nasal quality will be the real thing, however American the voice may sound to your unaccustomed ears. True nasal resonance is the result not of pushing the voice against or into the nose, but of drawing it out of the cavities behind the nose, cheeks and forehead, and pulling it backwards and more or less upwards in the manner of the baby's cry. The nostrils will feel so wide as to be positively negroid, and you will have the same prickly sensation as before sneezing. Everything inside will seem to be cleared right out through some imaginary back passage. But I cannot guarantee that the baleful catarrh which plagues so many of us will be eliminated.

In the early stages of acquiring nasal resonance you must be prepared to find the tone quality sounding, to your own ears at least, sarcastic, cynical, hard and unsympathetic. But remember that your condition is like that of a man who has never been out of Manchester in his life, and finds himself suddenly translated to the dazzling sunshine of the Italian Riviera on a June morning. In something so intimately expressive of personality as the human voice, instinct revolts against any

violent change, however much it may be for the better; especially
in this case since, despite its heady excitement, the nasal timbre may
seem to swamp much of the sympathetic tone-quality. It is a common
and a very natural reaction, but you must overcome it by bearing in
mind firstly the difficulty of hearing your own voice as it really sounds;
secondly, that woolly foggy tone could not possibly be the expression
of a truly emotional condition. Avoid sentimentality like the plague,
and aim all the time for positive Mediterranean villainy with stilettos,
high heels and long fingernails. The temperament of a Carmen must
be your inspiration rather than Mother Machree.

b. The frontal resonators*

With the help of the consonant *ng* sung with opened mouth, the
resonance cavities in the head, neck and chest can and should be made
available to give body and colour to each and every note throughout
the vocal compass. In practice their individual effectiveness varies
according to the pitch of the note, but the reader must not mentally
reserve chest resonance for his lower notes, nor the cavities which
provide head resonance for his high notes. All the cavities all the time
must be made to contribute their proper share. Whenever a note is well
sung, the whole head feels full of tone; not just one part of it but, with
the exception of the mouth, the whole head. This happy state of things
cannot be arrived at until you become actively aware of the position
and characteristics of all the vocal resonators, and not merely the throat.

The nasal cavity consists of long narrow passages running from the
nasal pharynx to the nostrils. Leading out from the nasal cavity, immediately below the eyes, are the maxillary sinuses. To judge by what
can be heard and felt in humming, these bony hollows must quite
certainly play a major role in imparting resonance to the voice.
Facial characteristics of singers confirm this. Good voices may issue
from every kind of face, but a very large proportion have a chubby
appearance round the cheek-bones which suggests large maxillary
sinuses; Caruso and Gigli are obvious examples, and potentially good
voices in complete strangers can be diagnosed in the same way before
they open their mouths. Two smaller cavities are the frontal sinuses
situated on either side of the top of the nose behind the eyebrows.

* I prefer to use the term 'frontal' rather than 'head' resonance, to guard against
the reader associating and possibly confining it to notes sung in head register.

Behind and between the frontal sinuses is the sphenoidal sinus. In addition to these and other cavities in the head, there is no doubt that the skull bones also vibrate and are sensitive to outside sounds such as tuning forks.

The immense resources of frontal resonance will only be realized if the singer applies an appropriate compression against correctly approximated vocal cords; in other words, when his tongue muscles are contracted and proper lung tension is previously built up. If then, like any mediaeval magician, he mentally summons it forth, frontal resonance will materialize to add radiance to the throat resonance. Its point of concentration seems to vary according to the pitch of the note. On high notes it will be low down at the place where spectacles sit on noses, and on low notes it should be on or even above the place where hair normally starts to grow. The middle notes will take care of themselves, but if you find them gruff or gravelly, treat them as low notes and feel your resonance high above the forehead. (See Fig. 5(a) and (b), pages 28–9.)

In describing these sensations I must make it clear that they are no more than subjective. Some singers are keenly aware of them, others not at all. If you are one of the others, there is no need to feel discouraged. At some time in the future you will recognize the feeling and, like an astronomer in search of a star, find it all the sooner for knowing what to look for. If and when this moment arrives, you will be amply rewarded by a greatly increased sense of security, and reluctance to abuse the voice. The low frontal position will banish the laborious scoops and agonized screams of which even the best of us have been occasionally guilty. The high frontal position is an equally admirable antidote to the gruff quality and excess of breath pressure, which spoil the low notes of all beginners. Together they are the perfect remedy for the unhappy singer who is still bedevilled by the hallucination of notes being literally high or low.

The technique of shifting the centre of frontal resonance from forehead to nose is one of the most valuable acquisitions in voice production. As a rule it is wise to associate it with the feelings of compression and suppression. Thus low and medium notes are sung with the centre of frontal resonance above the forehead and a feeling of suppression; and high notes at the bridge of the nose with a feeling of compression, the jaw being opened wide enough to accommodate the required note and vowel sound. In this way the tricky business of the vocal registers will be robbed of most of its complications.

EXERCISE 86

Sing on all vowels:

EXERCISE 87

Sing five notes up the major scale in mezzo-forte, starting on any note between A and C. To assist the feeling of the voice leaning towards the top and back of the head, it is helpful to make a slow, deep bow from the hips, so that on the top note of a phrase the head is at its lowest. In this way the point of resonance seems to swing naturally to a backward and upward point above and behind the ears. The process might be compared to the mechanism of a doll's eyes. Caruso learned to take high notes in this way, and taught it to John McCormack; Gigli did the same thing, even to some extent in concerts.

15
REGISTERS

Singers talk about placing the voice; but all we can really do is to place our perceptions of voice. High, medium and low notes find, and must be allowed to find, their resonance inside any of the various cavities capable of producing sympathetic overtones. The feeling that high notes seem to be predominantly in the head, and low notes in the chest, has given rise to the conception of registers; but it does not mean that you need to place notes of a particular pitch in one especial part of the body. So long as favourable conditions are provided, they will all seem to spring out of the lung tension and resonate in the throat, the upper part of the head and in the chest. Nevertheless every well produced voice contains groups of notes which seem to emanate more especially from one part of the anatomy, and to demand a particular degree of lung tension. These groups of notes are called registers. The singer does not place any particular note in the locality associated with a certain register, but he either induces or expects to encounter the sensations belonging to that register. As a result the note will sound in the register of his choice. It is as if a motor cyclist changed gear, not by means of clutch and gear-handle, but by inducing a different degree of wind pressure against his face, and a variation in the pitched and rhythmical sound of his engine. Only in the case of the man's falsetto and the woman's chest voice is it possible to make an adjustment as positive as a gear change on a car. These phenomena, which I call mechanisms, will be described in the next chapter.

a. The vocal registers

The particular locality in which a note appears to come to rest is determined by the amount of breath passing through the vocal cords at each vibration. As the pitch of the note ascends on a rising scale, or as a note gets softer in a diminuendo, the vocal cords in good production allow less and less breath to pass through the glottis, and it is the decrease of air flow that causes the sound to appear to come to rest in a relatively higher locality. The better the singer's production, the more pronounced will be his awareness of this. A forward breathy manner of singing will merely result in 'sing as you speak' sensations in the front of the mouth. On the other hand, if the suppression of the voice is exaggerated as in agonized groaning, no sensation will be felt except at the very bottom of the throat. The singer who is unaware of registers is seldom a good one.

In a matter which depends so much on personal sensations, it is hardly surprising that, ever since singing began, the registers have been a glorious stamping ground for controversy. Some teachers have given the voice two registers, some three, while others have noted as many as five or six. It is of course tempting to join the opposite camp and swear that if there are such things, it would be well to forget about them; but at no time in the history of the art has the reality of registers been seriously called in question. Confusion there has been in plenty, but the preponderance of opinion has favoured three. Certainly I have no inclination to quarrel with the pronouncement of one John of Garland who as long ago as the year 1250 wrote:

> It must be known that the human voice exists in three forms; it is a chest voice, throat voice, or head voice. If it is a chest voice, then it is in the low register; it ought to be placed in the lowest part of a piece. If it is a throat voice, it is in a middle position in relation to each, that is to the low and the high. And just as far down the chest voice is in the low register, so the head voice is high in the upper register. And, in regard to the way of singing, chest voices ought to be placed in their proper place, that is in the lower part, throat voices ought always to have the middle place in the upper sections.

The throat voice, or, as we call it now, the middle register lies more or less between the two E flats on the treble stave. Above the high E flat is the head register, and below the low E flat is the chest register. I need hardly say that these notes are the actual pitch in the case of women, and one octave above the actual pitch in the case of men. The table on page 201 shows the registers suitable for various parts of the voice:

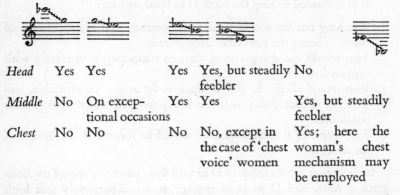

Head	Yes	Yes	Yes	Yes, but steadily feebler	No
Middle	No	On exceptional occasions	Yes	Yes	Yes, but steadily feebler
Chest	No	No	No	No, except in the case of 'chest voice' women	Yes; here the woman's chest mechanism may be employed

Registers have to be established partly by mental association and partly by the degree of lung tension which seems to be called for. The following diagram, which shows the practical range of each register for the generality of voices, can only be a very rough guide.

Skilled use of the registers is really nothing more than the proper employment of various techniques which have been already explained. They include the sensations of lung tension; the inducing either of compression or suppression; the swing back of the jaw on high notes; and the variation in the locality of frontal resonance. For instance, D on the second line of the treble stave can be sung either in middle register or in head register, and it is not easy on an isolated note always to be sure of launching it correctly in one or the other. To sing it in middle register, you have to condition yourself subconsciously to make the following preparations:

1. The lung tension must be appropriate for that note, with no thought of increasing the intensity in anticipation of notes higher than the E immediately above.
2. The predominant feeling is of suppression.
3. The jaw is not opened any wider than a finger's breadth.
4. The centre of frontal resonance is located high in the forehead.

If you wanted to sing the same D in head register:

1. The lung tension would seem to be greater, as if in expectation of the note being the start of a rising phrase.
2. You would use compression, though tempering it discreetly with suppression.
3. You would allow the jaw to open as far as was comfortable, and with the expectation that it was likely to open wider as the phrase continued.
4. The centre of frontal resonance would be located at the bridge of the nose.

In short you would think of D in middle register as a robust medium pitched note, and D in head register as a comparatively soft high pitched note.

The transition from one register to another on an upward scale may be compared to the act of changing gear on a car. The driver, finding himself moving at a speed unsuitable to his present gear, suspends acceleration and changes up or down. Only when the new gear has been safely engaged does he again depress the accelerator. During the period of gear changing he loses speed, and all the weight of his foot on the accelerator can only foul the engine. In the same way the singer increases his lung tension as he changes from middle into head register, but never his tone; in point of fact the two things are mutually contradictory. Emotionally everything suggests that an ascending passage in most cases should be accompanied by a steady crescendo. Technically it cannot be managed at the point where a change into head register is demanded. Any attempt to do so would keep the voice in middle register, and allow the emotional impulse of the earlier notes to degenerate into a shout. To avoid mishap you must trim your sails to the idiosyncrasies of your craft, singing the ascending passage with the controlled emotional restraint which the change of register demands. At the moment of the change there is a pronounced increase of lung tension. You may also like to feel an implied diminuendo, though this is a question of individual choice. Once in the top register, you can give the voice as much freedom as the music suggests.

In moving downwards the same lung tension should be maintained as on the higher notes. The mere feeling that one is descending to a lower pitch level causes an automatic reduction of the pitch tension, but keeps the lung tension at a level appropriate to the new note. Any conscious reduction of lung tension is death to good singing.

The beginner may feel that the establishment of the three registers will produce three different voices. In fact the impression which the listener receives is the exact opposite. Without correct registration it is impossible to build a homogeneous voice; the lower notes will be feeble and the high notes thin and unsteady. Only the middle notes will sound half-way good, and even these are liable to be dull and uninteresting.

b. Middle register

Registers are localities of acoustic sensation. One does not select a register as one selects a particular fingering for a phrase in a piano piece; in other words, one does not place notes in the head, throat or chest. All one does is to expect, in singing a passage, to experience a particular sensation which may be accepted as evidence that the voice is using head, middle or chest register. If this is clear, the reader will understand when I say that the distinguishing feature of middle register is its almost complete anonymity. Sensations in the throat and mouth are to all intents and purposes non-existent. Despite the overwhelming proportion of resonance provided by the throat, the singer should feel literally nothing between the top of the windpipe and the bottom of the nose; as far as he is concerned he has no jaw, mouth or throat, and in fact is no more than a series of cervical vertebrae climbing up into his skull. The only locality of acoustic sensation in the middle register of which he is aware are the cheeks and the back of the nose, and this is where he expects the voice to ring.

Middle register is the register which every male voice, trained or untrained, instinctively adopts on all medium notes. The female voice is characteristically unpredictable; but after some preliminary training it also will adopt middle register on medium pitched notes.

The habit of anticipating the correct register position—of expecting the voice to sound at a particular part of the body, but without taking any actual steps to place it there, is difficult to acquire, and hardest of all on the middle range of notes. In this part of the voice it is horribly easy to expect the tone to emerge like speech on the level of the hard palate. That is why there are so many singers who produce their high notes beautifully, but whose middle and lower notes are dull and un-interesting.

In forward production the voice is not only invariably associated with the middle register level, but deliberately placed there. How it is possible to combine this with the teaching of the three registers I cannot understand. If one places the voice on the hard palate on all notes, one automatically evokes the equivalent register adjustment of the larynx; in other words you will sing in middle register. Moreover, if you are unwise enough to place the note, instead of expecting sensations of resonance, you allow the breath to be master of the larynx; the cords will be loosely approximated, and the tone unsupported and shallow.

c. Head register

The locality of acoustic sensation embraced by the head register takes in the whole extent of the skull above a line drawn from the bridge of the nose down to the occipital bone which forms the base of the back of the skull. All this large area may be said to come alive when the singer expects to feel his voice inside it.

Just before entering head register the sensation of lung tension becomes noticeably greater, and the vocal cords shorten their vibrating length, so that only a tiny section of each cord is left free to vibrate (Fig. 25, page 207). The adjustment is not a conscious thing. One has no sensation of any movement of the larynx, and if you think you feel anything, it is nothing more than a variation in the movement of air escaping from the top of the windpipe into the throat. But to think aright gives those parts outside our conscious control the best possible chance of acting aright. Therefore it is wise to keep in mind that in head register the vibrating length of the vocal cords is shortened, and consequently there is an increased suppression of breath. The voice is not suppressed, but seems to be projected higher up in the head, just as a more powerful jet of water is created by closing more tightly the mouth of a running tap with a finger. The suppression causes a proportionately stronger kick back of the compressed breath. Psychologically the singer feels younger, more loverlike and less villainous, maternal or grief-stricken. He transforms himself, so to speak, from Rigoletto into the Duke, from Sharpless into Pinkerton, from Ortrud into Elsa. Since this condition is fundamentally emotional, it should when possible be the primary stimulus to making a change of register.

On entering head register there is a marked change in the sensation of voice. Together with the suppression of breath there is a feeling that the voice is being suppressed as well. This is hardly surprising considering how accustomed we are to a fairly unrestricted expenditure of breath when speaking. But it is quite illusory, and it is vital that the reader should understand this. Lung tension in head register will be greater, but the voice will seem to be smaller, albeit much more concentrated.

When singing in the middle and chest registers, we have the feeling that most of the vowels possess a characteristic which, for want of a better word, we describe as 'breadth'; and our habitual tendency is to regard 'broad' vowels as being vocally preferable to 'narrow' vowels. But we have already seen that good singing or speech both demand vowels which are concentrated and consequently narrower than the same vowels sung in forward production. Nevertheless the vowel still possesses breadth, so far as the singer's sensations are concerned. It can be compared to a ribbon of vowel tone—but a ribbon that becomes progressively narrower as the notes ascend in the scale and the sense of lung tension becomes more pronounced.

On entering head register the vowel sound can no longer be compared to a ribbon, however narrow. It changes to something as fine and concentrated as the filament of an electric lamp, and every bit as brilliant. When sung fortissimo a well produced ringing head note can easily make you feel quite dizzy—and often does so. The singer who can work with this small point of sound, while huge waves of orchestral tone are surging round him, needs a will of steel to hold him to his technique.

As one might expect, a soprano or a tenor uses head register much more habitually than would a baritone or mezzo-soprano. The first section of 'Where e'er you walk' sung in the original key of B flat contains only one G, but the tessitura is so high that the singer would need to keep in head register almost continually; in fact the only place in the whole song suitable for middle register would probably be at

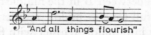
"And all things flourish"

A baritone or mezzo-soprano could sing the aria in this key, but their larger vocal cords were never intended to sustain head register over such an extended period, and both singers would rapidly tire. Accordingly they would be wise to sing the aria in A flat or G, using the middle register except in the phrases containing F or E; i.e. the final phrase of the first section,

"Shall crowd in-to—"

and

"And all things flourish"

The reader should now look through the easier songs in his repertoire, and come to a firm decision as to the register in which he proposes to sing each phrase, lettering the transitional point with an H for head, and M for middle register. When in doubt, head register should always be preferred. A change of register in the middle of phrases can be made in a downward direction without difficulty. In an upward direction it is comparatively easy on intervals of at least a major third. On smaller intervals such as scale passages the transition may be avoided, either by starting the phrase in head register, or by breaking off the phrase and completing the passage in head.

The reader will doubtless be fully aware that the shift in frontal resonance has no connection with the vocal registers and is simply a means of singing high or low notes in good production. But there is no doubt that a mastery of the frontal shift is of inestimable value in learning to move into head register. And not only that. Irrespective of the pitch of the note, a good nasal technique tends to keep the voice in head register, unless the singer deliberately wishes to give his voice a darker quality. As a result the voice will seem to have a freshness and youthful vitality, no matter whether it be a coloratura or a bass.

EXERCISE 88

(i) Sing single notes between B in the middle of the voice and E flat above, starting with full tone in middle register, softening into head register and returning into middle register with full tone.

(ii) Start the tone soft in head register, swell to full tone in middle register, and return to head register.

This art of swelling tone and diminishing it on a long held note is called the *messa di voce*.

d. The vocal cords and the registers

There is every justification for looking upon the vocal cords as violin strings, inasmuch as one mentally controls the pitch not by increasing the tension but by adjusting their vibrating length (Fig. 25). The process may be compared to the manner in which a woman makes up her lips; if she starts by drawing a short thin delicate line of lipstick, this would correspond to the short length and shallow depth of vocal cord brought into vibration in head register. If she then enlarges her lips and lengthens them, their appearance would correspond to the increased length and depth of vocal cord used in the middle register. If she again enlarges her lips so as to suggest a lady of easy virtue, they would correspond to the depth of vocal cord in the chest register. A natural singer makes his adjustments instinctively; the ordinary mortal can be equally successful if he applies his knowledge, sensitivity and musical taste aright. This means primarily that he expects to reduce the length and thickness of his 'string' as he goes up the scale. He assists the process partly by an act of thought, partly by varying the intensity of his lung tension, and particularly by maintaining the contraction of the tongue muscles. The contraction is probably no more intense on high notes than on low notes, but as the pitch rises there is a tendency for the muscles to relax.

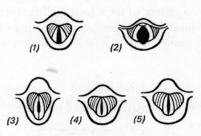

The vocal cords seen from above

(1) *Quiet breathing*
(2) *Inhalation*
(3) *Head register in the act of singing*
(4) *Middle register in the act of singing*
(5) *Chest register in the act of singing*

FIG. 25. REGISTERS AND THE VOCAL CORDS

No doubt the beginner will feel appalled at the new complications into which the registers have plunged him. It is not as bad as it seems. The important point is to be quite sure in which register one intends to sing any particular phrase. In the same way a tennis player must make up his mind at the earliest possible moment whether he is going to return a ball on the forehand or the backhand, on the volley or on the bounce; only then can he set about arranging his feet, his body and his racquet in such a way that the ball is likely to rebound with accuracy and effectiveness. As an alternative analogy, the singer is like a versatile dance band musician who, seeing a certain passage approaching, must decide whether to play it on his tenor saxophone, his alto saxophone or his clarinet. Decision is the first thing that is needed. Maybe he will use the register very ineffectively to begin with, but the technique is bound to improve so long as he remains determined to use at one time one particular register and no other. Uncertainty in this, as in the articulation of vocal sounds, is disastrous.

The sensitivity needed to master this technique may be long in coming, but at least you may be sure of a simultaneous improvement in your musical taste. You will find yourself preferring a vibrant tone to a loud tone, a flexible sound to one that cannot be modified, a light-weight champion to a prone heavy-weight. In these days there is a lamentable demand from conductors and coaches for loud tone. The singer must in this respect be strongminded, and remember that vibrancy should be his one and only objective. Gigli's pianissimo could be heard in the top gallery of the Albert Hall far more clearly than the loudest tones of most English performers because of the difference in vibrancy. Loud or noisy singing is bad singing, uncultured, insensitive and unmusical.

EXERCISE 89

Sing the following on all vowels in head register:

EXERCISE 90

In Exercise 26 (page 52) you had to visualize yourself as a tightrope walker. Having plumbed the mysteries of lifted cheeks, contracted tongue muscles and elastic-sided collars, let us revive this analogy. With cheeks hung securely aloft, you climb up to that frightening little eyrie which leads on to the high wire; in other words you build up your compression. With everything in order you step gently but firmly on to the wire, which is neither slack nor rigid but dynamically buoyant. In the same way you launch the note gently but firmly.

e. The medium voice and the upper registers

The notes between the upper F on the treble stave and the B below are of particular importance for robust tenors and for medium voices, especially baritones, since it is on these notes that the greatest range of dynamics is demanded. On the lower middle register from E flat to the B flat above, the tone seems to be flowing all over the throat; on and above B flat it gathers more and more against the soft palate, as if preparing for its high jump into the head register.

The potentialities for change of tone colour in this part of the voice can be realized either by anticipating or delaying the transition into head register. An early transition can be made on soft tones without difficulty. Remaining in middle register above the normal point of departure is practical only within a limited range which varies according to the individual. A robust voice can safely sing a G in middle register; a lyric voice would find this impossible, but could probably manage an F with no difficulty. It is a matter for each singer to decide for himself. In any case he must remember that a habitual use of the middle register on high notes is bound to lead to premature fatigue and possible injury to the voice.

The choice of register is governed by technical factors, but the singer's emotion is the deciding element. He may for instance sing a high F in head register as an ardent lover. Alternatively he may sing it in middle register with a suggestion of menace or of hopelessness. Opportunities for variations in tone quality are particularly common in the case of the baritone, who in opera has to convey a far wider range of emotion than do other voices. One day he may be cast as Silvio in *Pagliacci*, and as the ardent young lover he will rightly sing his high notes in head register. The next day he may have to play Tonio in the same opera, and as the rough despised clown he will sing most of his high notes in middle register. In the course of the week he may play Marcel, Scarpia, Escamillo, or Rigoletto. Whatever the role, he must decide what is the prevailing mood which should characterize his top notes. Naturally there are no operas in which the mood of the music and the character of the part clearly dictate one particular register throughout. Verdi's baritones are almost invariably passionate men in the grip of an evil destiny. Their dark moods of tormented jealousy demand a medium register carried as high as it can be comfortably taken. At the same time the normal tessitura is high enough to favour the use of head register whenever appropriate to the character. The aria 'Eri tu', for instance, from *Un Ballo in Maschera*, makes big demands on any baritone. Outraged despair and sorrow alternate with passionate love and a thirst for vengeance. To depict these rapidly changing moods on a highish tessitura is a challenge to any singer. Only when Renato looks back on the happiness which he has lost can he appropriately leave the middle for the head register. Verdi asked a lot of his baritones, but he knew a great deal more about singing than most modern composers. There are many F's in his scores which demand a full-blooded medium register, but he realized that only occasionally can G be sung in the medium register without endangering the singer's production.

Tenors and baritones are all sorts and kinds, and it is often difficult to decide whether an untrained or partially trained voice is one or the other. There is no real dividing line, but unless he is able to sing full-blooded F sharps in his ordinary medium register, a singer would be well advised not to aim for a career as an operatic baritone. However beautifully he sings, in most roles he will be rather ineffective; and subconsciously aware of this he will start forcing his voice. There is no way out of this impasse, except for him to modify his ambitions; but let him thank his stars that at least he possesses a voice for which there is abundant scope in concert, light opera and musical shows. There is of course a possibility that he is an unfledged tenor. Here he must move with the greatest deliberation. It is difficult not to be influenced by the artistic and financial opportunities which are open to a tenor voice and closed to a light baritone; but he must realize that such inducements are a mirage unless he really possesses a tenor range and quality. Lots of

[210]

baritones can shoot off A's and B's, and lots of tenors can barely manage a G, but in this respect such ability or disability is no convincing evidence. Any decision to shift one's ground should only be made with enormous circumspection, and with the help and supervision of someone who knows a lot about voices.

Disappointed baritones may derive a little consolation and amusement from a description of their breed which I came across in George Eliot's *Daniel Deronda*:

> The voice, sometimes audible in subdued snatches of song, had turned out merely a high baritone; indeed, only to look at his lithe powerful frame and the firm gravity of his face would have been enough for an experienced guess that he had no rare and ravishing tenor such as nature reluctantly makes at some sacrifice. Look at his hands; they are not small and dimpled, with tapering fingers that seem to have only a deprecating touch; they are long, flexible, firmly grasping hands, such as Titian has painted in a picture, where he wanted to show the combination of refinement with force.

EXERCISE 91

Sing these sentences

    i. Where e'er you walk.
    ii. Cool gales shall fan.
   iii. Trees where you sit.
   iv. Shall crowd into.
    v. Where e'er you tread.
   vi. The blushing flowers.
  vii. Where e'er you turn.
 viii. My heart's delight.

on the following phrases, first anticipating the transition to head register, then remaining in middle register.

[211]

f. Chest register

In practising the cat exercise (page 55) you brought a pressure of breath against approximated lips so as to produce a mewing sound. The mew was created not by the lips themselves, but by the rapid succession of puffs of air which escaped through the lips as they vibrated. Without an effective resonator in front of the lips, some readers may wonder how it is possible to make such a considerable noise. In fact the available resonators, consisting of mouth, throat and windpipe, are all situated behind the vibrating lips.

The existence of resonators behind or below the vibrator may come as a new idea; but it is important to remember that, just as ripples disperse in concentric circles from the place where a stone meets the water, so tone vibrates in every direction from the point at which it is created. The cat exercise is an irrefutable proof of this. In the voice the most important resonators are of course above the vocal cords. Even so, those below the cords must not be forgotten; they include the windpipe, and perhaps the bronchial passages which connect the windpipe with the lungs, as well as the breastbone and ribs. Together they constitute the resonators of the chest register. Being fixed resonators, they cannot be consciously controlled, and their effectiveness depends entirely on the degree of approximation of the vocal cords. If the approximation is poor, there will be no resonance to speak of coming from below the glottis.

In chest register the locality of acoustic sensation shifts from the head, and now seems to be in the place where the singer associates the birth of the tone, i.e. in the middle of the chest. The complete vibrating length of the vocal cords is used, and the lung tension is so relaxed as to be imperceptible. The singer, who in head register was a racehorse and in middle register a hunter, is now an easy-going middle-aged cart horse. Physically and mentally there may be a feeling of middle-age spread, but it must not extend to any postural degeneration; the stretch up of the spine and the continuous contraction of the sacrospinalis must be preserved at all cost. On the other hand it may be helpful, on the transition into chest register, to allow the weight to go back on to the heels. I need hardly say that this is the one time when such a fall from grace is permissible.

Chest register in the woman's voice is synonymous with the chest mechanism that is discussed in the next chapter. Women singers should accordingly skip from here to page 220, and then go back to Section g.

Even though their voices get steadily weaker in the lower range, tenors and high baritones should not ignore the existence of a chest register which in good production has a soft horn quality with the authentic core of brass. At the same time it is important that they should continue to make full use of the frontal resonators, which in chest register would be identified at a spot high above the forehead. Inevitably this means thinking of two distinct places at once; it would in certain circumstances be a difficult job, but I am sure my readers will have taken my advice and fully absorbed the technique of the frontal resonators before embarking on this chapter. Their virtue will be richly rewarded, for they will find it perfectly easy to think, accordion-like, both high and low at the same time. Very probably their low notes after systematic practice may surprise them, and give them an authentic thrill. Bass-baritones and basses who are proud of their low notes must do the same thing, and be careful not to press. The lower they go, the more they must aim for vibrancy, and steer clear of gruffness. Nothing is more thrilling than a truly sonorous bass voice; it suggests youth, gaiety and physical potency.

The reader must now have a second look at the songs in his repertoire. With a choice of three registers, he should letter each transitional point with H for head, M for middle, and C for chest register.

The present section completes the description of the vocal instrument. Stretching from the thoracic wall and extending through the ribs, breastbone and windpipe, it reaches the vocal cords, which are the only begetter of sound. Above the cords it enters the pharynx, which is the largest resonator and easily adjustable. Head resonators can be called into play by thought, but they are only effective if a sympathetic vibrational co-operation between throat and larynx has already been established. At some place between the bridge of the nose and the beginning of the hair line, the resonating tube seems to make a fairly sharp backward turn to a point a little behind the crown of the head. Here is the mouth of the vocal instrument, and once again I must stress the importance of realizing this. No singer who does not do so can get the best out of himself and his voice.

g. Interpretation and the registers

A clear understanding of the registers should be part of every good singer's equipment, especially as regards the middle and head registers. Without this understanding dramatic songs such as 'Erlkönig' would be impossible to interpret artistically, and the heavy demands of operatic arias would put an intolerable strain on the average voice. Difficult and tiring passages, such as the end of the Prize Song, will become practicable for the first time if the singer keeps not only his G's in the head register but all the lower notes of the phrases in which these G's occur. Admittedly he must sing them softly; but they will be sufficiently full for the demands of the music. Only an ignorant ass of a conductor or composer would want such notes to be sung loud in a comparatively quick passage containing G's and F's and a long held A. The singer's duty is faithfully to interpret a composer's or conductor's wishes, so long as the natural disposition of the voice is not abused. When this happens he must either re-edit the dynamic markings to suit the peculiar characteristics of the human instrument, or he must leave such music to be sung by freak voices and people who don't mind making nasty noises. Nobody can be a good singer unless he understands not only the potentialities but also the limitations of his instrument.

It would be foolish to pretend that the registers do not present many individual problems; however the following rules will apply to all voices:

1. Never sing any notes in a low register which might with equal effect be sung in a higher register.
2. When practicable, sing every note of a phrase in the same register. If this is impossible, change the register on the note preceding a leap up, and on the note following a leap down.
3. It is impossible to sing a medium note loudly in head register, or a highish note softly in medium register.
4. No register must be carried higher than is strictly comfortable.
5. In all passages involving a change of register, whether up or down, make sure that the diaphragm remains high and the tongue muscles contracted.
6. Associate the registers with your emotional point of view. They are the principal means at your disposal of painting the picture. Each

[214]

register is capable of conveying many different moods, according to the context of the song.

7. The singer must not try to make his voice a homogeneous instrument by blending the registers. He must feel that he is singing with three different voices, each of which is giving of its best. The impression which this makes on the listener is paradoxically that the voice is a single entity.

8. The singer will already have found how quickly muscles in various parts of the body can learn new patterns of behaviour. The laryngeal muscles are equally creatures of habit; but correct habits can be acquired only when all notes are sung almost invariably in their appropriate register.

9. The singing of high notes must always contain a physical and mental association of depth. This is what gives them their authentic thrill, so that every top C well and truly struck becomes an affirmation of the free spirit of man.

EXERCISE 92

(*a*) Sing down the scale, remaining throughout in head voice.

(*b*) Make a complete messa di voce, starting piano in head register, going to mezzo-forte in medium register, and returning to head register.

(*c*) make a messa di voce in reverse, starting and ending mezzo-forte.

(*d*) Go down and up the five note scale in head register.

(*e*) Go down the five note scale in head register; make a crescendo to mezzo-forte in medium register, then a diminuendo to piano in head register, and go back up the scale.

Do the same on all notes from E flat upwards on all five vowels.

There is perhaps no better way of realizing the potentialities in a voice than by watching and listening to a really good cellist. The intense and loving concentration with which he draws tone out of his noble but temperamental instrument is an object lesson to all singers. Like the voice the cello seems to have three distinct registers, each with its characteristic quality. Isolated notes sound so totally different, that it is hard to believe they belong to the same instrument; yet when they are joined in a leaping phrase, few sounds can be so utterly satisfying. The singer should follow the cellist's example, drawing from his instrument the most individual and exciting sounds possible on every pitch level. However variegated they may sound, his basic technique and sensitivity will ensure that the final result is musical.

16

MECHANISMS

The word 'mechanism' in this context may be defined as a particular
way of singing involving a conscious act of physical adjustment which
a singer has the choice of either making or not making. Irrespective of
range or sex, there is one and only one part of the voice where this
adjustment can be made. It is not an exact point, because the adjustment is conditioned by a number of different factors, but almost
invariably it occurs between middle C and the G above it. These notes
are the actual ones for both men and women, so that a man singing up
a scale which embraces these notes, and a woman singing down the
same scale, both encounter what may be called a point of departure.

a. The alto mechanism in men's voices

An untrained baritone singing up the scale on these notes, comes to a
point where he has a choice of doing two things. Either he can continue brazenly and uncomfortably up to G in his normal voice, or he
can drift into falsetto. This is a noise which may be comic or pleasing,
but either way will be ineffective, and quite inappropriate to the rest of
his voice and to his own personality. The true alto mechanism is no
breathy little pipe, but a tone of full-blooded contralto quality such as
is heard in English cathedral choirs. In Victorian days male altos were
popular as soloists and as leaders of quartets, but times have changed
and today they are seldom heard outside the cathedral choir stall.
Nevertheless, in the training of men's voices the alto mechanism plays
an important part which singers are unwise to neglect. In breath
management and vocal cord approximation the technique is precisely
the same as for the normal male voice. Tenors and basses are as a rule
nothing like such good alto singers as baritones. Even so, however
modest their range and tone quality, all singers should make use of
what they have. No matter what strange sounds they produce, they
will enormously increase the quality and the steadiness of their normal
voice. Of course, if they start singing exclusively in the alto mechanism,
their ordinary voices will soon disappear. Similarly women who

habitually sing in chest lose their ordinary voices, while their chest notes acquire surprising depth and range. I am assuming however that my male readers have no intention of becoming cathedral altos, nor that my female readers aim to excel as night-club singers, so that in both cases they will use their extraordinary voices to promote their general well-being.

It is not possible to sing a truly legato descending scale of four notes in alto voice, unless a correct technical preparation and follow-through is maintained—and let it be clearly understood that alto invariably means alto and not a quavery little falsetto. No forward production specialist can manage it. A high centre of gravity, raised cheeks and chest, retracted jaw and contracted tongue muscles, all these are indispensable adjuncts for a true alto voice. It is indeed significant that the average cathedral alto has a much steadier and purer quality and a rounder tone than have his colleagues in the tenor and bass sections. The voice itself has little individuality and is decidedly limited in range and power; yet it seems to remain as good as new through fifty odd years of cathedral services. This suggests that the male alto possesses an elixir of vocal life, but the explanation is much simpler. He cannot sing at all unless his technique is correct, and good technique keeps voices young.

The degree of lung tension needed to sing a high note in the alto mechanism is a great deal less than would be needed to sing the same note in the normal mechanism. This in fact is likely to be the cause of any difficulties you may find in singing in alto mechanism. But it does not mean that lung tension is not vitally necessary for true alto production. Without it the note would be no more than a flimsy falsetto of no power or significance.

Most people find that the G or A above middle C is the easiest alto note in their voice. Starting from here, sing descending scales of three or four notes. Cultivate a full round tone, making sure that the first note has genuine alto quality. Do not expect the range ever to be very wide. In any case, no useful purpose is served in singing high notes. The thing that will profit you is the power of maintaining a genuine alto on the notes just above middle C.

EXERCISE 93

Sing down in pure alto with a full tone on *A, E, I, O, U*.

(The notes of this and the following exercise are an octave higher than their actual pitch.)

EXERCISE 94

The notes with upturned tails are to be sung in alto and those with downturned tails in full voice. Do not go from alto to full voice without completely breaking off the tone.

Except by the male alto, the alto mechanism is very rarely used. The change out of chest is possible for high tenors on adjoining or widely separated notes by a technique which might be described as a refined yodel. No one should attempt it except a lyric tenor with a fully developed technique, and then only on very high notes. The arias of Rossini and Donizetti provide many instances where a transition into alto is appropriate, and indeed necessary, if these florid passages are to be executed with agility and lack of effort. Since they are for the experienced lyric tenor, and this guide is for the inexperienced of all voices, I shall provide no exercises. I must however warn young tenors that if they make experiments on their own account, they will be ruining their chances of singing full-throated top C's.

A baritone cannot change directly from chest mechanism into alto mechanism on a high note. But it can be done in a roundabout way via the falsetto. He starts in a full-throated medium register; as the tone gets softer, he finds it moving into head register. From there he allows it to go into falsetto by relaxing the compression, letting his 'bow and arrow' collapse. He can then, by lifting the chest, bring in the alto mechanism, which within modest limits provides an increase of tone. I need hardly say that this requires a considerable degree of technique. Falsetto used in this way can be most striking; used indiscriminately it is ineffective and definitely harmful, because it kills all chance of singing high notes easily and softly. To go from falsetto into full voice on the same note is impossible. A big downward leap as in yodelling would be the only occasion when it might be both possible and desirable; but since you will almost certainly not need to make such sounds in the whole of your career, it would be waste of time to practise something that is difficult, dangerous and extremely ugly.

For some reason, which only the psychoanalyst could disentangle, the very sound of the alto mechanism inspires most women with revulsion. To explain that it is merely a means of acquiring a sturdier and even more virile tone-quality is sheer waste of breath. Therefore it is advisable to practise the alto mechanism in a private room where female trespassers are not admitted.

In recent years there has been a marked revival in the popularity of the counter-tenor, though hardly sufficient to justify the enthusiasm of the writer of a detective story I recently read, in which the entire *Dichterliebe* in German was sung at a ship's concert on a British cargo liner with enormous success—by a counter-tenor! Nevertheless, although the pleasure he gives is usually very mixed, the phenomenon provides abundant food for speculation among listeners and singers. Generally speaking there are three distinct kinds of counter-tenor. First, there is the very high lyric tenor who can sail comfortably through whole pages of notes above the stave without turning a hair. His voice is not very strong, but it is always unmistakably masculine. For some curious reason this voice has always been popular among folk-singers in many parts of the world. Secondly, there is the baritone who deliberately chooses to exploit a naturally good falsetto, and sings in the alto mechanism described in this section.

The third type is really of the same category as the second, except that in his case he uses it unwittingly and in the belief that it is his true voice. Why he does this is nobody's business but his own, and it is rank injustice to suggest that he is faking his notes, or could sing otherwise if he liked. He cannot be bullied or coaxed into doing something of which he has no experience. The real voice materializes immediately he has learned to prepare and launch his notes correctly. More often than not it turns out to be a lyric baritone ideally suited for the more intimate styles of music making.

b. The chest mechanism in women's voices

Somewhere between middle C and the G above it both men and women have the choice of making or not making a conscious mechanical adjustment in their vocal technique. Singing up a scale which takes in these actual notes, a man can either continue in his ordinary production, or make this adjustment and use what I described as the alto mechanism. A woman singing down the scale from the G above middle C can also do one of two things. Either she can continue all the way in her ordinary voice, her notes becoming progressively weaker until they disappear altogether. Alternatively she can bring about a conscious physical change in her manner of production at the moment when she moves into chest register, the voice thereby acquiring a new, sturdier quality and a noticeable increase in power. Simultaneously the locality of acoustic sensation shifts from the head, and now seems to be where the tone has its origin, that is above the nipples in the region of lung tension. The condition is what I call the chest mechanism, the condition of being 'in chest', in contradistinction to the usual soprano mechanism. Unless she has a small high voice, the transition is as conscious and voluntary a process as changing down to bottom gear on a car. It will only happen smoothly provided she eschews all madcap notions of blending the registers. Such an idea is as nonsensical as to be simultaneously driving in two different gears.

Like the male alto voice the chest mechanism demands only a low degree of lung tension. This is probably why very many women have the utmost difficulty in realizing a true chest production. In the transition into chest they are pressing too hard. The beginner must employ lung tension but only very little, and she must encourage the transition by feeling twenty years older and fatter; on the note preceding the transition she mentally removes her corset, allowing a comfortable 'spread' between breastbone and navel, but keeping a long spine. This may sound suspiciously respectable; but the feeling of voice pervading the whole body is just as vivid as in the soprano register, and the exciting awareness of vibrancy even more intense.

The transition into chest mechanism varies greatly with different women's voices. A coloratura usually goes easily into chest on about F sharp above middle C, the change being scarcely perceptible either to the audience or to herself. Her quality after the change is strikingly similar to the corresponding notes of a flute, being highly effective above the octave from F on the top line of the treble stave, and then blossoming out on its bottom notes, with that tone quality which on a flute suggests a trumpet out of fairyland. Ordinary sopranos and mezzo-sopranos go into chest voice a note or two lower down and find the act of changing considerably more difficult. Indeed many beginners refuse to believe that it has anything to do with true singing. They look upon it as a kind of music-hall trick and are horrified at the idea of using it in serious work. One can hardly blame them for this. To their inexperienced ears the tone sounds so coarse and blatant that they feel as if their skirts had suddenly turned into trousers—men's trousers! In fact the quality of a woman's chest notes represents the masculine element in her voice. She will readily understand this and retort that it doesn't help matters. This is true of course; but it is up to you women to realize that as artists you have to interpret life in as many facets as lie within your powers. By neglecting the chest mechanism you not only deprive yourselves of part of your talent, but also prevent the soprano mechanism from realizing its full glory. Like an arm or a leg, a voice cannot give of its best unless all the muscles pertaining to it are allowed an opportunity of full contraction and relaxation.

In my experience very many women have no idea that such a mechanism exists. They may be forgiven for not knowing that most country women in Italy and many parts of Europe never sing in any other kind of voice, but how they could have lived such blameless lives as never to have heard any records or broadcasts of the fine women singers of blues and jazz, I do not know. Many teachers refuse to allow their pupils to make use of the subsidiary mechanism. This betrays a surprising ignorance of musical history, since chest voice has been recognized as an integral part of singing since the earliest times. It also reveals a curious lack of enterprise and imagination. An artist may have his blue period, but presumably he uses other colours at the same time; tragedy need not altogether exclude comedy, and even in England we have an occasional fine day. The result of this embargo is that the 'classical' side is represented by voices of limited range and carrying power, but of the utmost purity—and I am using the word in a Victorian and not, alas, in a technical sense. Meanwhile the singers in popular musical shows, night clubs and jazz sessions never use anything but chest voice. This is not to imply that the vocal quality of such singers is necessarily bad; their range is abysmally limited, but inside that range the best of them can produce a strong even tone of occasionally ravishing quality.

The popular singers have some reason for concentrating exclusively on chest voice. In no other way can they produce their strong trumpet-like notes on the lower half of the treble stave, and if popular music demands this sort of tone and allows them to dispense with all the higher notes, who shall blame them? Serious singers have no excuse at all. It is not just a matter of losing five or more powerful notes at the lower end of their voices, but of consolidating what may otherwise be an unreliable technique, since the employment of the chest mechanism compels an inexperienced singer to use her tongue muscles as she has never used them before. As a result the vocal cords produce notes which are invariably steadier and less breathy than anything in the normal mechanism. It is indeed significant that, despite an amount of work and a way of living which would appear to spell deterioration, the popular female vocalist who uses chest voice almost exclusively, seldom develops any serious wobble. The same lack of wobble is noticeable among cathedral counter-tenors who, in using their sub-sidiary mechanism, seem able to produce a steady stream of tone at an age when their bass and tenor colleagues have long since been obliged to retire. Obviously the employment of the subsidiary mechanism demands an efficient contraction of the tongue muscles. Doubtless also it braces up certain laryngeal muscles, which in the soprano voice are not as a rule sufficiently contracted. With very little training these muscles increase their elasticity and exert a control which immensely improves the quality of the voice throughout its compass.

If you have never sung in chest before, it is important to give the various unused muscles a chance to build themselves up. Practise the exercises little and often, and however delightful the discovery of the new voice may be, do not try any amusing experiments. Remember that you are not adding resonance to what is already there, but deliberately moving from one state to another. There is no more question of mixing mechanisms than of mixing gears on a car. The vocal engine will put up with more maltreatment than a car engine, but it will quickly deteriorate if you make any attempt to 'blend' the chest voice with your soprano voice.

The natural reaction of a great many women when they first use the chest mechanism is that it sounds so different from the rest of the voice that it could not possibly be used in serious music. Even if they get over their initial embarrassment, they continue to be haunted by a *pudeur*, which inhibits their technique and does them no credit at all. Any

Q

[223]

singer who feels this way should aim at realizing in each mechanism the full potential of which it is capable without reference to whether the quality of one part of the voice is going to blend with the other. The nearer she comes to achieving this, the better she will sing. Far too many teachers work from the opposite point of view. The fat luscious tone in one part is quietly ironed out in order that it may consort with some accepted theory of registers, and thereby 'blend' with another part of the voice which is comparatively ineffective. It is obvious where this whittling process leads, and it is in no way surprising that so many voices seem to lose much of their character and charm in the course of training. The vocal instrument was never meant to be a sort of well-tempered pianoforte, with each note throughout its compass no better or worse than its neighbour. Like its owner's face, it is a unique pheno-menon with its defects least obvious when good points are displayed to their best advantage. In this respect weak parts of a voice are more fortunate than facial defects, in so far as they will improve and to some extent take on the characteristic of the strong parts, provided the latter are allowed to burgeon as they wish.

No male teacher can properly demonstrate chest voice. For him the normal singing voice is in chest throughout his compass. The nearest he could get, in demonstrating the woman's transition from soprano into chest mechanism, would be if he sang in one breath G on the treble stave in a feminine alto followed by middle C in full voice. It would be a disgusting noise; but the change of mechanism would provide an extremely crude version of what a woman can do smoothly and beautifully. It is possible that man's inability to demonstrate the transition into chest voice has brought about the censorious attitude of many English teachers of singing. To hear them talking one might be back in the days when piano legs in drawing-rooms were considered indecent unless they were put into frillies! Obviously, if women wish to convey no more emotion than the pure voices of cathedral choir-boys in Eton collars, no more vitality than the waxwork heroines of Victorian novels, they must avoid all physical contact with chest voice and continue to warble their low notes purely and inaudibly. This is not the way to realize one's ambition. Every great international singer has made use of all that she had; how else could she bring to life the tender freshness of Gilda, the heartbreak of Desdemona and Mimi, the smouldering passion of Carmen and the grave dignity of Alcestis?

[224]

Put on their records and listen to their low notes. They all go into chest at about the same pitch, but naturally they vary according to the context of the music and their own idiosyncrasies. Listen particularly to your favourite singer on some phrase in which she jumps down about a fifth, landing on or around middle C. Play it over and over until you feel that it is part of your voice, associating each note with the mechanism she is using. Even if the quality sounds much the same in her ordinary voice and in chest, she will not be blending the two. Try and sense the physical feel of the higher notes and the changeover to the notes which seem to come off her breast-bone. If you cannot get it today, try again tomorrow, and the day after. There is no art in this; it is a knack, but fine knacks for ladies must be paid for in honest sweat.

On all notes in chest mechanism, frontal resonance should be identified above the forehead. This means thinking in two places at once, but provided Chapter 14, Section b was well and truly absorbed before tackling the problems of registers, the reader will encounter no special difficulty.

EXERCISE 95(*a*)

If your chest voice is as yet an undiscovered country, start by saying O and *A* in as deep a voice as you can manage. The tone should be neither loud nor gruff, but should have the same resonance as is found in bathrooms and swimming pools.

Now say the same vowel, but varying the pitch within about a third. The sound should resemble the revving up of an engine.

EXERCISE 95(*b*)

When these spoken vowels seem to come fairly successfully, try to put them on a sung note somewhere between B flat below and E flat above middle C. In doing this avoid any association with the usual manner of singing, and imitate as closely as possible a baritone voice on the same pitch, the tone being semi-staccato and of not more than moderate loudness.

EXERCISE 96

In singing a descending arpeggio of C major, beginning on the C in the middle of the treble clef, the first three notes are plain sailing; but if you continue down in the same way on to the bottom C, that note will be weak. Start again, and this time stop on the G; we are going to miss out the E and go straight to middle C. Visualize a powerful C which seems to issue from the lower end of the breastbone. Any idea of throat resonance is forgotten, and there is no feeling of voice above the place where the C emerges. Notes with upturned tails in this and the following exercises are to be sung in ordinary voice, and notes with downturned tails in chest. Practise on *A*, *E* and *O*, in keys between A flat and E flat.

In no aspect of singing are voices so unpredictable and so unreliable as in the use of the chest mechanism. If you have no chest notes, you must set to work and find one single one; then you must try to acquire a second and then a third. Aim for a compass of at least a perfect fifth on which you feel completely secure, the central note being middle C or thereabouts.

EXERCISE 97
Sing the following on all vowels in chest mechanism throughout:

These exercises should be practised with the utmost caution. Do not attempt any chest notes unless they feel perfectly comfortable. The compass of the chest mechanism will only grow gradually and will never be very extensive. On the other hand, unless you use the chest mechanism it will obviously never get any better.

In cultivating a chest voice the ideal is to build up a range of notes towards the bottom of the compass which can be easily and effectively sung in either mechanism. It is therefore important at the same time to acquire the technique of bringing the soprano mechanism as far down as you can manage. However promising the chest voice may be, remember this and practise Exercises 96 and 97 alternately with the following:

EXERCISE 98

Sing the following on all vowels in soprano mechanism throughout.

It is now necessary to establish a shorter series of notes which you feel you can sing perfectly easily in both mechanisms. In doing this you will find that the tone quality of your lowest notes in soprano mechanism will be greatly improved both in power and quality.

EXERCISE 99

Sing the following on all vowels first in soprano mechanism and then in chest. Make sure in which mechanism you are starting, and keep in the same one throughout.

EXERCISE 100

Sing the first note firmly in chest; break off smartly and, without breathing, immediately sing the upper notes in soprano voice. After a second break sing the final note in chest. Do not relax the tongue muscles at any time.

EXERCISE 101

On the octave descent do not relax breath pressure. The final note should feel considerably firmer, stronger and steadier, as a result of the muscles which you used in chest voice continuing tense and helping to maintain a firm voice production.

The reader should now get out her songs once more and mark any points where she thinks it might be wise to go into chest. When in doubt she should always remain in the soprano mechanism. Letter the transitional points as follows:

H for head register.
M for middle register.
C for chest register.

In conclusion, let me remind the reader that women's voices can be of an entrancing unpredictability. I have known one English singer of unimpeachably classical taste who habitually sang in a chest voice which in quality was indistinguishable from the average woman's normal voice. Between B in the middle of the treble stave and the E above she migrated unobtrusively into middle register, and around E she sailed into head register. Unquestionably the lower part of her soprano mechanism was so weak and uninteresting that it would have been rank folly to make her use it in orthodox fashion. Her case was exceptional, but not so very exceptional, and there are many singers whose voices simply do not fit into any accepted category. Teachers should realize this, and resign themselves to the bitter knowledge that just occasionally the pupil knows best.

Mechanisms

c. 'Chest voice' women

For want of a better term this is my name for female singers who use their chest register exclusively or very nearly so. 'Chest voice' is used extensively by folk singers and singers of blues and popular songs, but there is no reason for confining it inside such a narrow field. To English singers the sound of this voice is comparatively unfamiliar and often rather distasteful, but with practice it can be made strong, vibrant, perfectly steady and surprisingly beautiful.

If a beginner's soprano voice simply does not respond to ordinary methods, a six or eight week period of training the chest voice exclusively may bring about a startling improvement when work on her normal voice is resumed. If however the soprano mechanism is still so feeble as to be not worth training; or if her ambitions do not rise higher than popular songs and crooning; or if it is absolutely necessary for her to sing on stage, and she has not the time or money to develop her natural voice, then 'chest voice' is worth considering. But not otherwise.

It is not that I object to this voice. I derive a great deal of pleasure both from listening to it and training it, and that is more than I can say about counter-tenors! Maybe it is prejudice, but I am not alone in this. It is a deep-seated instinct and runs parallel to our attitude towards transvestism on the stage. A man masquerading as a woman is completely unacceptable except in broad farce. In contrast the woman transvestist can be a delight both to eye and ear. Her long and honourable lineage takes in Cherubino, Quinquin, Oscar and Prince Orlofsky,* to say nothing of the glamorous principal boys of English pantomime. In the same way, if she uses it correctly, her 'chest voice' does nothing to detract from and probably emphasizes her sexual charms.

Nevertheless sopranos should only be allowed to sing in chest voice in the circumstances mentioned. Furthermore they must make certain that their range is already at least one octave and a bit. If they decide to take the plunge, they must be prepared to go through a period of considerable psychological upheaval; this is to be expected, for no normal woman finds it easy to emphasize the masculine element in something so intimately personal as the singing voice.

* In *Figaro, Rosenkavalier, Ballo in Maschera, Fledermaus.*

Once through this uneasy stage, a 'chest voice' woman has little inclination to revert to soprano technique. There is no question of the voice being in any way damaged. Nor is it a matter of psychological inhibitions. It is simply that 'chest voice', once the knack is mastered, is so much easier and more effective that the singer will be disgusted with her limp soprano noises, and only too ready to jettison them. That is why a teacher should have a natural reluctance to allow a young pupil to adopt this voice. In practice, if not in theory, it amounts to a burning of boats. Consequently both teacher and pupil must be quite certain that there is no likelihood of an adequate soprano voice materializing.

'Chest voice' demands precisely the same basic technique as does normal singing. The range does not often extend beyond an octave and a fourth within the region of

Inside this short compass the chest voice woman needs to cultivate the finest technique possible. Throughout the lower and middle part of her voice she should localize the frontal resonance high up above the forehead. On higher notes which demand an opening of the jaw she simultaneously transfers her centre of frontal resonance down to the bridge of the nose. The point where the jaw is opened on a rising scale is an octave below the normal point; i.e. somewhere around E or F above middle C, but it is governed, as in the soprano voice, by the need for keeping the tongue muscles contracted.

A chest voice can be trained in a much shorter period than a soprano voice, but the singer, hampered by a short compass and conditioned by a highly individual tone quality which does not blend with other voices, needs to exercise much more creative imagination in gathering together and working up a repertoire. Do not confine it to the usual guff. The whole world of folk song and traditional song is yours, as well as a great many classical songs of the French, German and Italian repertoire. But with such a restricted tessitura songs must be very carefully chosen. Almost certainly they will need fairly drastic transposition in an upward direction, and here you must make sure that the piano arrangement does not sound tinkly. Popular and traditional songs will need to be transposed up about a fourth higher than their published key. The songs of the classical repertoire were generally written for a tenor or soprano, and would probably need transposing about a tone or a minor third up. 'Where e'er you walk' would probably be in C, and 'Drink to me only' in A. Naturally in some songs the piano accompaniments would need a little adjustment to avoid a too tinkly treble, but as a rule the effect of such transposition, on a Schubert song for instance, is infinitely less disastrous than a transposition two tones down to suit a bass voice. Incidentally the slightly uncomfortable feeling caused by women singing songs such as Schubert's 'Ständchen' which were obviously intended for men is completely absent; they sound absolutely right and appropriate.

Finally I would like to reassure readers who are afraid of ruining their voices as a result of taking the chest register above the normal range. So long as the basic technique is understood and properly applied, chest voice women thrive on hard work. Within a modest range, their voices are steady and powerful. Far from sounding forced or artificial, they constitute a sturdy and whole-hearted affirmation of the glorious certainties of life.

17

AGILITY

a. The trill

The trill is not an affair of learning to sing adjoining notes with extreme rapidity. Nor is it the kind of vague tremolo which suggests the call of a discouraged goat. Possibly it is caused by a rapid contraction and relaxation of the wall dividing the windpipe and the gullet, but in any case the movement is entirely subconscious.

Small larynxes are more amenable than large ones; but all women and most men should practise the trill, for in no aspect of music is the nature of the vocal instrument so vividly realized. Hovering between two notes the singer seems to transform himself into a gigantic bird. For the time being self-criticism is forgotten, along with the shackles of the spoken word, and the tyranny of written music.

EXERCISE 102

Sing on all vowels:

The *sforzandi* must be made by momentarily increasing the energy with which the sensation of pressure is applied at the top of the chest; as a result the note will rise momentarily in pitch. The diminuendo between the *sforzandi* should be quite pronounced, but be careful not to slacken the normal compression. Concentrate wholly upon the sensation of pressure at the top of the chest, and pay as little attention as possible to the actual sound of the voice. In this and the following exercise the physical condition is very similar to sobbing.

EXERCISE 103

Sing on all vowels:

[232]

In the second bar of all these exercises the singer should keep the lower note continually in mind. He does not deliberately sing the upper short notes, but increases his sensation of pressure against the chest and allows the voice, as it were, to break momentarily. In certain respects the technique is the direct opposite of the yodel, in which there is a momentary relaxation of the sensation of pressure.

The secret of the trill is to think only of one note. On a whole tone think of the upper note; otherwise intonation is apt to be flat. On a semitone think of the lower note. Sooner or later you will find one or two notes on which the trill seems to come easily. Concentrate on these two notes and then on adjoining ones.

b. The appoggiatura

The appoggiatura originally served to disguise what, for those days, was considered an inexcusable modernism. According to *Grove's Dictionary* 'it consists in suspending or delaying a note of a melody by means of a note introduced before it, the time required for its performance, whether long or short, being always taken from the value of the principal note'. The average student tends to think of the appoggiatura as a quaint tradition, like the Changing of the Guard at Buckingham Palace. This is all wrong. The vocal appoggiatura is a simple device enabling the singer to declaim his words with the utmost eloquence and dramatic fervour, and at the same time to feel confident that his intonation will not be disturbed. Appoggiaturas in fact are the very antithesis of the musical antiquarian's hobby horse; they are part of any serious artist's tool kit. As a general rule they are needed on the penultimate syllable of any phrase in which the verbal sense calls for an accentuation followed by a decrease of tone on the final syllable. If the two notes are sung on the same pitch, there will be such conflict between the demands of the words and music as will lead inevitably to bad singing. At best the final note will be uninteresting; more probably it will be slightly out of tune or verging on speech technique.

Although it is to be found in all kinds of instrumental music up to the time of Beethoven, there is no question that the appoggiatura originated in vocal music and that its existence was due, not to the demands of aesthetic taste, but to the simple exigencies of the vocal organ. In these days the appoggiatura is usually omitted on the ground that it was not written out note for note by the composer. It is a thoroughly wrong-headed reason. The early composers implicitly realized that certain passages in their works could not be properly performed without appoggiaturas, and that the singer, by reason of his technical experience, was the person to decide where they should be inserted. This is particularly relevant to sung English in which an emphasis is generally placed on the first syllable of two syllabled words, and on an early syllable of multi-syllabled words. You have only to read aloud any page of this book to realize that appoggiaturas are needed a great deal more urgently and frequently in an English translation of a song or aria than in the original French or Italian.

EXERCISE 104

Sing the following first without an appoggiatura as in (i); then with, as in (ii). Imagine them inside an emotional context which calls for more or less of an accentuation on the middle syllable. On the (i) examples you will find it difficult to sing the words expressively without tending to go off pitch.

EXERCISE 105

Go through any recitative from a Mozart opera or Handel oratorio, and make up your mind where appoggiaturas are needed. Practise them with the emotional as well as the musical necessity for them in mind.

c. Scales

The human voice has its own characteristics, its likes and dislikes. It does not readily accept any interval wider than one note beyond the octave. It has a preference for the intervals on which the common chord is built, i.e. for major and minor thirds, fourths, and to a lesser degree for combinations of these intervals such as fifths, sixths and octaves. Diminished and augmented forms of these intervals are also easy, so long as they are used in contrast to the normal intervals and not to excess. No matter whether the intervals are simple or complicated, the ear abhors monotony. Even though a whole tone is the easiest of all intervals, it finds an unrelieved series of whole tones or half tones comparatively difficult to manipulate. It is on this basis that the western scale of five whole tones and two half tones has been built. The oriental ear is more partial to small intervals. Almost invariably it uses quarter tones, and is content with a music which does not often extend beyond the interval of a sixth. Within that compass it can find expression for the highest emotions, in a style which for a western ear rapidly becomes excruciating.

For most singers quarter tones are impractical. Semitones are easy to sing, but the listener does not distinguish them readily unless they are pitched with the utmost accuracy. Because of this infirmity of the western ear, scale passages must be sung non legato. This does not mean marcato or staccato, nor does it mean that the notes are detached. They are legato, but as tonally distinct as the legato scale of a good pianist who is not making use of the pedal. On a scale of C major the singer needs to watch the intonation at E and F, and at B and C. At these places he will be inclined to smudge the clarity of the notes as would an inexpert pianist with a weak and uncertain fourth finger. The pianist needs to build up the fourth finger until it acquires sufficient power and independence to come into line with the others. The singer's problem is not so very different; with the help of his tongue muscles he must make sure that every semitone is as clearly defined as are the whole tones. With practice along these lines a percussive sensation at the larynx may become so noticeable as to make the singer suspect that he is literally hammering on each note and breaking the legato. There is absolutely no fear of this happening; it is in fact a guarantee that breath compression is being maintained, and that the notes are distinct and clear.

The scale must be visualized as a whole, as if you were the hand of a stop-watch travelling smoothly and rhythmically round a clearly defined circle. Every note is sung with the top and the bottom notes in mind, and an awareness that at a suitable moment you migrate into the register appropriate to that top note. Except in the case of a very light coloratura voice, which can easily manage the change-up, the chest register should never be used by women in scales or in any passage requiring agility. Coming down the scale, exactly the same care should be taken as in a diminuendo to keep a constant lung tension.

EXERCISE 106

Sing the following on all vowels:

d. Arpeggios

In contrast to scales, arpeggios with their comparatively wide intervals demand the most consummate legato. The beginner, uneasily aware that this must make him scoop from note to note, may feel tempted to compromise with some kind of semi-staccato technique. This can only produce a tone which is superficial. To move from C to G in a legato passage the singer, while increasing or diminishing the vibrational speed of the vocal cords, must keep a consistently sustained tone. In this way the voice, like a factory siren, travels smoothly and rapidly through the intermediate notes. The resulting scoop, which can be heard on a gramophone record played at slow speed, need not disturb the listener's sense of a perfectly executed phrase, provided the interval

[236]

is not more than an octave, and the transition is made as rapidly as possible. A voice which, by some superscientific means was able to eliminate all trace of scoop, would sound cold and inhuman. But the singer should beware of exploiting the scoop in the interests of expression. There are moments when it is both appropriate and desirable; but they should be few and far between.

EXERCISE 107

Sing the following on *A*, *E*, *I*, *O* and *U*:

We are all familiar with the pianist who practises hours a day and never gets any better; there are singers who do the same and always get worse. Nothing is more infuriating than a pupil who says he has been practising for two hours on end. He might just as well admit that he was deliberately practising badly. Not even an experienced artist can work concentratedly on technique for longer than twenty minutes at a time. In any case there is no need to plough through all the scales and arpeggios in major and minor keys. Far more beneficial at this stage are the operas and oratorios of Handel. No other composer's works are so gloriously invigorating and beneficial to every type of voice. Stemming from the old Italian opera tradition, his florid passages are a continual challenge to our agility and breath control, and the wonderful flow of inspired melody, which invariably accords with the dramatic demands of the words, keeps our musical senses keyed up without entangling them in thickets of chromaticism.

18
VERY HIGH AND VERY LOW NOTES

a. Very high notes

Brought up not to raise their speaking voices above a certain decorous pitch level, English singers have a natural tendency to produce their high notes in the same position and with the same quality of tone and vowel as their low notes. High sopranos may get away with this sort of technique, but not the lower voices. Almost invariably an ascending scale of an untrained English-speaking singer deteriorates into a bleat or a shout. His efforts to compensate for these shortcomings are usually confined to pulling the abdomen in on high notes; this prevents the abdominal muscles from compressing as easily as they should. Equally ineffective and much more injurious is the fashionable method of protruding the abdomen as if it was a battering ram. There should in fact be no conscious contraction anywhere between the triangle below the breast-bone and the navel, no matter how high or low, loud or soft the note may be. At the lowest part of the abdominal wall, in the middle of the pubic bone, the singer needs occasionally to induce a pronounced muscular contraction, but only on his highest notes. At this place a shelf of hard muscle will seem to protrude forward and upward. The contraction, which must never be induced except when the singer is already in head register, occurs immediately before the top note of a difficult phrase in which a note above medium height appears, or where there are upward leaps of intervals greater than a major third, or at the end of a series of ascending notes. Whatever the context, the contraction must be maintained to the end of the sung phrase.

Many singers try to make the contraction by pulling in their buttocks. As a result the pelvis is tilted, but that is all. There is a feeling of a contraction extending all over the front of the pelvis as far as the front hip-bones, but none to speak of on the pubic bone itself. This concentration on the buttocks seems to pervade the work of innumerable singers in learning the position of readiness and the 'bow and arrow'. It is fairly ineffective; the front cannot be manipulated by recourse to the back. The reader must jettison his puritanical instincts and 'dig' firmly enough at the pubic bone for him to feel a consistent muscular pull in that region.

On very high notes the singer's 'mouth', which is normally a little behind the crown of the head, is shifted downward to a point at the back of the head on a level with the top of the ears, Fig. 26(*a*). At the same time the consciousness of nasal resonance at the bridge of the nose

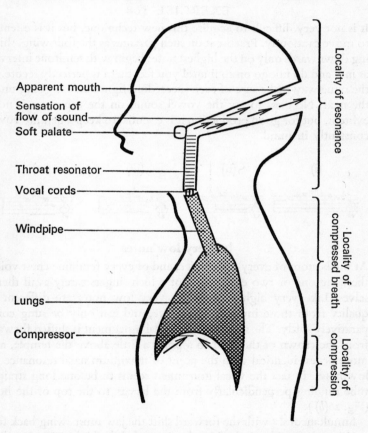

Apparent mouth

Sensation of
flow of sound

Soft palate

Throat resonator

Vocal cords

Windpipe

Lungs

Compressor

Locality of resonance

Locality of compressed breath

Locality of compression

FIG. 26(*a*). APPARENT DIRECTION OF THE VOICE ON VERY HIGH NOTES

disappears, and the jaw swings open to a position even wider than has been described on page 82.

The tone quality on these very high notes is markedly different from those immediately below, and no attempt should be made to sing them any fuller than is strictly comfortable. To the singer they will sound distinctly more feminine, but this must not tempt him to alter his basic technique in any way. He remains a full-throated tenor or baritone and to the audience, at any rate, he will sound like one.

EXERCISE 108

It is not very difficult to acquire this new technique, but it is essential to move cautiously. Practise it on such passages as the following, shifting downwards only on the highest note; begin with semitone intervals as in i, and do not go on to ii until you feel that i is perfectly secure. In the same way make sure of each succeeding figure before going on to the next. Needless to say the vowel sound on the top notes is non-existent, but for good production it is essential to keep a definite vowel constantly in mind.

(i)	(ii)	(iii)	(iv)

b. Very low notes

At the bottom of every male voice, and of every feminine chest voice, there are one or two extra notes of which singers rarely avail themselves. Like very high notes, these very low notes are different in quality from those immediately above, and can only be sung comparatively softly. The mouth of the vocal instrument is shifted forward from the crown of the head to a point a little above the temple, and more or less identical with the point of maximum nasal resonance on low notes. In fact the vocal instrument seems to be one long straight tube running perpendicularly from the larynx to the top of the head (Fig. 26(*b*)).

Simultaneously with the forward shift the jaw must swing back to a position almost identical with what is needed for high notes. Needless

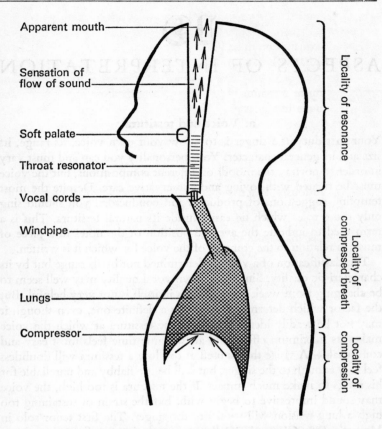

Apparent mouth

Sensation of
flow of sound

Soft palate

Throat resonator

Vocal cords

Windpipe

Lungs

Compressor

Locality of resonance

Locality of
compressed breath

Locality of
compression

FIG. 26(*b*). APPARENT DIRECTION OF THE VOICE ON VERY LOW NOTES

to say the vowel disappears in exactly the same way, though the actual
vowel is kept constantly in mind.

EXERCISE 109

Sing on all vowels:

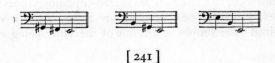

19

ASPECTS OF INTERPRETATION

a. Voice and tessitura

Your first duty as a singer is to know your own voice, its range, its size and its general character. Your personality you can and must vary in order to portray the moods of different compositions, but the voice must be treated with loving and conservative care. Despite the most tempting suggestions of producers and conductors, you should sing only those roles which lie easily inside its natural tessitura. This is a term used to indicate the average position of the notes in a piece of music in relation to the compass of the voice for which it is written.

The classification of a voice is determined not by its range but by its characteristic quality. Since your own vocal quality may well seem to be changing from week to week, this in itself is not very helpful. But the factor which determines quality is a definite one, even though it may not be readily identifiable; it is the tessitura at which the voice makes its maximum effect, and at the same time feels most easy and comfortable. A voice that is used at too low a tessitura will doubtless feel easy enough to the singer, but will be too flabby and unreliable for his songs to make much impact. If the tessitura is too high, the voice may sound impressive to begin with, but the strain of sustaining too high a lung tension will soon tire the singer. The first tenor solo in Mozart's *Don Giovanni*—'Dalla sua pace'—is a perfect example of this. It never goes above the baritone high G, but by far the greater part of it lies between the high G and the B natural. So high a tessitura calls for a degree of lung tension that neither a dramatic tenor nor a high baritone could support without a sense of strain.

It is this combination of vocal effectiveness and freedom from lung strain which determines the category in which a singer belongs. The voices of nearly all beginners are a little relaxed. At their first lesson most sopranos seem to think they are mezzo-sopranos, tenors that they are baritones, and baritones that they are basses. After a while the natural tessitura rises simply as a result of the voice being exercised,

[242]

and both pupil and teacher may be tempted to push it higher than it was intended to go. However wide the range, this is utterly wrong. Stretch a voice persistently at the ends, and like a piece of elastic it will gradually weaken in the middle, and lose its vibrancy and flexibility. It is all very well for fiddles and trumpets, but a voice, if it is to remain in healthy condition, must be given music in which the bulk of the notes lie a little above the middle of its range.

The following is a convenient method of determining which key of a particular song is most likely to suit your voice. Let us suppose you are a mezzo-soprano with your central note at G. You wish to learn Handel's 'Where e'er you walk'. In the original key of B flat the top note is G and the bottom note F, and the question is which of the keys available, B flat, A flat, G or F, is most suitable. Certainly, with the top note only E in the key of G, no lower key need be considered. The only safe way of deciding is by practical experiment. Unfortunately no music shop that I have ever encountered keeps all published songs in every available key, and allows its customers to try them out on the spot. The next best way is to take a perfect fifth from your central G to the D above; this interval may be said to constitute your middle range. If you then count the notes occurring above D and below G in the major section of 'Where e'er you walk', the score in the three different keys would be as follows:

> B flat: above 18; below 7
> A flat: above 8; below 12
> G: above 1; below 20

Clearly the key of B flat is high; G obviously too low; while A flat seems to be nearly perfect. There are, however, certain considerations which may lead us to diverge from the apparently obvious choice. First, as a mezzo-soprano, the best part of your voice will be in its upper reaches. Secondly, the song is a gentle lyrical invocation, a *canto spianato*, but with more than a hint of *canto fiorito*; such songs are invariably more effective in the high part of the voice, whereas dramatic or declamatory songs, which need clear vowels and emphatic consonants, are more suited to the lower part. Thirdly, as top note the single F seems very short commons in a lyrical song with never a hint of underlying melancholy. These considerations should persuade you to compromise and, regardless of the accompanist's feelings, sing the aria in A. You will then be faced with a fresh problem, for it may be that copies of 'Where e'er you walk' in A are not obtainable. Nevertheless it is essential that songs should be not only clean and readable, but also in the key in which you propose to sing them. Many accompanists are justly proud of their skill in transposing, but they should not be given a chance to display their prowess in public. No matter how brilliantly and accurately they play, they will perforce be concentrating on two things at once. Don't allow them to do it!

Flat keys can often be changed into sharp keys and vice versa by a little skilled work with pen and razor blade. For instance the key of A flat can be changed into A by scratching out the flats in the key signature and substituting three sharps, and turning flats into naturals, and naturals into sharps. Obviously this sort of thing can only be done in comparatively simple music which is being transposed a semitone up or down. Usually it is a matter of sitting down and making a transposed copy. Your first attempt will not be very successful, but skill as a copyist is such an invaluable accomplishment that it is well worth the trouble of acquiring. It will save—and incidentally could earn—you a great deal of money; it will enable you to sing practically any song you like in any key; and it will guard you against the shortcomings of accompanists who think they can transpose.

b. How to study a song

Having acquired the song in the right key, the first thing is to write, or preferably type the words on a separate page of a looseleaf notebook. This enables you to keep the words of all the songs which you are currently singing in the right order. The lines must be written in their original poetic form with spaces between the verses. If they are in a foreign language, take care of the spelling, and do not attach the wrong gender to a noun, otherwise you will never again be completely sure of its sex. All this is important because you are building up a visual memory of the words in their original shape; and the less you know of the language the more valuable the visual memory can be. The greatest pains should be taken over correct pronunciation and accentuation. This can only be done by listening attentively to the radio and gramophone records, and enlisting the help of friends who are familiar with the language. Do not depend on your teacher; you are paying him to teach you singing, not languages.

[244]

In learning both words and music from the vocal score, visual memory plays an extremely, perhaps even an overwhelmingly important part, but the reader must be on his guard against being influenced by the spacing of bars. For the sake of clarity and appearance, a busy accompaniment calls for bars of considerably bigger dimensions than one in which the accompaniment is sparse. The inexperienced singer must on no account be influenced by these variations, particularly if he is encouraged to do so by the struggles of an inexpert pianist. Aesthetic considerations also demand that the concluding bars should come at the bottom of a page; consequently the last line or two of a song may be sometimes more and sometimes less generously spaced than the earlier lines. It is surprising how easily these variations in spacing can subconsciously influence the interpretation of the most intelligent people, so that for no other reason in the world they make a *più* or *meno mosso*. The spacing of words can also affect the standard of legato singing. The look of such a printed line as 'That damsel's complaint startled Frank' with its serried ranks of consonants, particularly if the syllables are widely spaced, constitutes a pressing invitation to indulge in bumpy forward production. Visual memory in short is a precious possession but it has its dangers, and nothing is so salutary as to feel that one is singing a song with absolutely no conscious recollection of the printed page.

Having dealt with the words in isolation, stand up and practise each line on a single note. Beat time while you are doing this, and do not allow yourself the slightest latitude in time values. Next, sing the musical phrase on the Italian vowel *A*. Only when you feel that the words on a monotone and the musical phrase on *A* are both perfectly easy and comfortable should you sing the words and music as they are written. If the song is a quick one, slow it down sufficiently to be sure that not a single mistake creeps in, and if the rhythm is in any way complicated, conduct it or beat time with your foot; this will ensure that you keep a steady but flexible rhythm, and an awareness of the musical flow of the piece. In many cases it will also compel you to think in smaller units of time; instead of 4 in a bar, you will be forced, by the technical exigencies of conducting, to think in terms of 2 or sometimes 1 in a bar; waltz tempi will frequently be transmuted from 3 in a bar into 1, and 6/8 tempi will become 2 instead of 6. Moreover do not forget that a large part of your work will be with conductors, and that later on there may be many occasions when you yourself are called upon to conduct. So if you do not know how to wave a stick, learn to do so with the help of a mirror, a ruler and a child's guide to conducting.

In early stages it is advisable to divide the song into sections, and since nearly all songs consist of several verses there is no difficulty in this. Having made your divisions, work on one section at a time. Once you know two successive sections, they should be practised together as one section, and thus in time the whole song is mastered.

However interesting in itself the accompaniment may be, the singer should not allow either his technique or his interpretation to be in any way influenced by it. A folksong may be arranged in a dozen different ways; one version may consist of a few stark chords, another may be rich and lush, others may be contrapuntal, polytonal or even made mysteriously out of tone rows. The singer should study all these varieties with critical interest. But however smooth or bumpy, bare or busy the accompaniment, it must not affect his performance. Words and the vocal line are the only considerations which should be allowed to condition his technique and his interpretation. No voice was ever intended to blend with a pianoforte, or in any way to imitate or echo its percussive quality. It remains its singing self, while the accompanist comments, agrees, observes, speculates, and renders all those little services for which he is justly esteemed.

Do not consciously put in expression. This is like pouring sauce over a dull pudding. Your job is to make the pudding tasty by feeling the musical shape of the phrase and the expressive quality of the words. You have to recreate the essence of the song as it sprang to life in the composer's mind, to recover the inspiration which gave it birth and to convey it to the audience. The more successful you are, the less you need bother about expression; it will come of itself.

c. Tempo and the whole man

No matter in what style an aria is written, it is wrong to treat it as a piece of instrumental music with a tempo conditioned by exclusively musical considerations. Tempo is probably the most vital factor in determining the effectiveness of an interpretation; it is the singer's first response to the emotional mood of his song, and the actor's to the mood of his recitation. No one has the right to play fast and loose with a composer's markings, but within the general indication of *andante*

[246]

for instance there is room for a large number of delicate variations of pace, one of which will suit a particular singer better than any other. At this speed he can impart the maximum degree of rhetorical eloquence to the words of his song.

Naturally every instrumentalist chooses a tempo which accords with his individual temperament, but singing is a function of the whole man —soul, mind and body. The instrument is not merely his larynx; it is himself, and a good singer will instinctively adopt the rate of delivery which seems to bring the bodily processes into the closest possible harmony with his mind and spirit. The moment he is forced to adopt a tempo that puts the slightest strain upon his natural lung capacity and resilience, that imperils what might be called the respiratory equilibrium, his performance will suffer. It will suffer not simply because he is running out of breath or has insufficient time to breathe, though doubtless these factors are symptomatic evidence that something is amiss, but because his singing has become an expression of a partially disintegrated personality. The sense of unease may be so slight as to be barely recognizable by the singer himself, but the damage will be done. A memorable performance can only come from one whose body, mind and spirit are all in harmony. The body is the instrument of feeling; it responds to the stirring of the spirit, while the mind watches to see that the bodily response is never so violent as to cause the voice to become stifled. In this way the whole man is in the singing.

d. Perils of interpretation

As soon as the reader sets about the task of creative interpretation, his technique will be in jeopardy. He must not faintheartedly shut his eyes to anything but technical considerations, but in view of the added complications he would be wise to settle on a judicious compromise. Let him therefore keep under the most ruthless scrutiny every line of any song which could be called informative.

A somewhat blatant instance of this occurs in the sea-shanty 'Shenandoah' in which one verse runs as follows:

> O Shenandoah, I love your daughter,
> Away you rolling river!
> The Indian camp lies 'cross the border,
> And away we're bound to go,
> 'Cross the wide Missouri.

You will find it extraordinarily hard not to sing the third line as though you were giving directions to an inquiring tourist. Such a conception must be firmly expunged and the line delivered as if it were the expression of your emotional reaction to this enthralling piece of information.

The more precise and concrete the images which are suggested by the words, the more closely you have to watch your technique. The highly poetic words of 'Where e'er you walk' or 'Drink to me only' present no special difficulties, but a song like Vaughan Williams's 'Linden Lea' is a trap for anybody who is not an experienced artist. The first two verses, being little more than a simple and precise description of English scenery, are a sore temptation for the average singer to turn himself into a poetic commentator on country life. Yet somehow he must convey the emotional impact which the apple tree, the mossy moot and the bubbling stream have made on his immortal soul. The difficulty of maintaining this conception is probably why the majority of cultured performers prefer to sing songs and arias from other countries in the original language rather than in translation. Usually they have not sufficient acquaintance with the language adequately to convey the poetical content of the words. Yet audience and singer are more often than not agreed that it is infinitely preferable to sing '*Che gelida manina*' rather than 'Your tiny hand is frozen'. Indifferent to the stale charge of musical snobbery, they will point out the difficulties of singing in English. Nevertheless the incidence of awkward consonants and elusive vowel sounds are no more than contributary factors. The real reason is that, compared with '*Che gelida manina*', it is difficult to sing 'Your tiny hand is frozen' in a completely emotional way.

Rudolfo has only just met Mimi and her cold hand gives him an admirable opportunity for starting a flirtation. All this he conveys in his acting, and it would be wrong to suggest that at the beginning of his aria he has any deeper feelings. But if he allows dramatic implications to overwhelm his vocal instincts, the production will become superficial and inexpressive. No matter how it may conflict with the dramatic sense, good singing has to be an expression of the basic emotions. These include love, hate, anger, ecstasy, jealousy and grief, but not that of meeting a nice girl and starting a flirtation. Faced with this dilemma the singer, who is not yet conditioned to his new technical approach, must help by converting the flirtatious implication of 'Good heavens, you are cold; give me your hand and I'll warm it for you' into some such emotional process as the following: 'The chill of her hand has made my heart burn within me. Let me warm it in mine so that its beauty may kindle love within my breast.' Small wonder if these shy-making sentiments are miles away from the conception of the average English opera singer. The more he thinks of his words and tries to bring their meaning to life, the worse his technique will become. As a result, he sings his aria with its informative account of his daily life considerably better in Italian of which he understands merely the general drift, than in the English which he uses for everyday communication.

A second and even more important resolution for the newly-fledged singer is to make the first and last syllable of every phrase a properly produced musical sound. A sentence such as 'the love that's growing' possesses strong emotional associations, yet the beginner will find it extremely hard to sing the first vowel and the last with un-exceptionable production. In conversation he would pretty certainly swallow both vowels. Singing in his accustomed manner he probably does the same thing and, if he listens carefully, he will be shocked at the dull and dry sounds which introduce and round off many of his phrases. Therefore let him apply, but not too literally, the advice of Sir Thomas Beecham who said: 'The important thing is to begin and finish right; the audience never notices what happens in the middle.'

e. Gesture and technique

To a great extent operatic gesture should be governed by this same conception of emotional reaction. A certain amount of fussy 'business' would thereby be eliminated to the benefit of all concerned, but the style would remain realistic and expressive. A great deal of apparently good operatic acting is ineffective because the singer's gestures and posture in no way spring from his emotional impulse, but are dramatically conceived. In these days there are many such performances; on first hearing they seem unexceptionable, but in repetition they boil down to a series of contrived tricks.

The problems of dramatic gesture are outside the scope of this book. At the same time the reader should be warned that if he habitually makes gestures which by implication contradict the physical movements demanded of his technique, he will certainly come to grief. Good singing is based on emotion, and emotion gives birth to gesture.

If the impulse to make such gestures were suppressed, emotion would also be suppressed. But these gestures must consort with the physical movements of the singer's body which create the emotional impulse. Motivated gestures of love, hate, scorn, rejection, hope and pleading do not as a rule come under this category, because they have a dramatically inspired emotional basis. It is the little telltale, unconscious gestures which betray the incompetent artist.

A few examples will show what I mean. The singer who keeps his arms continually by his side or behind his back and the singer who holds his hands in front of him at waist level or even lower down, are not likely to be much good. In these positions they cannot possibly have a feeling of a high centre of gravity and a relaxed diaphragm, both of which suggest a feeling of upwardness.

The singer who continually waves his arms about is not likely to be aware of the sensation of lung tension. This is a sensation which breeds an atmosphere of quiet dignity and authority; fussy gestures are eliminated, and the overall impression is of a simplicity and single-mindedness which come as a blessed relief to the usual operatic sema-phore.

The singer whose hands are continually rising upward with out-spread flaccid fingers, as if to scatter rose petals, is probably a victim of forward production methods. Like the arm waver he can have no idea of suppressing breath and approximating the vocal cords. If he were to express this aspect of technique in gesture, his hands would be some-where near the breastbone, with the fingers flexed in a downward gesture towards the body.

The singer whose hands wave in time to the music, or who appears to be delivering upper cuts or kidney punches, can obviously have little idea of maintaining a truly receptive resonating cavity. By infer-ence he has no conception of the art of bel canto, or indeed of any truly musical legato.

The walk and body posture in standing, sitting and moving are the singer's secondary means of conveying character and emotion. Rigo-letto and Tonio are both of them unpleasant, misshapen people; the warp of their souls and bodies should be conveyed at every entrance or exit, but the actor's characterization must not interfere with his ability to produce sounds which are always musical. His neck and spine must remain long, even if they appear to be twisted, and his face must always be a singer's face. These are the only limitations on the singer's freedom of movement, and nobody could say they are particularly formidable. If the reader honestly feels restricted, it will be his own fault; he will have misunderstood or wrongly applied my instructions.

The same principle holds good in the singer's attitude to interpretation. Even when there is a printed direction to sing a passage *parlando*, he must not revert to speech technique. He can convey what the composer wants by emphasizing consonants, producing a more forthright or a more intimate tone, or by breaking up the legato line, but he must not sing the passage as if he was speaking it. The temptation is particularly strong in places where the melodic line is uninteresting as in recitative, or when the words are important, or in dramatic songs such as 'Der Doppelgänger'. In the same way the artist must eschew any attempt to create verisimilitude at the expense of vocal quality. Most operas end in a death scene, but even when death is a long time coming, the singer must never sound sick. To ape the actual voice of a real-life Violetta or Mimi is not singing at all; it is vocal mimicry. The actress who portrays these dying women must do so in her entrances and exits, and in her pose while other artists are holding forth. When she herself is singing, her voice must be musical and her body crackling with rude vigour and lung tension.

f. Personal involvement

It goes without saying that since the vocal repertoire is wider and more varied than that of any musical instrument, it requires of the singer an equally varied interpretative approach. This book does not pretend to discuss all the problems connected with interpretation. There is however one point which singers should consciously recognize but seldom do. This is the distinction between music which is subjective and that which is objective.

We live in an essentially non-romantic age. This does not mean that it is prosaic or in any way unromantic. Non-romantic however it certainly is. Byron, Heine, Chopin and Delacroix are all admired, but their attitude to art, which was primarily the subjective one of personal and emotional involvement, does not come easily to the artist of today. Forewarned by the revelations of Dr Freud, we do not consider our individual selves of sufficient importance to warrant such displays of emotion either in our lives or in our art.

Musical interpretation is still dominated by the conception of personal involvement. It is understandable, because much of the repertoire in general circulation belongs to the nineteenth century in which romanticism flourished. The music of this period requires in performance a correspondingly romantic approach, and has generated in many of its interpreters a deplorable lack of restraint and discrimination. Bad pianists yearn over their noisy keyboards, and good ones in all innocence induce in themselves entirely non-existent emotions. Teachers, by adjuring their pupils to feel the music and put their souls into it, commit a double misdemeanour. No man can teach another to feel something, and in talking like this they are defaulters in respect of their true function, which concerns technique and musical interpretation. In a subjective romantic approach both of these aspects must be subordinated to personal feeling. There can be no question of paying more than a marginal attention to anything else, consequently a technical mastery is called for such as is seldom achieved by students.

The failure of teachers and performers to discriminate between music which is romantic or subjective, and music which is non-romantic or objective, results in their pumping false sentiment into non-romantic music which of its very nature demands a cool, sympathetic and exclusively musical approach. The old Italian arias for instance and the works of Bach, Handel, Haydn and Mozart do not demand the same intimate subjective approach as the songs of Schumann and Fauré. Naturally all vocal music suggests a more subjective approach than does instrumental music. Nevertheless a great deal of the vocal repertoire is evocative; it calls for an active imagination and a sympathetic knowledge of the style and period of the composer, but no personal sentiment. For a teacher to tell a student to feel this kind of music is no more or less than an invitation to tell musical lies. Any work of art which is predominantly objective must be performed with the keenest ear for tone quality and variations of colour, rhythm and tempo, and with a respectful though not necessarily reverent regard for traditional readings. A sympathetic and active imagination is needed also, but no more personal involvement than would be found in an actor who plays Macbeth.

It is of course impossible to draw a simple line between music which is subjective and music which is not. Individual temperament and the circumstances of performance would not allow this. There are however certain basic guides. First, the more demanding or complicated the music, the more risky a subjective attitude is likely to be. The claims of technique or musicianship in such cases call for so much concentration that personal involvement would not be practical. The singer who tried to defy this rule would sing either badly or dully, probably both. No doubt, being himself personally involved and feeling the music deeply and sincerely, he would finish his piece convinced that he had sung it superbly. Experience will teach him otherwise!

In the second place dramatic music should always be treated objectively. This is so even in the music of Puccini which, heaven knows, seems to demand the closest possible personal involvement. Any opera performance is of course a co-operative activity, calling for a sympathetic and imaginative, but always objective, approach. Operatic arias in concert programmes should be performed in a similar spirit, evoking the dramatic situation rather than using it for the expression of personal feelings.

Thirdly, while an intimate acquaintance with the language in which one sings is desirable in all music, in subjective music it is absolutely essential.

Finally, performances must either be subjective or objective. They cannot be mixed. If your performance is technically defective, then you have to eschew romantic attitudes, cutting out personal sentiment, and keeping attention concentrated on technique, musicianship and the example of tradition. Only when you feel yourself in technical control should you consider whether the piece you are interpreting is one which really calls for a subjective treatment. If you decide that it is, then abandon objectivity, trusting to your subconscious to keep the technique and musical interpretation on an even keel. In this way you have the power to turn the dreariness of the average *Lieder* recital into an exciting and revealing experience. Alas, this happens all too rarely. The discipline of learning a technique is generally too hard and long for the naturally emotional artist, so that as a rule we hear performances of two kinds; either beautifully sung and very musical renderings of subjective music which, because it is not personally felt, are stone dead; or else performances so badly sung and ineffectively communicated that they make no impression at all.

Objective music must be performed objectively. Subjective music must be performed subjectively, but only if the singer is so much a master of his technique that he can safely entrust it to the subconscious mind. The problem is to decide where subjective music begins and ends. Much depends on the individual, but I would say that unless you can feel yourself personally involved when singing the music of Schumann and Fauré, you had better leave them alone. The same applies to Brahms and to a great deal of Schubert, Wolf, Strauss and Mahler. Traditional songs and folksongs may be performed in so many different ways that it would be useless to suggest in what category they belong; it depends on the individual interpretation. Perhaps the most subjective of all performances can be found among the best singers of negro spirituals, blues and unaccompanied folksongs.

The artistic impact of personal involvement is often unwittingly destroyed because the singer is in too much of a hurry to perform the work he is studying. Words and music must be given time to settle down and take root inside his being. They are a living thing; they must be cherished but not forced in any way. Conscious decisions about interpretation kill any chance of truly personal involvement. Like making friends with a wild animal, you need patience, sympathy and love. If you wait in the right spirit, the inspiration will come, but only when you are ready for it.

It is possible that the last three sections have been a little confusing. 'Vocally,' says the reader, 'I am told to be consistently emotional, but in my performance, gestures and general attitude I have to be more or less unemotional. How is that possible?' If this is your question, you have been forgetting that the emotional condition needed for singing is essentially an artificial one. It is induced by the combination of a compression of breath and a properly formed resonating cavity. Once it is induced it must be maintained till the end of a sung phrase. But except in the technical act of producing sound this emotional condition must not be allowed to overwhelm your mental approach. To be a great interpreter you need an ice-cold brain and a heart of fire.

20
STAGE-FRIGHT

The worst thing you can do is to pretend that panic is not there or that you can suppress it by willpower. Your job is to come to terms with it, so that it will not seriously interfere with your performance.

The commonest and most potent cause of stage-fright is an awareness, conscious or subconscious, of technical shortcomings. Nothing reveals the cracks in your armour so infallibly as an audience which is not as enraptured as you expected. All the praise of an easy-going teacher, an admiring accompanist or doting mother, is spot-lit for what it is worth; for a few seconds you see yourself in an artist's nakedness, and realize that you are only at the beginning of the long journey to Bannockburn. Contrariwise, nothing banishes stage-fright so effectively as the knowledge that, even if your voice is not marvellous, at least you have done your homework.

All public performers are victims of stage-fright, and singers particularly. This is not in the least surprising, for the singer's instrument is himself; not just his larynx, his tongue and his diaphragm, but his whole self—mind, soul and body. Moreover the greater his artistic integrity, the greater the nervous strain. When he opens his mouth in a crowded hall, he has no certain knowledge what sound will come. The instrumentalist on the other hand knows very well. His violin does not suffer from catarrh or colds; it does not have a digestion which makes mischief at the wrong moment; above all it does not suffer from that awful nervous tension which, in afflicting the greatest artists in their greatest triumphs, is no respecter of persons, times or seasons.

a. Public performance

There are other less obvious causes of stage-fright which, once recognized, can to some extent be faced, grappled with, and well and truly hustled from the field. These aspects are very rarely mentioned, yet they can be much more potent than the occasional cold. So far from being a temporary handicap they grow like parasitic monsters, killing or withering the hopes, dreams and happiness of those who are their prey. It is these little monsters which we need to examine, before they have time to do any serious damage.

Public performance is an outlet and a sublimation of several instincts of which you will be the last person to be aware. These instincts stem from varying causes, and can be found in every person who aspires to be a public performer. Kept in a right proportion they have a truly beneficial effect; but if they are present to an undesirable degree they can wreck the most promising career. No artist has ever lived without a certain exhibitionist instinct. This is perfectly healthy if he wants to become a good singer, to make a fine reputation, to be liked and respected by his friends and public; if he is ambitious in an ordinary sensible way. But if he goes around telling himself that he means to be the greatest singer in the world, to spread the doctrine of music far and wide, and to bring love and enlightenment to the nations through his art, that singer is in for trouble. He has set himself a preposterous standard which he cannot possibly reach. When the time comes he will be prostrated by nerves and sing badly. Even if he sang at his best, he could never hope to reach his own lunatic level. Accordingly he concocts a nice little alibi and tells everybody that for one reason or another he was not doing himself justice.

There are a good many people like this in the musical world. Many of them are the sons and daughters of quite sensible but rather too demonstrative parents. A mother who has cherished artistic ambitions in her youth—and few have not—will be delighted with the unusual gifts of her offspring, in whom she sees a compensation for her own disappointments. Eagerly she does everything to foster and develop the budding talent, and the awful result is that the young hopeful grows up with the idea that unless he turns into a Caruso he will be a ghastly failure. And he is a ghastly failure, not only because his standards are impossibly high, but because he harbours an unconscious instinct to avenge his parents for inducing and encouraging this attitude. The poor wretch is of course unaware of the underlying reasons for his comparative failure, and not unnaturally attributes it to nerves. Young people are extremely impressionable and not very logical; they are taken to hear a great singer or to see a great dancer, and the unspoken suggestion that some day they will be doing that very thing is planted in their subconscious, and watered by an enthusiastic parent. In other cases the parent actively discourages the child, either by insisting that it follow some other career, or by pouring cold water on its best efforts. No doubt the parent is right; but in certain cases he sows the seed of such an inferiority complex that the child grows up determined to have his revenge by becoming the greatest singer in England.

This sort of thing may happen, not from excess of encouragement or discouragement, but simply from inculcating the feeling that the child must reach some wonderful level of achievement in its profession to satisfy family pride. The child may work its head off, but with no genuine artistic motive behind all this energy the result will be negligible. Everybody to a slight degree has had some experience of one or other of these relationships, and practically everybody emerges with affections undimmed and a healthy attitude to their work. Unfortunately the profession of singing, with its double attraction of self-expression and exhibitionism, is particularly liable to awaken such cloud-cuckoo ideas as I have described. Almost certainly, if you search your heart, you will find traces of their influence. Do not be ashamed of what you uncover but make up your mind to put your work and ambitions on a truer, sounder basis. If you are physically and mentally capable of being a good singer, you should have the gumption to realize that ambitions to be the greatest singer in the world are bogus and that the reasons for harbouring such notions are selfish and wicked. Get rid of these ideas, and remember that you are a perfectly ordinary human being, with a bigger throat than most people and a small talent for music.

And at your next few concerts insist that your parents sit well out of sight at the back of the hall!

b. Putting ourselves on exhibition

However diligently we have worked on technique and rehearsed our programme the public exhibition of good voice-production comes near to conflicting with very many of the unwritten edicts of civilized society. We know, of course, that the whole aim of art is to express emotion and to convey it to other people in such a way that similar emotions are aroused in them. At the same time we are uneasily aware of the taboos of contemporary civilization, particularly the one which says: 'Thou shalt on no account display thy emotions in public.' This puts the singer between the devil and the deep sea. If he smothers his emotions he will sing badly and disappoint his audience, and if he sings with spontaneity he transgresses one of society's cherished rules. How much worse when he is giving the concert himself, and has had the temerity to invite the public to witness this betrayal!

Don't think for one moment that any singer is likely to reason things out in this way. He just feels nervous. He may be calm and confident when he starts, but perhaps a third of the way through the ordeal the appalling question 'What am I doing in front of all these people?' rears up at him. In all probability its appearance coincides with a point where the audience is friendly and he has successfully negotiated his more formidable difficulties. Quite unconsciously he has relaxed some of his concentration and become, according to his temperament, over-confident or self-conscious and miserably nervous. While the latter mood is on him the best efforts are in vain, and the mightiest applause is dust and ashes.

Every soloist is an occasional victim of these feelings, but perhaps the singer who uses the technical methods described in this book suffers more than anyone since the instrument on which he plays is his own body. Indeed the whole art of singing exhibits characteristics which are not altogether usual, for there can be no reader so young and innocent as not to have felt that the contraction of the abdominal muscles brings with it certain sexual associations and that these are intensified by the breath compression and subsequent emotional condition which make up the foundation of good voice production. Add to this the pre-dominantly erotic character of most song literature, and no one need wonder why there are so few good singers; the most superficial acquaintance with modern psychology provides reasons galore.

In face of this gloomy diagnosis, it is your duty as an artist to show the public your worth. You know that these physical gestures are the essence of good singing, and in themselves produce a feeling of truly creative vitality. You know too that the underlying moods of your songs are based on the noblest and most beautiful instincts that exist, instincts which will continue to make life worth living in a world that seems to be following the Gadarene swine to their doom. If through nerves you fail to do yourself justice, you are committing a double misdemeanour. You are betraying yourself and leaving the audience unsatisfied and discontented. For an ordinary person this would be bad enough, but for an artist it is deplorable because it means that he is not doing his job properly. In other words he is a bad artist, and nobody is so dispensable as a bad artist. Contrariwise nobody is so intrinsically valuable as a good artist, irrespective of whether he earns twopence. If he makes a thorough-going success of his job, he can beat his wife, sponge on his friends and diddle the tax-collector, and he will still scrape his way into Heaven.

Having delved into the murk of psychology the reader is perhaps waiting impatiently for my own special elixir for curing stage fright. He will be disappointed. Apart from the rather negative hints in Chapter 22, I cannot help him. But for the singer who tends to become self-conscious half-way through a song, there is one golden remedy. And here let me say that self-consciousness in this context includes all the qualities that give rise to stage-fright and a good many others besides—over-confidence, under-confidence, lack of concentration, an analytical unemotional approach, lack of vitality; and perhaps commonest of all, lack of technique. The remedy is to re-read Chapter 6, Section e, and to blink the very moment the feeling of self-consciousness threatens. But of course blinking cannot bring about or restore a desirable state; it can only help to keep something which is in danger of being lost.

21
WE WHO SING

a. Vocal health

The less you bother about the condition of the throat and vocal cords, and the more you bother about applying and maintaining a correct vocal technique, the better it will be for yourself, your throat, your cords and your career. This is particularly important in connection with the launching of the note. There is no doubt that the misapplied *coup de glotte*★ has been responsible for much damage to voices, and a superficial reading and careless application of the instructions in these sections could easily lead to exactly the result which I have been at pains to avoid.

It stands to reason that if you start singing before you have built a sufficiently reliable technique, or undertake roles or songs which are outside your natural tessitura, you will come to grief. This will be only too likely if your voice is good, for managers and conductors do not understand vocal technique. All they know is whether they like a voice, and how the music should be sung. Accordingly, once they get hold of the right voice, they stuff their own interpretation of the part literally down the poor singer's throat. All goes well for the time being, but after a few months of this sort of treatment the voice shows signs of deterioration. Don't let this happen to you. You may be ambitious, but there is no credit in singing a few notes before you disappear into oblivion. However willing the spirit, the voice cannot survive continuous abuse. Within its natural tessitura it is strong; elsewhere it is weak and incapable of standing the strain. All singers know this subconsciously and should have the strength of character to act on this knowledge. They will be accused of laziness, vanity, timidity and worse, but ultimately they will be respected for their common sense.

However careful he may be to equip himself with a reliable technique and to limit himself to work which suits his voice, the singer is

★ See Appendix.

[260]

still prey to those bodily afflictions which plague the best of us. Commonest of all, the common cold is a particular bane, not only because it attacks an important part of the vocal instrument, but because against its onslaught there seems as yet to be no defence, albeit an abundance of hopeful remedies. Having caught your cold, there is no need to become a hypochondriacal fusspot; even with a really bad one you can safely do some quiet singing, but only in short spells and in the middle of the voice. With a good technique it is surprising how little effect on tone quality nasal congestion seems to have. The unavoidable discomfort however is liable to affect concentration as regards both technique and general musicianship. Therefore keep the nasal passages as free as possible by inhalations of Friars Balsam. The paramount reason for avoiding colds is that so often they accompany or are the prelude to sore throats and laryngitis. In the case of a sore throat you should not, and indeed will not want to sing a note more than is strictly necessary until the soreness has disappeared. Aspirins, gargles, inhalants, chest rubs, hot drinks and Turkish baths all help to bring relief, but only if the voice is rested at the same time.

The moment you find yourself achieving spectacular low notes and barely encompassing high notes except in full voice, stop altogether. It is a sure indication of laryngitis. A certain amount of congestion in the subsidiary resonators, in other words a cold in the head, cannot do much harm, so long as it does not persist. Similarly an inflammation of the pharyngeal resonator, which means a sore throat, is so painful that you will take steps to get rid of it. These are infections of one resonator or another. But laryngitis must be regarded with the utmost seriousness, since the vocal cords are the singer's life blood. Unfortunately for our vocal health, we feel nothing whatever at the cords nor in the laryngeal muscles. Even when no laryngitis is present, these muscles are frequently so overworked that a singer, at the end of an arduous performance, is liable to attack a highish note that simply does not materialize. He literally loses his voice as a result of the laryngeal muscles being so tired that they are unable to respond to a perfectly efficient preparation. This is distressing because it is unexpected, but in most cases it is a symptom of wrong technique. It is damning evidence if it happens long before he is physically tired.

The minimum period of complete rest following an attack of laryngitis should be three days at least, during which not only all singing should be cut out, but smoking and any kind of unnecessary talking. Smoky stuffy atmospheres should be avoided. Beer or wine you may drink so long as you shun talkative company. The same remedies as for sore throats may be employed, although they will not provide much more than psychological relief. Far more efficacious are solitude, rest, fresh air, and good food. This may be impossible in the middle of a busy professional life, but you can at least set it up as an ideal. During the three days following recovery, you should sing quietly for very short periods and only in middle range. If laryngitis is slow in clearing up, or of frequent occurrence, do not hesitate to see your doctor, especially if the speaking or singing voice remains abnormally deep or changed in any way. We are all occasional victims through no fault of our own, but chronic laryngitis is a condition which can only result from debilitating disease, overwork, excessive smoking and drinking, or misuse of the vocal organs. The first two factors may perhaps account for one in fifty cases. The remaining forty-nine sufferers would be well advised to spend a part of their enforced silence in a thorough and honest reconsideration of their technical methods and of their habits of life. Faulty technique and excessive pub-crawling are equally symptoms of ignorance, negligence and over-confidence.

There is a frightening description of what can happen when a voice is misused in the memoirs of the American soprano Grace Moore. As a result of incompetent training, she literally lost her voice in the middle of a lesson. Dr Marafioti, to whom she was recommended, and who had looked after Caruso and many other Metropolitan Opera singers, told her: 'Signorina, you may never sing again. Acute laryngitis and severe strain are apparent. Your future recovery lies in rest and complete silence. Even one word may endanger any chance of recovery. Come back and see me in three months.' A three months' entirely solitary existence by a lake in Canada was followed by another three months during which she was allowed only to speak Italian words under his personal supervision at a short daily lesson. At the end of this long period she was considered fit enough to sing for a few minutes every day.

While in the throes of laryngitis or recovering therefrom, you are likely to become horribly depressed. Indeed, a feeling of depression is often the first sign that all is not well; but at least the realization that this is apt to precede, accompany and follow laryngitis does enable one to endure with philosophic fortitude. At such times the prudent female singer would do well to bolster her morale by treating herself to a new hat, good food, and an afternoon cinema.

Any kind of smoking is bad for the throat and in the long run has a serious effect on the vocal cords and lungs. If you enjoy it there is no reason to cut it out entirely so long as you keep within moderate limits. Smoking also causes catarrhal conditions, so if you suffer in this way it is worth the effort of giving it up altogether.

Needless to say, alcoholic over-indulgence is undesirable. Wine and beer leave no permanent damage but gin and whisky in excess are extremely harmful to the vocal cords, as any saloon-bar habitué will unwittingly testify. Since all alcohol slows up physical and mental reactions, any artist is a fool who does not rigorously keep off it until his work is finished.

Old-fashioned gas fires give off a certain amount of fumes which make throats very dry, particularly when some of their elements are missing or broken. Coke and anthracite stoves also give out fumes. Electric fires are preferable, but even so the best kind of heating is a coal fire which circulates the air in a room. There is no need however to be over-fussy, so long as the room is well ventilated.

There are two further enemies about which the singer should be warned. Candles can dry up throats in the most devastating manner. Naturally one does not meet them often nowadays, but occasionally an artistic hostess may inflict them upon a long-suffering performer. A far commoner source of danger is strong smelling flowers such as hyacinths or lilies. Their irritating effect on the throat and nasal passages varies from person to person, but I believe that most singers are to some degree affected. All such flowers should be taken out of the room before you start work. If you find them on the concert platform, try to get them removed without hurting anybody's feelings, and in any case keep your head turned as far as possible away from them. The same applies to bouquets, which should be reverently laid on the upstage side of the piano within smelling distance of the pianist, whose fingers will be in no wise inconvenienced.

Sore throats are frequently accompanied by inflamed tonsils, and vice versa. Somewhat illogically doctors at one time tried to solve the problem by removing every tonsil they encountered. Nevertheless sore throats continued to occur, and today the tonsil has been granted a partial reprieve. If they are chronically unhealthy, tonsils will cause continual sore throats unless removed without delay. This is not very common. Generally the fate of tonsils comes in question when they are found to be larger than usual. There can be no hard and fast rule, but if a singer suffers from repeated attacks of tonsilitis they had better be removed. Provided the operation is skilfully managed, one can and should start singing gently as soon as healing has taken place; this would be after ten days or a fortnight. The idea that the shape of the resonating cavities or the quality of the voice will be affected in any way is quite erroneous.

No reader of this book needs to be reminded that good health, good singing, good articulation and good looks are all to a large extent affected by the condition of the teeth. Make a habit of seeing the dentist every six months. If you tell him you are a singer, he will be encouraged to make your teeth look as nice as possible. All fillings which are likely to be visible should be made of porcelain. Certain toothbrushes and toothpastes are definitely bad for the teeth, so take the dentist's advice and don't fall for the most glossily advertised product. Since the condition of the teeth reflects the condition of the rest of the body, it is particularly important for them to be examined if you have been suffering from any physical or emotional disturbance. The prospect of false teeth is horribly unwelcome, and I am frequently asked how they affect one's singing. So far as I am able to judge from other people's experience, they make no difference. Pupils come back after three weeks and seem to have no trouble either in pronunciation or in production, though naturally the usual periodic adjustments have to be made. I feel sure however that with the methods which emphasize bringing the tone on to the hard palate and front upper teeth, singers would not be nearly so happy. As it is, new teeth may constitute an added inducement to keep the tone where it belongs.

See that you get lots of air and exercise, and plenty of rest. Don't wrap up more than you need. Keep your feet dry and sensibly shod. Don't stand around in draughts. Don't talk when coming from a hot atmosphere into a cold one; and avoid as far as possible going out, and particularly talking, in fog. Try to get your eight hours' sleep every night, and don't be shy of indulging in odd snoozes on other occasions. In professional life you have to woo sleep in strange beds at even stranger times, and it should never be done with the artificial help of pills. The same applies to the digestive apparatus. Train the bowels to be clockwork in their action, for no one can sing decently when they are constipated, and stage-fright can play havoc with internal arrangements.

Other things being equal, a healthy throat and larynx means a healthy person. If you are over-weight, under-weight, ill or run-down, the throat and larynx are likely to reflect your general physical condition. Consequently it is essential to live as happy and healthy a life as possible. An actor may be running a high temperature yet go through his performance as well as ever; no singer could possibly do so except with the help of undesirable stimulants.

Finally, if you ask me what are the best recreations for singers, I would say anything which will help you to acquire and keep a good posture and breathing technique. On this basis I should recommend swimming, if possible in the sea; rowing, riding, golf, skating and fencing. And of course, I must not forget the best of all recreations, which is singing—but not too much!

b. Singing ladies *

Women find the exercises in Chapter 2 considerably harder than men. They do not have the same interest or pride in physical achievements, nor are their bodies so well adapted for such things. It is only natural that, finding more difficulty and experiencing greater fatigue in doing the exercises, they should tend to pass them over. It is misguided of them since none of the exercises are difficult in themselves, and nearly all are designed to eliminate that body sag which is much more common among women, and ensures comparatively poor breathing and breath control.

One of the reasons why the general standard of singing seems to have been considerably higher in Victorian times is that in those days women were trained to hold themselves upright. Tight corsets, while doing considerable harm by encouraging women to breathe from their upper chests, must have helped to maintain erect posture. Furthermore Victorian taste, as seen in old volumes of *Punch* and the *Illustrated London News*, clearly approved of tall, somewhat statuesque women. Even more convincing evidence of the influence of good posture can be seen in the general appearance of great singers. The impression they give of

* 'A Prima Donna is a singing lady.' (General Knowledge paper.)

[265]

maturity, poise and dignity is a sad contrast to the fashionable sag of the contemporary female.

Singing is an energetic business, and all singers should eat heartily. Inevitably they will get fat unless they eat sensibly, cutting out the odd snacks of biscuits, sweet cakes, chocolate and gin, which ruin so many figures. Some fat people may have good voices, but it is not true that singing makes people fat! Admittedly the expansion of the chest is increased and the part immediately below the breastbone becomes slightly more conspicuous. Below the navel there is no reason for spreading. The abdomen derives immense benefit from the contraction of the abdominal muscles, but it must not be constricted by tight foundation girdles. Naturally, if muscles are prevented from working, they will become lazy. Singers must accordingly provide themselves with garments which support but do not constrict.

People are going to look at you as well as listen to you, and their first impression is how you carry yourself. You can do things to your face to make it look glamorous, but your body must stand on its own legs in every sense. While most of the audience are too far away to get more than a general impression of a face, every man and woman in the hall will be critically assessing the way you stand, the way you walk and the way you sit. If you know how to do these three things really gracefully, your clothes will show to their greatest advantage, and in an opera or musical play the audience will be more than half convinced that you are a good actress! For this reason work on the exercises in Chapter 2.

There is no need to remind you of the importance of clothes in a professional career. From the moment you appear they will be under close scrutiny, and therefore part of your education should be the cultivation of a good dress sense. With the objective detachment which so distinguishes your sex, you should take stock of your figure and colouring with all its beauties and blemishes, and learn how to make the very best of yourself. At concerts you should not only criticize what the women are wearing, but go on to decide what, under the existing conditions of lighting and elevation, they ought to have done to bring themselves more into harmony with the furnishings of the hall and the music they were interpreting.

When you go for auditions remember that you will probably be shoved on to a stage and viewed from a long way away. Subtly contrasting shades and tastefully unobtrusive adornments will go for nothing, yet at the same time you want to be remembered as an artist and a person of taste. This means simple contrasting colours and good materials. Either wear a little hat or nothing on your head, be sure that your hair is tidy, and do not wear a lot of clattering bracelets. Make-up should be extremely efficiently but discreetly administered; if you do not wear make-up as a rule, it is advisable to do so on this occasion, for you will probably be seen from a distance in a cruel light, and in any case managers are so used to seeing people in make-up that they expect it. Cut out running repairs except in extreme emergencies, and above all don't smother yourself in scent!

Since the most serious-minded manager has an eye for a woman's legs, shoes and stockings must be worthy of standing up to his scrutiny. Always buy shoes of good quality, making sure that the heels are in alignment so that you can stand and walk correctly. In a great many mass-produced shoes the heel is set too close in, so that the weight of the body is brought on to the inside of the foot, causing the knees and hipbones to have an inward instead of an outward thrust. New shoes should be tried on with the greatest care, since a badly fitting pair can affect a singer far more than a congested nose.

Never wear glasses at auditions or interviews. Managers will be justified in assuming either that you are unable to see without them, or that you have no instinct for the stage. In any case, they are seriously handicapped in visualizing your potentialities in possible roles. Learn to do without glasses as much as possible, and eschew the silly fashion of wearing sunglasses in all weathers. If you are extremely short-sighted, it would be wise to consider the possibility of contact lenses. From both an optical and an aesthetic standpoint they are wonderfully good and well worth their considerable cost.

During the monthly period you must use your own discretion about taking things easy, but always do some work. Practice sessions may be shortened, but the standard of work must remain on its top level. Physically you will find that things do not come quite as easily, and that you need to expend rather more conscious effort. Mentally you will not be quite so quick on the uptake; since this is something of which you will not be aware, unremitting concentration is the only remedy.

Much the same advice applies during pregnancy, but again it is impossible to make any hard and fast rules. As time goes on it is naturally somewhat more difficult to take deep breaths, but there is no reason why breathing should be seriously affected until the last few weeks.

Many women have found that the experience of childbirth brings a new richness and power into their voices, and indeed there can be no cause for astonishment that the greatest experience in a woman's life should, at its culmination, be reflected in that part of her which expresses her deepest emotions and desires. At the same time very many wives, happily engrossed with husband and family, find that they have little desire to continue their career. Not only this, but they seem to lose their delight in singing for its own sake. It may distress both them and their husbands, but there is a very simple psychological explanation. The singing of their earlier days served as an outlet for many of their subconscious emotions. It was in great part a means of expressing the need of a husband and family. Now that the need has been satisfied, the urge to sing is largely dissipated. Tolstoy in his novel *War and Peace* describes with marvellous insight how Natasha Rostow was content after her marriage to give up her singing:

> We know that man has the faculty of becoming completely absorbed in a subject however trivial it may be, and that there is no subject so trivial that it will not grow to infinite proportions if one's entire attention is devoted to it.
>
> The subject which wholly engrossed Natasha's attention was her family; that is, her husband whom she had to keep so that he should belong entirely to her and to the home, and the children whom she had to bear, bring into the world, nurse and bring up.
>
> And the deeper she penetrated, not with her mind only, but with her whole soul, her whole being, into the subject that absorbed her, the larger did that subject grow and the weaker and more inadequate did her own powers appear, so that she concentrated them wholly on that one thing and yet was unable to accomplish all that she considered necessary.

Times have changed, but men and women remain much the same. No matter what the future holds in store, if your technique is founded on a rock, it will not be washed away by absorbing family duties. Not only will it remain your faithful weapon, it will also to some extent become the inspiration for fresh adventures, since you will hate to feel it lying idle. But learn the foundations of your technique while you are single and don't let it gather more than a very little rust.

Many people have the idea that at the menopause or change of life the voice begins to deteriorate. This is completely untrue. Some women go through an unhappy period and for them a sound technique is indispensable, if they wish to preserve their voices; but if they know how to sing there is no reason why they should not remain as good as ever for another twenty years.

In the course of your work you are bound to come in close contact with tenors and baritones. If you are sensible, you will treat them as friendly colleagues working together on a serious job. The conditions of professional life with its nervous tensions and subsequent reactions make this a difficult rule to abide by, but the slightest departure from it is certain to bring about a deterioration in your own work, and heart-ache for your colleague's wife or girl-friend, who in any case does not have a very easy time. The average woman's ideal is to have a nice settled home with a nice settled income, and an unambitious contented husband who comes back to it at the same time every evening. The artist's wife never achieves this. Furthermore she knows that he finds in his work some mysterious thrill which she can never share, and to make matters worse he frequently realizes this thrill in company with another woman! However confident she is that her man loves her alone, the poor girl is bound to be a bit jealous. It is up to you not to give her the slightest reason for becoming more than a bit jealous. Make friends with her, ask what she thinks about the works you are rehearsing, praise her cooking and do everything to keep her in the picture.

Singing ladies are most fortunately placed beside their sisters. The instrumentalist, the composer, the poet, the painter, the doctor and the barrister must all compete with men, and only too often in these professions women find themselves outclassed. The singing lady has a clear field, for the public very sensibly vetoes male sopranos.

c. Growing girls and boys

The years before puberty need not be regarded merely as a period of vocal prematurity. Like their bodies and minds, children's voices are quick to adopt right and wrong habits which are never entirely shaken off. Bad habits can ruin voices for life, while good habits acquired in early years could easily sow the seeds of that ethereal angelic quality which we associate with the famous sopranos of the old school. But let no choirmaster jump to rash conclusions, for singing demands a combination of natural gifts and hard work which are rarely found in the same person.

Characteristic of most English children is the extremely breathy quality of their singing; a quality which is enhanced by the average conductor's insistence on clear diction and the placing of notes as high up and forward as possible. True singing is the enemy of breathiness. It has no sentimental associations, but suggests something disembodied. In the best sense of the word it is a heavenly thing. No subtleties of musical interpretation can compensate for its absence, yet I doubt whether it is ever completely acquired in all its glory by any singer except at an early age. The revolution in technique is too big to be successfully undertaken by anyone whose career is in midstream. The attempt in itself will bring about a tremendous all-round improvement, but the gulf between the old and the new technique is too wide for any but the youngest and most agile, although for them it is a comparatively easy jump. Train a boy soprano to use his larynx in the right way, and the young rascal may easily give us a fleeting glimpse of Paradise.

The glimpse, alas, is all too fleeting, for in these days conductors of school choirs find themselves in a situation which appears to be growing steadily more difficult, owing to a startling acceleration in the process of adolescence. Over the last hundred years the average onset of puberty in boys and girls of all classes in all countries has been occurring at a progressively earlier age. Forty years ago every church in the country had its boys' choir; today there are scarcely any outside the cathedrals. The moralists put this down to the influence of television and football pools, but the true reason is that whereas sixty years ago the average age when a boy's voice changed used to be about sixteen, it is now about two years earlier. For the conscientious choir-trainer this must be a deplorable situation, but let there be no mercy upon him should he try to bolster up a tottering soprano-line by keeping a boy in the choir after his voice begins to change.

At the onset of puberty the larynxes of both sexes give evidence of physical development. With boys the thyroid cartilage increases in size and the vocal cords grow tougher and longer and heavier. During this period, that is to say as soon as there is the slightest tendency for the voice to deepen in quality or tessitura, to crack while singing or croak while speaking, a boy should drop all choir and solo work. Good male adult voices invariably are voices which never broke, but which gradually deepened, so that at no time were they incapable of singing. Choirmasters have no excuse for not noticing every case of laryngeal development, since it coincides usually with a marked physical growth and invariably with the development of facial hair. Anybody who does not notice such changes has no business to call himself a teacher. Yet it is certain that nearly all choir-trainers, teachers and organists have shown either a callous disregard for the well-being of the adolescent male voice, or an equally unforgivable ignorance. Innumerable voices have been permanently damaged, impaired or coarsened as a result of boys being allowed to continue singing after the vocal change has begun. The boys themselves are never to blame; they can have no experience or knowledge of their condition, and look to their teachers as responsible guides who, when occasion demands, are expected to lay down the law in no uncertain terms. In most cases, the teachers will have been so anxious to ensure a fine performance of whatever is pending, that they will not have bothered to think of the effect on the future of the individual voices in their care. Perhaps one or two will now realize that they have probably wrecked goodness knows how many potentially beautiful singing and speaking voices, all of them with an expectation of at least fifty years.

It is impossible to say how soon a boy may start serious lessons after his voice has changed. The period of growth varies in different bodies. As a rule baritones and basses may start considerably sooner than the tenors, who as usual are rather fragile plants. In any case it is important not to make a hasty diagnosis. A boy who appeared to be an obvious candidate for the army may suddenly decide to become a medical missionary, and voices equally surprisingly change direction. Both teacher and singer must be prepared for this, contenting themselves with describing the voice as a potential tenor, baritone or bass. In the course of training its true identity will disclose itself. Since the technical work is in all respects identical, there is no question of wasting time. Dozens of singers have started their careers as baritones and ended up as tenors. Others have gone the opposite way. Big voices in particular take a longer time to arrive at maturity, and dramatic tenors and

T

sopranos often reveal their true identities only after years of training and stage experience.

Although they do not suffer the same growing pains, the larynxes of girls also go through certain physical changes. They do not increase in size, but there is a notable development in the sturdiness of the vocal cords and their controlling muscles. Until then girls' and boys' voices may be looked upon as essentially similar. Some small girls seem to have completely adult voices from an extremely early age; even so, until the onset of puberty, their voices should not be treated differently from those of other girls of the same age. Compared with boys the girls have a very easy time, and one never meets a musical woman who does not possess a singing voice of some kind. At puberty they can continue singing without risk, and a year after they have started menstruating, say from fifteen, they may safely be treated as adults. By learning to make full use of the chest mechanism, their voices will immediately acquire a new depth and extended range. The vital thing is that the instruction they receive should be on the right lines, and no reader needs to be told how rare good teachers of singing are. If they are not available, it is better to wait rather than waste time and money with the wrong teacher. Bad teaching can ruin a voice. The voice to all intents and purposes may be as good as ever, but the bloom will have gone as surely as a peach is spoilt which has been shaken about in a bucket.

The timbre of the speaking voice is only a very rough indication of the character of the singing voice. A highly-strung mezzo-soprano may speak on a highly-strung speech range and the world will assume she is a high soprano; alternatively she may be a tweedy horsy type, and choose her speech range on such a low level as to suggest not so much that she is a contralto, but a baritone in petticoats. Naturally most voices use a speech range appropriate to them, but life is full of surprises, and frequently a speaking voice tells more about a singer's psychology than about the roles which he is fitted to undertake. Some throat specialists claim that the size and character of the vocal cords is an infallible guide; but diagnosis on these lines is an uncertain business. It is also dangerous, for the young singer, being a child of his time, is only too willing to bow down before the marvels of medical science. Voices are live things, and the outcome of so many different physical and psychological phenomena that no specialist is entitled to do more than give his professional opinion, which the singer may consider interesting, but by no means infallible.

While I am in favour of girls and boys beginning serious training at a much earlier age than is usual, it should not be thought that starting at twenty-five is too old. Provided you are in the habit of lifting up your voice in song, you can begin at any age you please up to sixty; and if you study along the right lines, the reward is certain. But don't put it off longer than you can help.

22

THE SINGER IN ACTION

a. Auditions

In applying for an audition, do not talk about your startling talents and versatility, but try to give factual information which you think necessary and nothing else.

Let me give examples of the information you should provide in various instances:

1. *Straight concerts, oratorio societies.*
   (*a*) Your voice, your approximate age.
   (*b*) Where you studied and for how long. If you have been in Europe it is sometimes an advantage to mention that you had lessons from Boguslavsky in Paris, even if Mr B. is quite unknown and you had only two lessons!
   (*c*) The names of any conductors or organists under whom you have sung as soloist and the works performed.
   With your letter enclose a specimen recital programme showing the sort of work you like doing.

2. *Opera companies*
   (*a*), (*b*) and (*c*) as above.
   (*d*) Your dramatic training and experience both in opera and straight plays.

3. *Managers and agents for Operetta, Musical Comedy, Concert Party, Revue*
   (*a*) and (*d*) as above.
   (*e*) If you can dance at all, state what style and your experience.
   (*f*) Your height and colouring.
   Enclose a postcard-sized photograph, with your name, address and telephone number on the back.
   Names and addresses of people in this world can be found in the publication *Spotlight* which is obtainable at public libraries.

[274]

4. *Chorus and Churchwork*
   (*a*) and (*b*) quite briefly.
   (*g*) Say you can read music.

As a rule managers are not interested to hear about work you have done in churches or choruses, however distinguished, but it is of some help if you can say that you understudied in certain roles.

Write, or preferably type your information clearly and briefly on one side of a quarto size sheet of white unlined notepaper, and enclose a stamped addressed envelope.

The kind of information that is not wanted is that you can play the violin, are a champion fencer, can paint scenery, do shorthand or act as a trained nurse. It suggests that you may be a dab at these accomplishments, but as a singer you are a dead loss.

Photographs should be of postcard size or one size bigger, and look like professional jobs. Misty amateur efforts or glossy magazine productions are not appreciated. At all stage and operatic auditions it is wise to bring photographs of yourself in any roles you have sung. These too should have your name, address and telephone number clearly written on the back.

Unless you have some marvellous press cuttings from first-class London newspapers, it is wise not to bother about them overmuch. Provincial notices and carefully edited extracts cut no ice at all. When however you have something really good, buy or otherwise appropriate as many copies of the paper as you can. Then at future auditions, if circumstances are favourable, take out a fresh-looking cutting and present it to your interviewers with a modest smile.

Tape recordings are being increasingly used by agents and managers in the light music field. The reader should therefore have available one or two small-sized tapes which he feels are representative of his work; naturally, like the photographs, they must be of professional standard.

I need hardly say that it is most unwise to start applying for auditions until both you and your teacher are absolutely convinced that you are ready for them. Once you have written, be prepared to go along at a moment's notice and sing whatever is appropriate to the engagement which you hope to obtain. If you sing a Bach cantata at an operatic audition, or a Gilbert and Sullivan number for a position in a church choir, it can only mean that your repertoire and musical taste are unsuitable, or that you have no imagination or consideration for the person who is hearing you. He wants to have an idea of your voice, your style and personality, so that he can decide not only whether you are good enough but, what is even more important, whether you are likely to fit in with his company.

For some auditions you will be asked to bring an accompanist; these are much less nerve-racking because the chance to rehearse will enable both of you to get acquainted with each other's idiosyncrasies. Accompanists are invariably kind and co-operative people, but make sure that the one you engage can also play the pieces as you wish them to be played and will turn up a quarter of an hour before the time arranged in reasonably respectable clothes. For each audition it is only fair to pay him a modest fee, as well as standing him a meal and his expenses.

Bring at least two contrasting pieces. If you are in doubt as to what sort of music is wanted, let your audience choose. They should be pieces with a clearly defined tune, and not lasting longer than three minutes. In most cases listeners simply want to judge the quality of your voice. Anybody who knows his job can decide for or against you in half a minute or less; in fact it is only politeness as a rule that prevents him from thanking you at the end of half a minute. Unless there are sound reasons to the contrary, audition pieces should always be sung in English, but take care that translations are good, otherwise your listeners will be justified in concluding that your taste is not of a very high standard. Sing what is grateful to the voice; Handel, for instance, in preference to Bach or Mozart. Don't sing anything with silly or esoteric words; your audience will listen to them and not to you. In any case clearly enunciated words are immensely important, for when two or three are gathered together, the odds are that at least one cares nothing for vocal quality, but likes to hear the words and judges you accordingly. Unless you have your own accompanist, do not bring songs in manuscript, and avoid any with difficult or showy accompaniments. When the person who is auditioning you is playing himself, it is asking for trouble because however brilliant he is he will be forced to give some of his attention to reading the music; this will justifiably annoy him, for if he plays all the notes he will not be listening to you properly, and if he contents himself with a bald approximation he may easily confuse you. The same applies when a pianist is provided, for he may well be a very imperfect specimen and the piano even worse. Furthermore acoustics can play the devil in an empty hall or theatre, particularly if the piano is down there in the orchestra pit and you are up here on stage. It may seem to swamp your voice so that you are tempted to shout, or it may be practically inaudible. Above all to thine own self be true, and don't sing anything that is not well within your range and suitable to your personality.

Almost certainly, if you are auditioning for a choir or chorus job, you will be asked to do some sight-reading. This is an essential acquisition for anyone who hopes to earn his living by singing. Whatever you are given to read, try to decide, on the evidence of the time signature, the words and the music, whether the rhythmic beat should be one in a bar, two in a bar or what. As a rule the composer's intention is fairly clear, but not always; as for the Italian instructions, they can help, but often they are so ambiguous as to be misleading. Having made up your mind—and remember that there can be two opinions about every piece of music—conduct the piece as unobtrusively as possible while you sing. In this way you will prevent yourself panicking and going faster and faster or, in your anxiety not to make mistakes, dragging to a snail's crawl. Occasional mistakes do not matter, though it is advisable to have a careful look at the key signature before starting! What is much more important is to show that you are a musical person with a good sense of rhythm. Needless to say, beating time is permissible only during a sightreading test. Nothing in performance is so distressingly obvious as a tapping foot, a jigging knee, or a jogging elbow.

If you are asked about yourself, say where you studied and for how long. Do not say that you won any gold medals at school or played any leads there. Managers are not interested in academic triumphs because they know that it is the business of academies to keep students profitably employed; but if you worked with the local repertory company or amateur opera, you will be wise to slip in a modest word or two about this. In any case the information you give is not nearly so important as the impression which you make in imparting it.

Auditions are held sometimes in order to find good singers, and sometimes for all sorts of reasons. The manager may want a bald fat man, or a brunette of five foot four with a large bosom; and if your voice was the equal of Caruso or Melba, he wouldn't be interested. Even if he is simply looking for voices, yours may be too powerful, the quality too rich or the technique too good to blend with the other voices in his company. Having engaged and rehearsed these others, it is common sense to present them under the best possible conditions. Very probably he will regret having to turn you down, but he will be acting wisely if he does so. Every singer in the world has been turned down at some time in their lives, including Caruso and Melba (by the d'Oyly Carte Opera Company).

b. Before you go on

You are about to walk on in front of some hundreds of people who not only have paid money and taken time off to hear you, but who look upon you as something special. Go to any variety concert, and invariably you will sense an unusually sympathetic atmosphere when the singer is due to appear. If he fails, 'Well,' they say, 'he did his best.' On more auspicious occasions the extraordinary demonstrations at the end of a concert by a great artist suggest that he has transmitted something precious and unique to each member of the audience. Anybody who listens to a real singer experiences in a small way the same sensations in throat and belly that I have described in this book. They are good sensations, healthy and life-giving. That is why an audience, who amid the orgy of present-day bleating has heard a record of Caruso or Galli-Curci, is still ready to greet with enthusiasm the appearance of an unknown young singer.

When you step on to a platform, you are answering a challenge for which you have been preparing yourself by years of work. It is foolish therefore to risk spoiling your prospects by making an unfavourable impression before you even open your mouth. Yet this is what a great many artists do. Of course one learns by experience; but since platform deportment is mostly a matter of imagination and common sense, it is worth a little attention.

Your first duty is to be in the best possible voice for the great event. Alas, there is no way of securing this blessed state, but you can at least make sure of getting a reasonable allowance of sleep, food and drink. Over- or under-indulgence in any of these three necessities of life affects voices as fatally as a sore throat, so make sure that you have your proper quota of all of them the day before and on the day of the concert.

Give your voice a good work-out the day before the concert, but on the actual day use it very little; ten minutes in the morning is enough. After that do not sing at all until you are dressing for the concert. It is a great temptation to go on rehearsing till the last moment, but this is a sure sign of a bad singer. Think mentally through the music if you must, but rest the voice; this means not only that you should not sing, but that you should do no more talking than is reasonably necessary. I know of course that the rigours of professional life seldom allow such favourable conditions.

Having done all you can to ensure that you are in good voice, the next point is to arrive at the right hall on the right date at the right time with the right clothes. There was once a famous man who was forced to send his agent an S.O.S. reading: 'Am at Market Harboro; where ought I to be?' Every performer can tell stories almost equally harrowing. They may be comic in retrospect, but they are grim when they happen, and a most inauspicious prelude to an artistic performance. Allow plenty of time therefore for catching trains and buses; take it for granted that they will arrive late, and you may be reasonably certain of reaching your destination preferably an hour, and at least half an hour, before the advertised time. Nothing is more upsetting to a breathless young artist than to be greeted on his arrival by black looks from a harassed manager. Furthermore public appearances are apt to play merry hell with the digestive apparatus. To make matters worse many halls are designed so as to place the lavatory at the farthest possible distance from the artist's room, the architect being under the impression that musicians are too pure for such lowly needs. They aren't! The needs of performers are often extremely urgent, especially in the case of singers who for obvious reasons cannot give of their best unless their bladders and bowels have been emptied.

More than likely, on your arrival you will be greeted by some aged relative or odious school-friend whose uproarious reminiscences of your childhood will set your face in disorder and your mind going off at tangents. It is your duty to be as politely tough with these well-meaning saboteurs as you decently can. If you have come with friends it is their duty to keep well-wishers at bay until you have finished your job. Their secondary duty is to absent themselves. You may not mind their staying, but the other artists do, particularly the accompanist who will be anxious to look through the music and cope with last-minute instructions.

If it is an evening concert, you will have eaten a fairly substantial meal about five or six o'clock. Don't have anything afterwards, least of all any of the nuts and sweet biscuits which many concert societies thoughtfully provide. If they offer you something to drink, use your own discretion, but in any case drink very little. If it is tea or coffee, wait till it gets reasonably cool and put in very little sugar. These precautions only apply to the half-hour or so before you go on. You are then, so to speak, on the job, and your vocal organs must be in the soundest condition possible.

You will naturally have taken care to look your best; this means, not only that you are properly dressed, but that you are prepared for emergencies. It is remarkable how inanimate objects conspire against the most conscientious of artists. At one and the same concert a shoe-lace will break, a vital trouser button will come loose and a stud will disappear. The only way to anticipate such grim coincidences is to make sure that every garment appears to be in sound working order; then to start dressing in good time, and to set out for the hall in even better time, carrying with you a battery of extra combs, safety pins and anything else which might come in handy.

If you have the music, check it through beforehand; if the accompanist has the music, make sure on arrival that it is all there and in the right order. Torn or ragged pages should be reinforced with transparent tape. It is also a good idea to stick the loose sheets of a song together. We have all seen long-suffering accompanists struggling to keep erect music which is in the last stages of collapse; this is not only cruelty to a noble breed, but an invitation to the audience to watch the accompanist. And serve you right!

Before the concert walk on and off stage several times. Some stages slope much more than others, some are slippery, some have steps or odd bits of projecting scenery; on others you may find it a squeeze getting round the piano, particularly if you are a soprano with a train. All this is not mere fussiness, for you have to step out, possibly into a dazzling and temporarily blinding spotlight, in high heels if you are a woman, and present yourself as a figure of beauty, dignity and confidence.

And now the great moment is at hand. This is when the most experienced of us suffer from butterflies in the stomach, but they can be kept at bay so long as you allow the respiratory cycle to continue unchecked in a smooth rhythm for at least a minute or two before going on stage. This means that you do not talk, you do not hold the breath, you do not even think through your music; neither do you take huge breaths, or let the breath escape slower or quicker than it naturally wants to. Your condition in fact is in complete contrast to anything which you are preparing to do. You are a healthy, instinctive vegetable, and nothing more or less. In this way you will come undisturbed, uninhibited and utterly fresh to the act of singing. Just before you enter, make a slow, smooth cat stretch, starting from the knees and continuing up to the crown of the head.

God bless you!

c. On stage

As a rule you will be coming on from the right side, but right, left or centre, walk straight out to your point of operation as if you mean business, and have been doing this sort of thing since you were six. Be aware of the audience, but do not look at them until you are in your correct position, however tumultuous the applause which greets your entry. When you have reached centre stage, bow graciously from the hips. Do not bow more than once unless it is a big hall and the welcome is in proportion; in that case you may bow first to the left and then to the right, but only if the audience and the applause are sufficient to warrant it. The applause represents a welcome from a friendly house. Since you have done nothing as yet, your single bow represents no more than an acknowledgement. Remember the audience is intensely interested in you, and if you pretend to be confident they will be aware of it long before you open your mouth.

Your first entrance tells the public what to expect more surely than the most expensive advertising schemes. It is your job therefore to create an immediate harmony between the audience's impression of you as a personality, and the programme which they are to hear. Whether it is a single song or a whole evening's programme, your deportment should be simple and yet composed, even stylized. You have to make yourself consciously look the personality which you in your heart of hearts want to be, a sublimated version, so to speak, of what you are in everyday life. Only then will you find it easy to express through your personality the changing moods of the words and the music. This sublimated version of yourself must be in terms of

your own physical characteristics. If you have a long neck, the one
thing you must not do is to tuck it in. The voice production will be
ruined, but aside from that you will be telling a lie about yourself. You
need to carry the impression of length downwards, so that instead of
looking like a giraffe you look willowy. It might be done by joining
the hands and holding them considerably lower than you normally
would, but in any case it is a matter of individual taste. If you are a
woman, you have the immense advantage of being able to dress in such
a way that your defects become an adornment, though no dressing can
do more than help the conscious impression of a fine artist which you
build up in terms of your physical appearance. Yvette Guilbert, who
has been immortalized in the drawings of Toulouse-Lautrec, was an
adept at this kind of thing. She was never a beauty, and her voice
towards the end of her career was a strange noise, but her stage-
deportment was unforgettable. This is how she describes her entrance
and exit:

> Je faisais mon entrée en scène très lentement, et très simplement,
> les bras allongés tout naturellement pour augmenter mon impression
> 'de longueur' et de sveltesse, mais ma sortie de scène était autre. Je
> ramenais mes bras devant moi afin que, dégageant 'mes flancs', ma
> silhouette vue de dos fut très fine, très mince, dégagée de toutes
> lignes supplémentaires. J'avais alors cherché et trouvé la silhouette
> correspondant à mon répertoire 'pince sans rire', composé alors de
> chansons 'immobiles', d'esprit chat-noiresque.

During the few seconds while the audience is settling down, look
round the house in a friendly relaxed way and if there is a gallery look
up and allow your eyes to take in all the people upstairs. Do not loll
against the piano, and don't smirk. The few seconds may easily
lengthen into something like thirty while two old ladies totter down
the aisle and pass some dozen people. Don't start glaring at the poor
things. It is bad manners and the audience who would otherwise be
sympathetic will not like you for it. Just continue looking round. If
the wait seems unendurably long, turn to your accompanist and tell
him in a whisper what day of the week it is.

Do not begin until you are certain that stragglers have stopped moving about. Right from the start make it plain that you expect silence;
otherwise you are being unfair to the music, to yourself and to the

99 per cent of the audience who have no intention of whispering and fidgeting. Somehow you have to establish a bond of friendship; but friendship will not materialize unless you make it clear to them that a lovely treat is in store which will not come off unless they are perfectly quiet. This is particularly important when the hall is large and the audience sparse.

The moment the audience is settled, nod to your accompanist as a signal to begin the first song and immediately bring your eyes to a short-sighted blur so that nothing can stand in the way of an utterly relaxed diaphragm. Listen to the introduction and show the audience that you are listening and looking upon it as an integral part of the song.

From that moment you are on the job. This means that to all intents and purposes you and your songs are all that matter in the world. Having read this book, you will be far too busy to be nervous. You will also know that, so far from letting your voice go out to the person at the back of the gallery, with the help of your technique you are quickly gathering him up to yourself and compelling him to share in the music.

During interludes and postludes listen attentively, and do not relax concentration until a second or two after the end of the song. The moment after—not the moment before—applause begins, smile and bow to the centre. You can then bow left and right if the applause warrants it but not otherwise. At the end of your group shake hands with the accompanist or conductor and make him share in the applause. Then walk straight off without looking anywhere except the way you are going. With concentration relaxed, you could easily spoil everything by tripping over a plant.

If you get an encore, let it be an appropriate pendant to whatever you have been singing. Encores should never be long, and should preferably be short and simple, for they are not part of the programme, and there is invariably a slightly restless feeling in the audience. Do not insult your public by showing off your superlatively eclectic taste in the choice of encores, or by singing rubbish. At every concert you will be asked to sing 'One fine day' and 'Ave Maria'; both are deeply moving things, but remember that this unending request in no way represents the taste of the audience as a whole, but comes from a few simple-minded people. If you give them what they want, your efforts will inevitably be greeted by volleys of applause! A well-known piece always incites an audience to clap. Because people know 'Ave Maria', they like to show other people that they know it, and they convey this valuable piece of information by clapping. The poor wretches who do not happen to know it and feel a bit ashamed of their ignorance, hastily cover up their cultural gap by clapping too. Soon everybody is cheering, and the singer is convinced she was terrific. But do not forget that in giving the public what they want, you have to run the gauntlet of the hi-fi addicts; these enthusiasts will quite certainly possess gramophone records of Gigli, Toti dal Monte and Flagstad in the same pieces, and will be comparing you bar by bar with these illustrious artists. One pupil of mine actually had six versions of 'Your tiny hand is frozen', while his girl friend boasted seven of 'Love and Music'.

Instead of 'Ave Maria', sing one of the songs which you love, and which you know you can sing well. But do not take everything for granted. Once the major part of the ordeal is over, there is an awful risk that concentration will lapse for a moment, despite your utmost watchfulness; even more so when persuaded to repeat a song in the middle of a programme. If this should happen in the one song or aria which everybody knows inside out, it is doubly disastrous. I remember one such instance when a young soprano, who was supporting one of the world's greatest baritones, had finished her solo group, and as an encore was pleased to give us 'One fine day'. So delighted was she to have come through her ordeal with success that she stopped concentrating. An audience of thousands was concentrating perhaps harder than they had done heretofore, while she was busy congratulating herself. Half-way through she dried so completely that in spite of audible assistance from accompanist and audience she was unable to carry on. In clattering high heels she had to walk round the piano and begin again from a position behind the accompanist's left shoulder. Since this melancholy exhibition took place in England, the victim was acclaimed during the interruption and at the end with salvoes of applause. But she will surely never forget that evening.

d. After you come off

Congratulate the composer, conductor, accompanist and fellow artists; and apologize for any mistakes even if it was somebody else's fault.

Shake hands with everybody who speaks to you; don't just thank your admirers, but tell them how kind they are. While it is important to seem friendly, natural and 'not a bit conceited', it is a great mistake to be all modesty and coyness. Whatever you think of yourself, the public must look upon you as a personality with an exciting 'artistic' background!

Tell the organizers how much you have enjoyed the evening, addressing them if possible by their names, and being careful to include their wives.

If they want to entertain you afterwards, accept the invitation as part of your job; this will involve a lot of hand-shaking and chat, with some not very potent drink but lamentably little to eat. If your hostess is sympathetic there is no reason why you should not drop a hint in her ear that you are ravenous and would like some bread and cheese. But do not stay in the kitchen longer than a very few minutes, or your absence will be adversely commented on.

Refuse to do any more singing, but listen graciously to any home-made entertainment.

Keep a store of chocolate or some such emergency ration. Singing is a hungry business and the vagaries of professional life make meal-times appallingly uncertain.

e. The way ahead

This book is concerned almost exclusively with technical problems. Questions of musicianship, interpretation and artistry cannot be discussed and settled in the same way. Such qualities flourish or wither according to the way you live and work, the friends you make, and the books, music and pictures which influence you. In fact they depend on what you yourself are.

Technique must be learned; musicianship must be acquired through your own efforts. Gustav Mahler summed this up devastatingly when he said that tradition is slovenliness (*Schlamperei*); by this he implied that the work of any performer who merely copies the interpretation of a teacher, or the gramophone record of some celebrity, or the manner in which a piece of music is habitually performed, is worthless. Every young artist must find his stimulus among the interpreters of today and yesterday; he should spread his net as widely as possible, caring nothing for the inflated pretensions of 'tradition', studying his heroes closely and critically, but not insulting them with thoughtless imitation. Inspiration is found only in the composer and his work, no, matter whether he be an intimate friend who has just completed his Opus 1, or a fat, short-sighted young man who a century and a half ago in the city of Vienna enriched our lives with a whole new world of song. In the rush of learning and memorizing new works it is very easy to forget this. Performance is not reproduction or even interpretation. It is in the most literal sense re-creation, and it is by immersing themselves in a composer's works that singers can acquire that awareness which enables them to share his emotions and re-create what those emotions inspired. This priceless gift can only be realized through an instrument which is loved and played as it would wish to be played. Few of us have any great depths of spiritual insight; yet at least, if you have laboured to make technique your devoted handmaiden, you will be equipped to make the journey of your choice. How far you travel along the golden road depends on you and you alone. Most of us fall by the wayside, but some go on. These happy few are the artists. The world may not recognize them, but the world needs them. Maybe, at the sound of their voices, old Hans Sachs himself will look down from his heavenly cobbling, for once again:

> Es klang so alt, und war doch so neu,
> Wie Vogelsang im süssen Mai!

APPENDIX

Manuel Garcia and the *Coup de Glotte*

As I explained in the Preface, this book was initially inspired by the teaching of Manuel Garcia, whose name will always be associated with a technique of launching notes called the *coup de glotte* or 'glottal shock'. The very mention of this phenomenon is apt, in England, to set up a horrified revulsion. Much of this irrational behaviour is due to the unfortunate English translation, which suggests nothing so much as strangulation in a dark alley. If we cannot use the original term, for heaven's sake let us think up an equivalent that is less convulsively opprobrious.

But there is more to it than just an unfortunate translation. Religions, systems of thought and methods of teaching tend to be perverted in all innocence by enthusiastic disciples. Garcia's teaching was no exception. One of his most eloquent disciples used to demonstrate the *coup de glotte* with the aid of a gun, but such eccentricities need not be associated with a man who was clearly one of the world's great masters. The brother of Malibran and Pauline Viardot, the teacher of Jenny Lind, Marchesi, Stockhausen and Santley, may have lived to be a hundred, but was not such a doddering old idiot as to teach his pupils to launch notes in a way which people nowadays refer to as the *coup de glotte*. Careful reading of his somewhat delphic treatise suggests that what he called the *coup de glotte* demands an intermediate movement between the inhalation and the attack. Quite certainly he never intended anything like the violent and explosive attack which, as doctors and teachers rightly point out, is bound to do serious damage to vocal cords. This is how he described it in his *Traité Complet de l'Art du Chant*:

> . . . the neat articulation of the glottis that gives a precise and clean start to a sound. . . . By slightly coughing we become conscious of the existence and position of the glottis, and also of its shutting and opening action. The stroke of the glottis is somewhat similar to the cough, though differing essentially in that it needs only the delicate action of the lips (i.e. *the vocal cords*) and not the impulse of air. The

lightness of movement is considerably facilitated if it be tried with the mouth shut.

Once understood, it may be used with the mouth open on any vowel.

With all respect to a great pioneer, Manuel Garcia was peculiarly unfortunate in his choice of words. The sense in which he uses 'articulation' would not be recognized by any dictionary, though the reader will be correct in understanding 'articulation of the glottis' to mean the approximation of the vocal cords. Less obscure but far more regrettable is his comparison of the *coup de glotte* to a cough. The word 'cough' is defined by the *Oxford Dictionary* as 'a violent expulsion of air from the lungs with the characteristic noise'. From the medical standpoint 'the act of coughing comprises a short inspiration followed immediately by a closure of the glottis, and a forcible expiratory effort. A high pressure is thus created within the lungs and lower air passages. The glottis then opens suddenly, allowing the air to escape in a blast'.* It would be difficult to object to either of these descriptions, and we can hardly wonder that as a result of his rash comparison, Garcia's system has been associated not only with violence, effort and abruptness, but with the implication that air is forced through an open glottis.

The French word *coup* is also an unfortunate term, though in this case Garcia was hardly to blame. When associated with another substantive it does not mean shock or blow, as most people seem to think; it means a sudden swift movement and nothing more or less. By reason of its association with particular words, such as *coup d'état* and *coup d'oeil*, it has acquired dozens of shades of meaning. Sometimes by reason of the accompanying word there is an implication of violence, at other times an implication of delicacy. It all depends on the word that follows 'coup de', but basically *coup* means 'split second motion'.

In his later book *Hints on Singing*† the author tried to undo this dual misconception by writing a footnote in which he says that:

> . . . the stroke of the glottis is meant to describe a physical act of which there should be merely a mental cognizance, not an actual physical sensation. The articulation which gives the precise and clean

* Best and Taylor, *The Living Body*, p. 259 (Chapman & Hall, 1958).
† Manuel Garcia, *Hints on Singing* (Asherberg, Hopwood & Crewe, 1894).

start to a sound is not felt in the throat (i.e. the larynx) of the singer. It is felt in the sound itself, the attack on the note, beginning clear, clean and true upon the middle of that note without preliminary movement or action of any sort beyond the natural act of singing.

The footnote was reinforced by an observation of the editor that:

The suggestion of an analogy between the stroke of the glottis and the act of coughing is intended simply to aid the student in locating the position and realizing the function of the glottic lips. There is no need even to think of its application when articulating or attacking a vocal sound.

No doubt the old man felt that some such footnote was needed to dissociate his teaching from the heavy-handed efforts of his more ruthless evangelists. But it is a thousand pities that he was persuaded into writing, or allowing someone else to write, this nonsensical footnote with its talk of mental cognizance. An unmistakable sensation is and must be present on a good vocal attack. It is every bit as unavoidable as the twang of a bow-string when you shoot an arrow into the air, or the click of an electric light as you switch it on. Once it is established, the sensation is forgotten within a few days. If nothing is felt at the glottis, it is certain that the throat and larynx are in a condition of normality, in other words in no condition for effective voice production.

Let us forget about the footnote and consider Garcia's original words in the light of the technique which I have described. He says that the stroke of the glottis is somewhat similar to the cough, and that the lightness of movement is considerably facilitated if it be tried with the mouth shut. Normally the act of coughing is sufficiently violent to make you on social occasions eager to suppress your cough as much as possible. Nevertheless, with increasing physical discomfort, a time may come when the abdominal muscles contract so as to produce a compression against the larynx. You are, however, able to withstand this pressure long enough not only to provide yourself with a silencer in the shape of a hand or handkerchief, but also to expel the released air with none of the explosiveness of less formal occasions.

The normal violent cough is an example of the perverted *coup de glotte* which induced Garcia to write his footnote. The polite concert cough, which follows along precisely the same lines as have been described in this book, is surely what Garcia intended, particularly when he goes on to suggest that you try it first with the mouth shut, in other words, that you grunt. In this way the act of singing is initiated with the same smoothness as when one puts a car in motion by releasing the clutch, though of course at infinitely greater speed. The operation can be made so quietly that, even over the microphone, it is no more noticeable than the impact of a violin bow against the string.

An even smoother attack can be achieved if the singer falls in with the conception of allowing the vocal cords spontaneously to vibrate before coming in contact with the compressed breath. In this way, and so far as I know, only in this way is it possible to make the *coup de glotte* as firm and yet as gentle as a lover's caress.

INDEX

INDEX

'ham', 191
Handel, 65, 154, 166–7, 186, 192, 237, 243
hard palate, 78, 159, 160
harmonic series, 64
harmonics, 63–8
head, crown of, 19, 20–1, 23, 45, 213
head register, 200–1, 204–7, 209
health, vocal, 260–5
heating, 263
heavy and light consonants, 153–6
heels, 12, 13, 14, 15, 212
Herrick, Robert, 180
high notes, 19, **147–9**, 197, 199, 215, **238–40**
  geometrical compasses analogy, 149
high spots, 183–4
Hints on Singing (Garcia), 288–9
hips, 12, 13–14, 16
hosepipe analogy, 12, 19
humming, 121, 161, 162
  and nasal resonance, 194–6
hydro-electric dam analogy, 129
hyoid bone, 68–9

inhalation, **34–9**, 41, 43, 50–3, 186, 187–8, 191–2
  bicycle pump analogy, 32, 39, 51
intensity, 59–61
intercostal breathing, 37–8
interpretation, 72, 139, 140, 170, 180, 181–2, 184–5, **242–54**
  gesture and technique, 249–51
  perils of, 247–9
  personal involvement, 251–4
  and registers, 214–16
  short-sight analogy, 184
  studying a song, 244–6
  tempo and whole man, 246–7
  voice and tessitura, 242–4
intonation, 124–7
intrusive 'er', 165
  intrusive 'h', 163–4
  inward gulp, 163
Italian vowels, 70–1, 103–6, 133, 138, 147

jaw, 68, 79–82, 86–7, 94, **147–51**, 240
  geometrical compasses analogy, 149
John of Garland, 200

knees, 13–14, 15–16, 22

language, 4, 70, 108–9, 182–3, 248–9
laryngitis, 261–3
larynx, 20, 26, 27, 41–4, 69, 79, 80, 129, 270–1, 272
laughter, 83, 84, 91, 100, 173
legato, 49, 107, 163, 166, **168–73**, 182
light and heavy consonants, 153–6
light music, 5–6
Lind, Jenny, 140
'Linden Lea' (Vaughan Williams), 154, 248
lip consonants, 161–3
lips, 29, 55–6, 111, 112–13, 114, 140, 141, 142–3
looking downwards, 146
loss of voice, 262
low notes, 197, 199, 240–1
lower ribs, 187
lung tension, 129, **134–40**, 144–5, 147, 151, 153, 164, 176–7, 191, 197, 218
  hydro-electric dam analogy, 129
  and registers, 199, 201–3, 204
  squirt analogy, 130
lungs, 32, 33, 39–40, 46, 58

McCormack, John, 198
Mahler, Gustav, 285
Marafioti, Dr, 262
marcato, 173–5
Martin-Harvey, Sir John, 178
maxillary sinuses, 196
mechanisms, 199, 217–31
  alto, 217–20
  chest, in women's voices, 220–8
  'chest voice' women, 229–31
medium voice and upper registers, 209–11
menopause, 269
menstrual period, 61
messa di voce, 138, 207
mewing analogy, 55, 56, 212

[297]

relaxation, 39–40, 45, 50–3
and breathing, 186
repertory companies, 4
resistance, platform of, 127–9
resonance:
frontal, 123, 196–8, 201, 206, 213,
225, 230
nasal, 78, 194–8, 239, 240
tonal, 102–3
vowel, 102–3
resonator, 24, 26–9, 59 *et seq.*, 145
tiger face analogy, 82
respiratory cycle, 51, 129, 280–1
rest, 264
rhythm, 183, 185
rib reserve, 6, 48–9
ribs, 212, 213
and diaphragm, 36–41, 48–9
false, 38
floating, 38
lower, 187
true, 38
umbrella-frame analogy, 36
upper, 187
ripples on water analogy, 62, 212
rising from chair, 22

sacro-spinalis, 47, **53–8**, 59–60, 89, 91,
127, 212
bow and arrow analogy, 54–5, 56,
100
Santley, Sir Charles, 26
scales, 235–6
Scholes, Percy, 59
Schubert, Franz, 181, 183
Schumann, Elisabeth, 150–1
scooping attack, 126, 197, 236–7
seagull analogy, 58
'Shenandoah', 247–8
short-sightedness, 95, 177, 184
shoulders, 10, 46
sighing, 73
sight-reading, 277
sing-song, 177
Singer and Accompanist (Moore), 3
singers, listening to, 4–6

singing ladies, 265–9
sinus, 196–7
sitting, 21, 22
Sleeping Beauty analogy, 70
slurring, 168–9, 171, 172, 179
smiling, 83
smoking, 263
sobbing, 173
soft palate, 26–7, 28, 78–9, 147, 148
consonants, 156–7
soprano, 205, 221, 223–4, 227–8, 229–
30, 272
sore throat, 261, 263–4
sound, 56–7, 59–60
waves, 61–3
Spanish dancer analogy, 9, 55, 100
speaking, 114
pitch, 126
voice, 176–9
speech, stage, 6–8
speech technique, 176–9
sphenoidal sinus, 197
spinal column, 14–15, 20, 53–5
Sprechgesang, 181
squirt analogy, 130
staccato, 175
stage appearance, 280–4
stage experience, 4
stage fright, 255–9
stage speech, 6–8
stage technique, 114
stairs, going up and down, 23
studying of song, 244–6
style, 181–4
subjective music, 251–4
suppression, **129–32**, 134, 197, 204
swimming, 265
syllable accentuation, 114

tape recordings, 275
technique, 251
teeth, 29, 111, 112–13, 114, 158, 162,
264
tempo, 246–7
tennis-player analogy, 208
tenor, 205, 209, 210, 213, 219, 271

0092770

VWS

This book is to be returned on or before
the last date stamped below.

15. JUN	18. JUN	-3 MAY 2000
08. FEB 96		25 APR 2001
7 MARCH	07. OCT 97	11 MAY 2001
18 APR 1996	13 JAN	21 JUN 2001
16 MAY 1996		CANCELLED
15. APR 97	-6 MAY 1998	CANCELLED SEP 2002
21. APR 97	17 JUN 1998	CANCELLED NOV 2002
19. MAY 97	-7 SEP 1999	-9 JAN 2009
28 FEB 1998		-7 APR 2011

LIBREX —

B 54485